chicken

NEW HOLLAND

First published in 2012 by
New Holland Publishers
London • Sydney • Cape Town • Auckland
www.newhollandpublishers.com

Garfield House 86–88 Edgware Road London W2 2EA United Kingdom
1/66 Gibbes Street Chatswood NSW 2067 Australia
Wembley Square First Floor Solan Road Gardens Cape Town 8001 South Africa
218 Lake Road Northcote Auckland New Zealand

Copyright © 2012 New Holland Publishers

All rights reserved. No part of this publication may be reproduced, stored in a retrieval system or transmitted, in any form or by any means, electronic, mechanical, photocopying, recording or otherwise, without the prior written permission of the publishers and copyright holders.

A catalogue record of this book is available at the British Library and the National Library of Australia.

ISBN: 9781742573588

Managing Director: Fiona Schultz
Publishing Director: Lliane Clarke
Design: Stephanie Foti
Production Director: Olga Dementiev
Printer: Toppan Leefung Printing Limited

10 9 8 7 6 5 4 3 2 1

Follow New Holland Publishers on
Facebook: www.facebook.com/NewHollandPublishers

contents

Introduction 5

Fingerfood 13

Salads 35

Sandwiches and Wraps 57

Curry Chicken 73

Stir-fry Chicken 91

Main Meals 101

Index 190

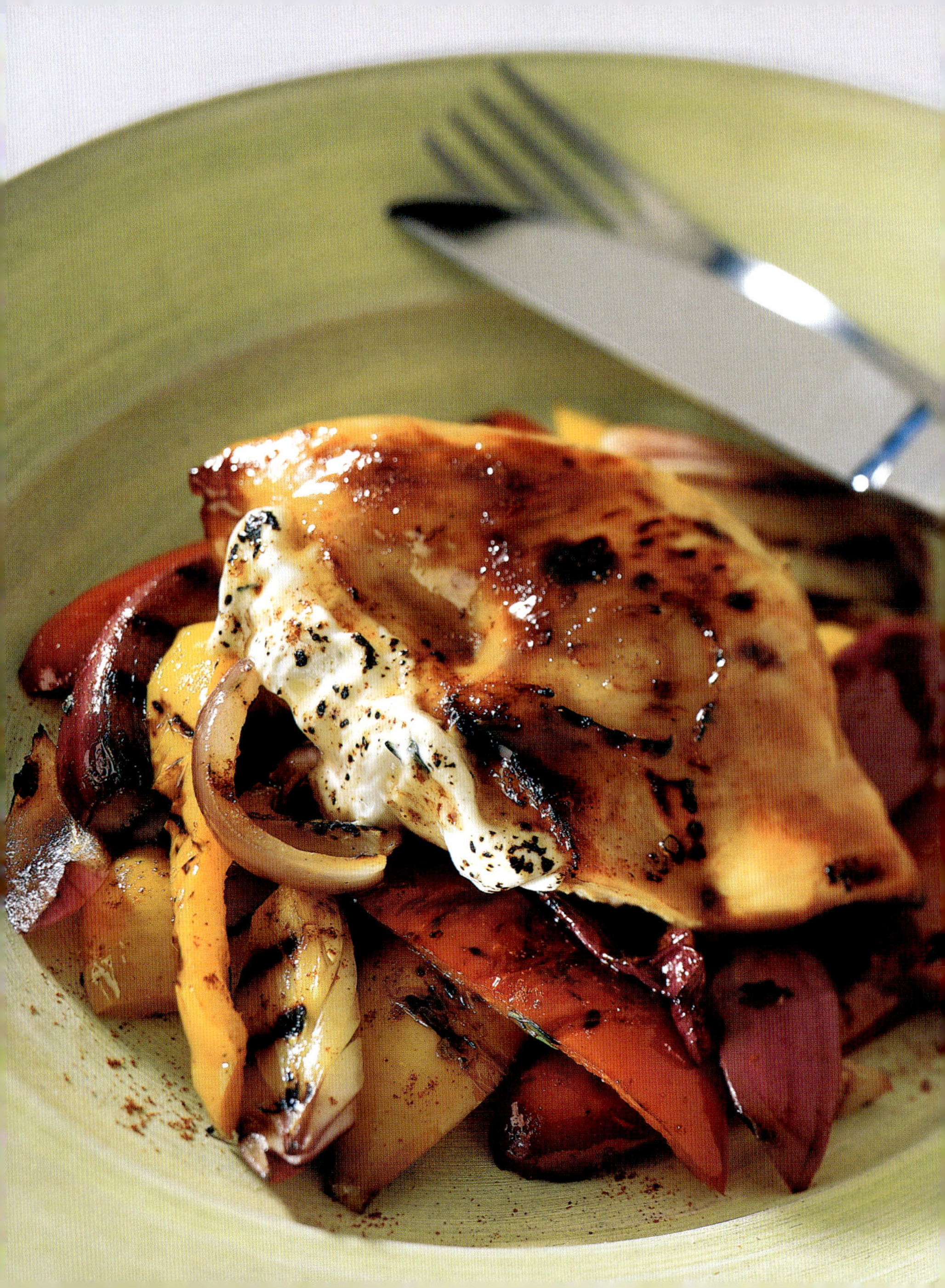

introduction

Chicken can be found on the menus of many cultures throughout the world, which have each added aspects of their culinary heritage to this versatile meat. However, it wasn't very long ago in Western countries that poultry was considered a luxury food and only consumed on special occasions. Things have changed greatly in the last 50 years, with chicken now being one of the major sources of protein in the Western world.

As chicken has become more and more popular, people have experimented more and more with different cooking methods and combinations. With the rich diversity of cuisines available to us, our repertoire of chicken dishes has expanded considerably, and continues to expand. Dishes from many different cultures, such as tandoori chicken, chicken cacciatore and Hawaiian chicken, are just as popular as the traditional roast.

As with beef, lamb and pork, different cuts of chicken are more suited to different methods of cooking. Thighs are the fattiest cut of chicken, and make excellent curries and stews. Breasts are drier and are particularly well suited to the barbecue or frying pan, and to salads. Tenderloins are perfect for shish kebabs or wraps. And while chicken skin may not exactly be a health food, it's still hard to resist on a crispy roast or spicy tandoori.

Chicken is one of the best sources of high-quality protein, and is also incredibly versatile. This is why there are so many popular chicken dishes throughout the world. Through the pages of this book you will experience the new flavour combinations that have resulted from our culinary cultural exchange, presented in simple and quick-to-prepare recipes.

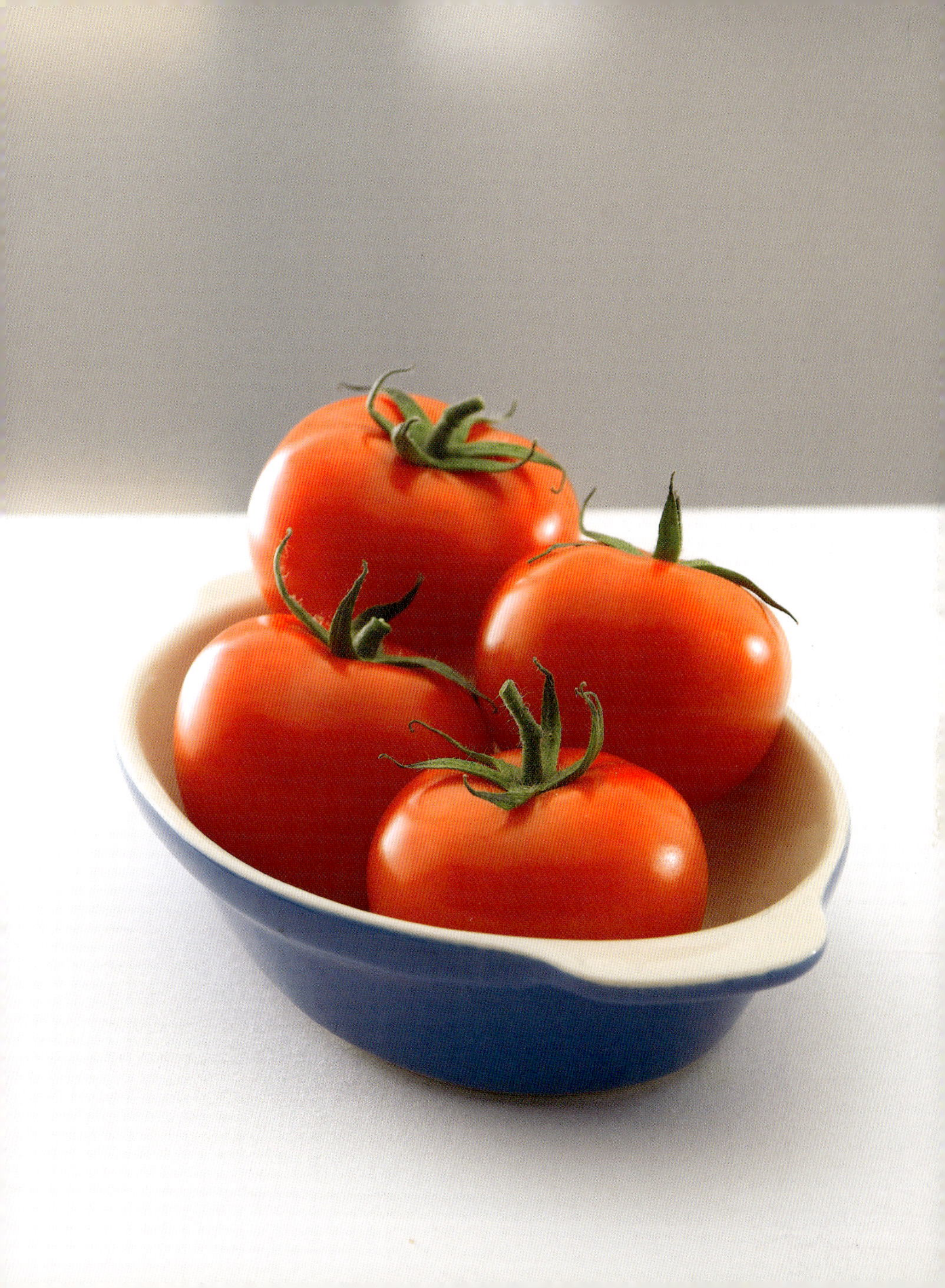

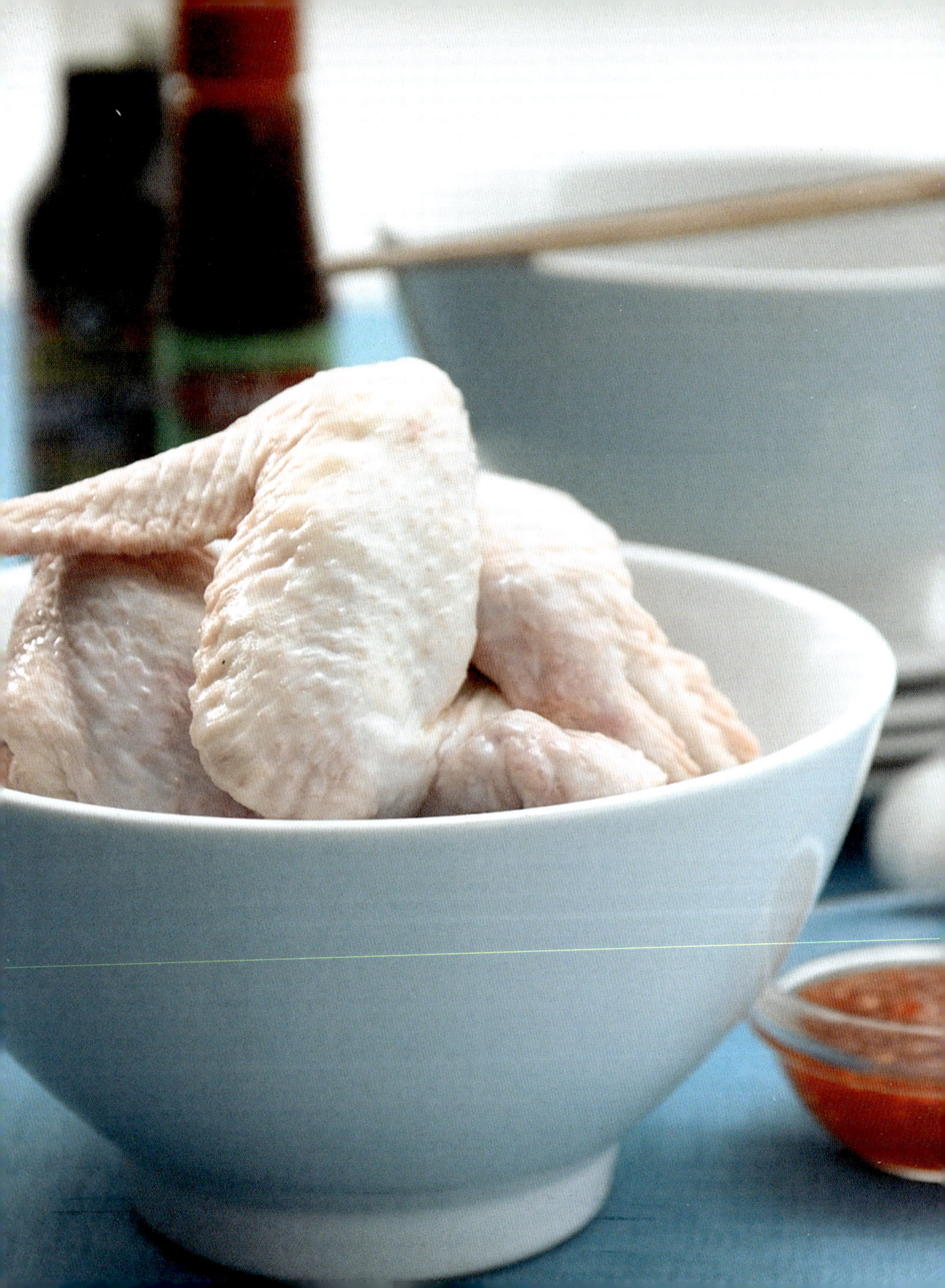

Whether you're a novice or an experienced cook, you will find these recipes to be the perfect blend of simplicity of preparation and sophistication of flavour, and you will enjoy not only eating them but preparing them as well.

We've brought together the world's best chicken recipes — fiery curries from Asia and India, as well as classic French chicken casseroles and finger licking barbecue favourites. Most feed four, but can be easily adapted to your needs. Most of the ingredients are easy to find in good supermarkets.

Whatever your cooking experience, whether you are cooking for family or to impress friends, you will be sure to come back to these recipes again and again.

The key to cooking chicken...

- Cuts on the bone and with skin are more tasty and are ideal for braises, roasting and stews.
- Skinless breast meat is perfect to poach for salads, to stuff and pan fry and stir-fry.
- Wherever possible, buy free range chickens which are superior in taste and are raised in a more ethical manner than battery hens.

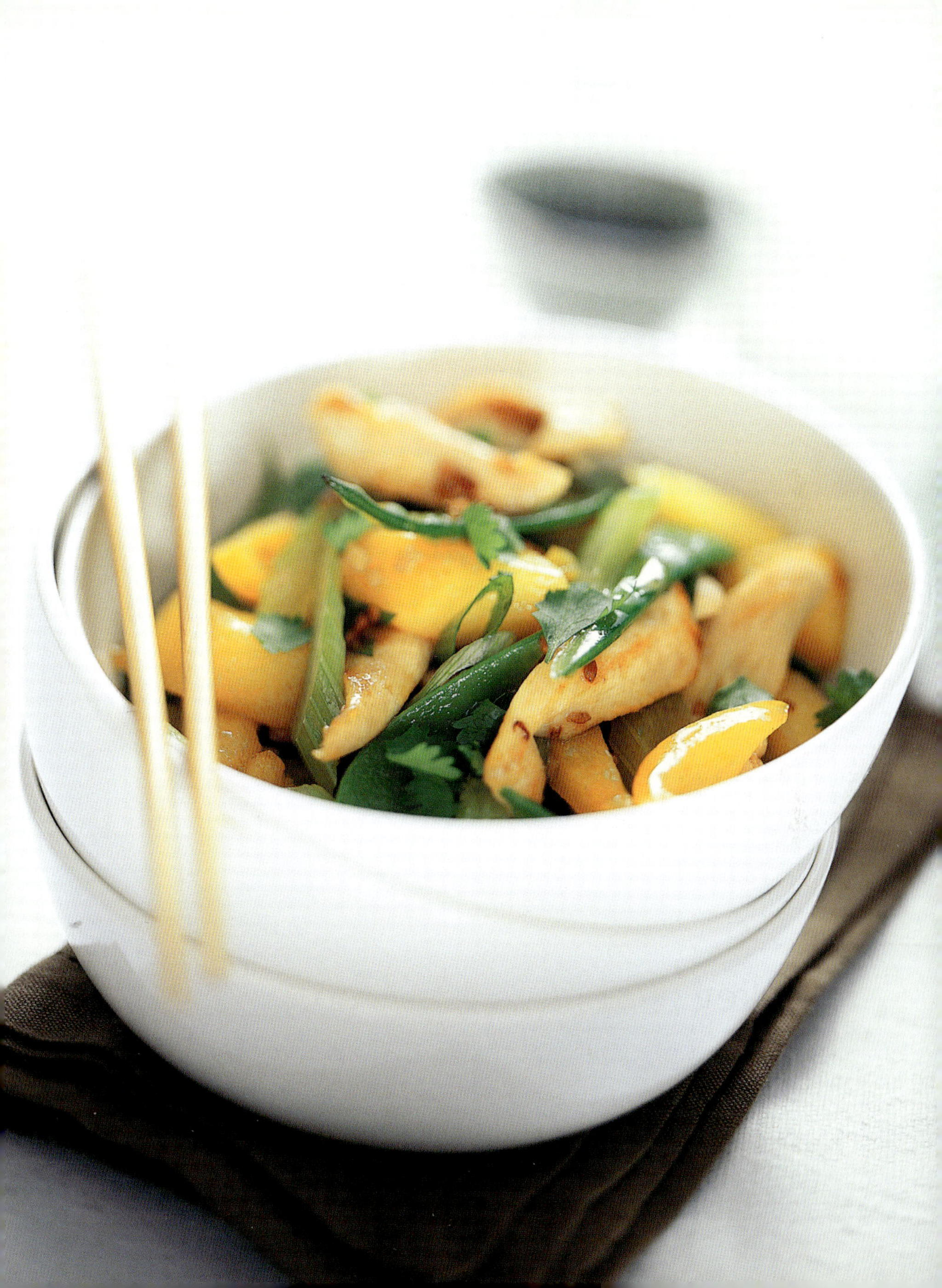

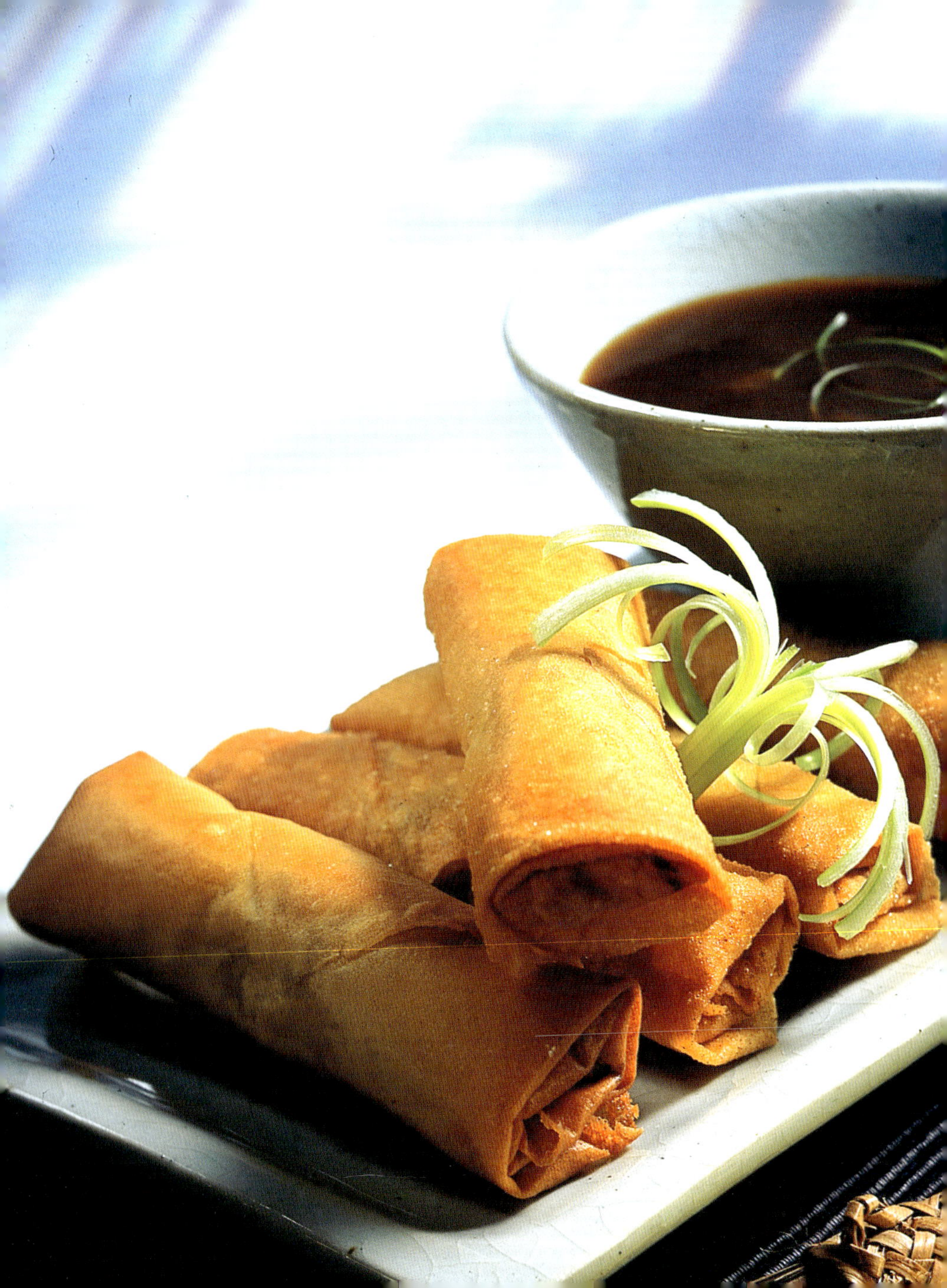

fingerfood

Samosas

MAKES 30

9oz (250g) chicken mince
1½ cups vegetable oil
2 medium onions, finely chopped
1 clove garlic, crushed
2 teaspoons curry paste
½ teaspoon salt

1 tablespoon white vinegar
½ cup water
2 teaspoons sweet chili sauce
¼ cup cilantro/coriander, chopped
1 packet frozen spring roll wrappers

1. Remove the chicken from the refrigerator and bring to room temperature. Heat a wok, add a little oil and fry onions and garlic until soft. Add curry paste and salt and fry a little. Stir in the vinegar. Add chicken mince and stir-fry over high heat until it starts to turn white. Break up any lumps. Reduce heat, add the water, cover and cook until most of the water is absorbed, about 6 minutes. Uncover, add chili sauce and cilantro. Stir until the water has evaporated and mince is dry. Remove to a plate to cool. Rinse wok.
2. Cut 10 spring roll wrappers into 3 even pieces. Place a teaspoon of filling at bottom end and fold over the pastry diagonally, forming a triangle. Fold again on the straight and continue to fold in same manner. Moisten the inside edge of the last fold with water and press gently to seal. Repeat with remaining wrappers.
3. Heat the wok and add oil until approximately 6 ins/5cm deep. Heat oil but take care not to overheat. Add 3 or 4 samosas and fry until golden. Remove with a slotted spoon to a tray lined with absorbent paper. Repeat with remainder. If samosas become too dark, immediately remove from heat to drop the oil temperature.

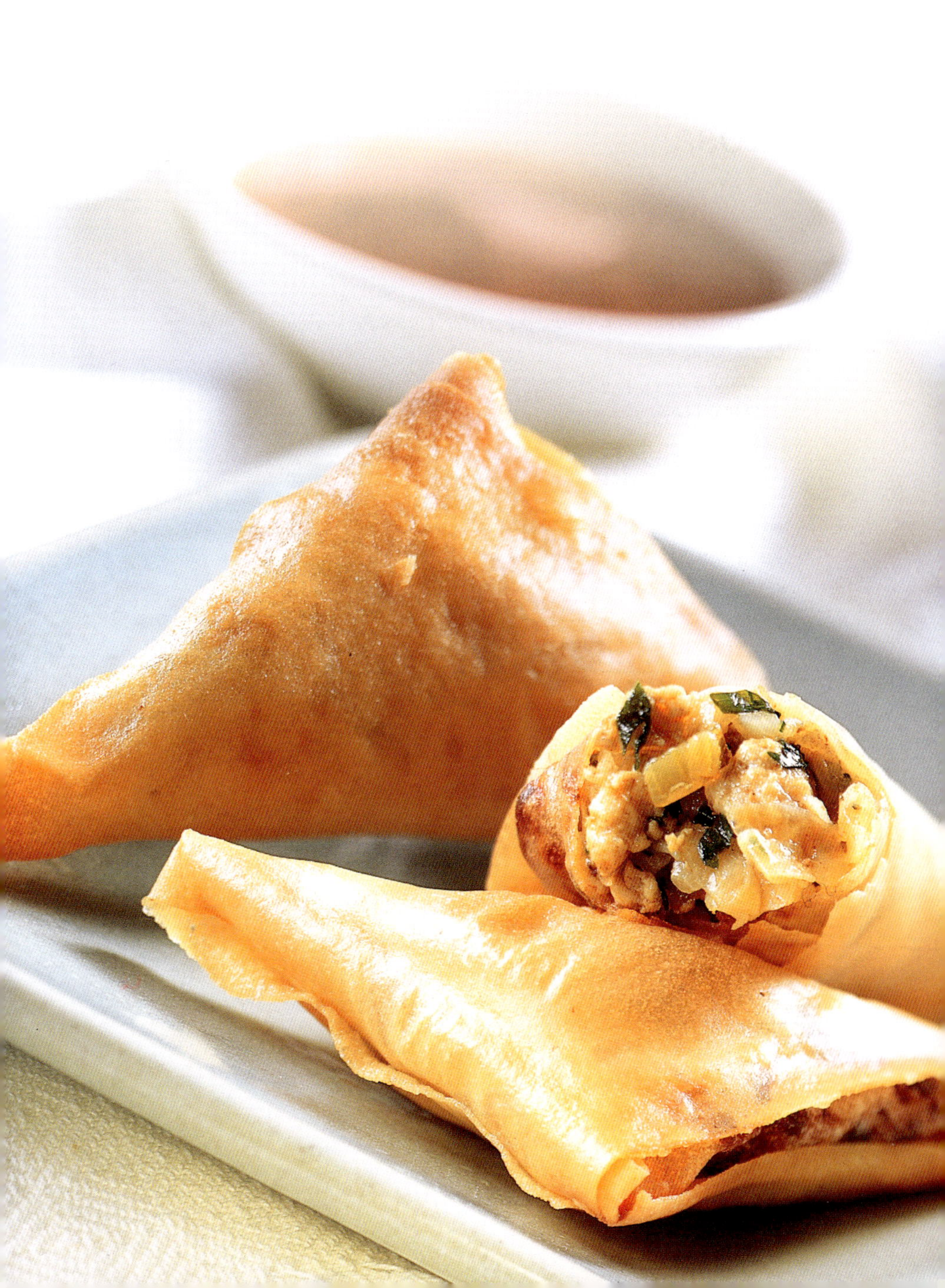

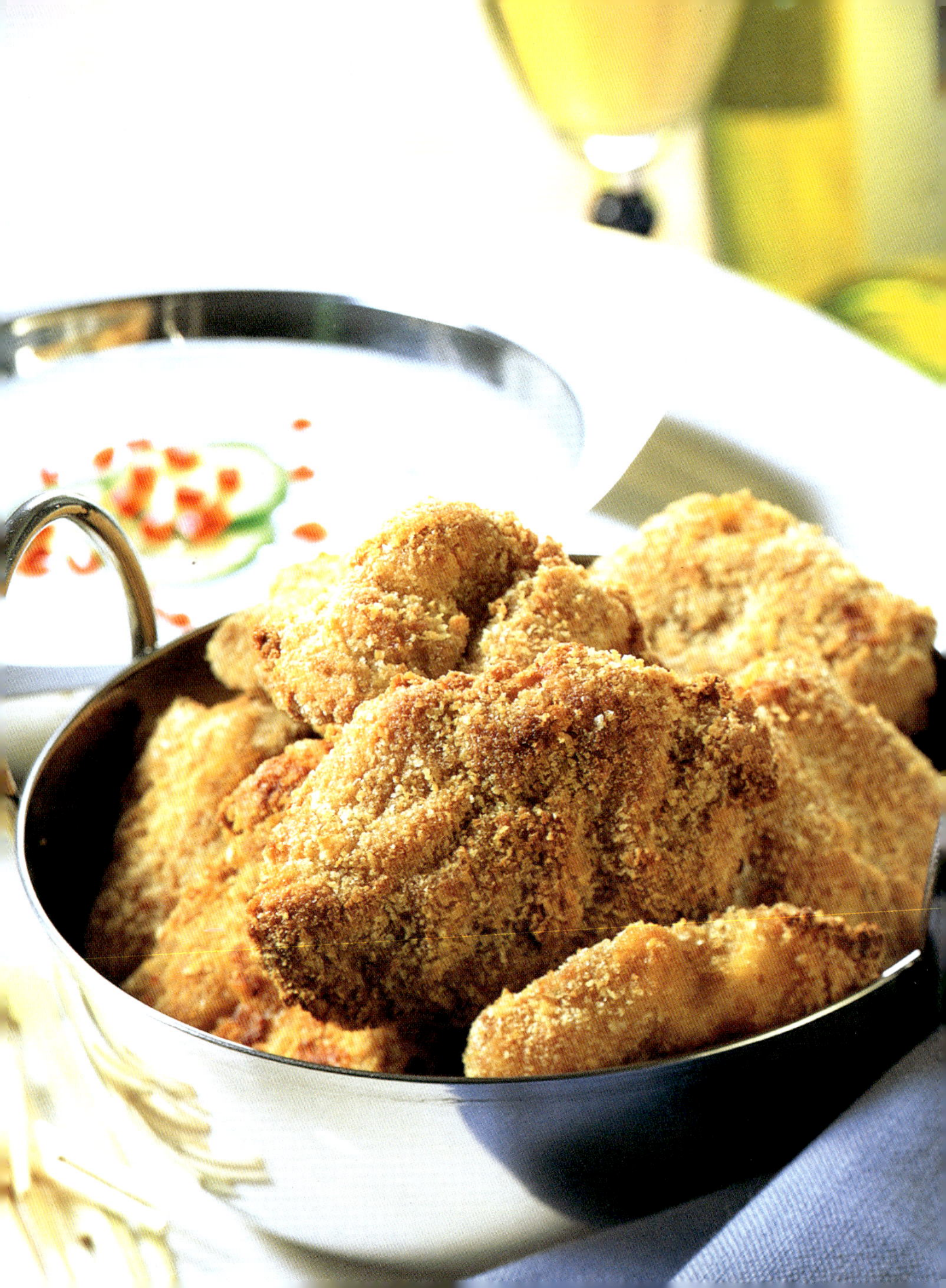

Vindaloo chicken nuggets

MAKES ABOUT 32

2 lbs/1kg chicken thigh fillets
salt and pepper
1 tablespoon lemon juice
2 tablespoons vindaloo curry paste
1 cup all-purpose/plain flour
2 eggs, lightly beaten
1½ cups dried breadcrumbs
canola oil spray

Yoghurt and cucumber dipping sauce
1 Lebanese cucumber, grated
1 cup plain yoghurt
salt and pepper
1 tablespoon lemon juice

1. Cut each thigh fillet into 4 pieces. Place in a bowl, sprinkle lightly with salt and pepper then pour over the lemon juice. Toss with spoon to mix through. Rub the vindaloo curry paste well into each piece with your fingers. Cover and refrigerate 2 hours or more.
2. Preheat oven to 390°F/200°C. Coat the chicken pieces in flour, dip in the egg, then cover in breadcrumbs. Lightly spray a large flat tray with canola oil spray and add the nuggets. Lightly spray the surface of the nuggets. Bake for 15–18 minutes.
3. To make the dipping sauce, place the grated cucumber in a strainer and allow to stand a few minutes to drain off excess liquid. Mix into the yoghurt with seasoning and lemon juice.
4. Serve hot nuggets with yoghurt and cucumber sauce.

Chicken and almond triangles

MAKES 21

1 lb/500g chicken mince
1 tablespoon olive oil
½ cup slivered almonds
1 medium onion, finely chopped
½ teaspoon salt
1 teaspoon ground cinnamon
1 teaspoon paprika

2 teaspoons ground cummin
2 small tomatoes, chopped
¼ cup raisins, chopped
¼ cup flat-leaf parsley, finely chopped
¼ cup dry white wine
1 packet filo pastry
canola oil spray

1. Remove chicken from the refrigerator and bring to room temperature. Heat oil in a frying pan and sauté the almonds until pale gold. Quickly remove with a slotted spoon and drain on absorbent paper. Add onion and fry until soft, stir in salt and spices and cook until aromatic. Add chicken mince and stir-fry until almost cooked. Add tomatoes, raisins, parsley, almonds and wine and simmer, covered, for 15 minutes. Uncover and cook until juices are absorbed. Allow to cool.
2. Thaw the pastry according to packet instructions. Count out 14 sheets, repack and refreeze remainder. Cut into three even strips. Stack and cover with a clean tea towel.
3. Preheat oven to 360°F/180°C. Take 1 strip, spray one side lightly with canola oil, then put another strip on top, and spray again. Fold in half down the middle, making a long, thin strip. Spray once more. Place a teaspoon of filling on bottom end of each strip. Fold right-hand corner over to form a triangle then fold on the straight, then on the diagonal, repeating until end is reached. Repeat with remaining.
4. Place triangles on a tray sprayed with oil. Spray tops of triangles with oil and bake for 20–25 minutes. Serve hot as finger food.

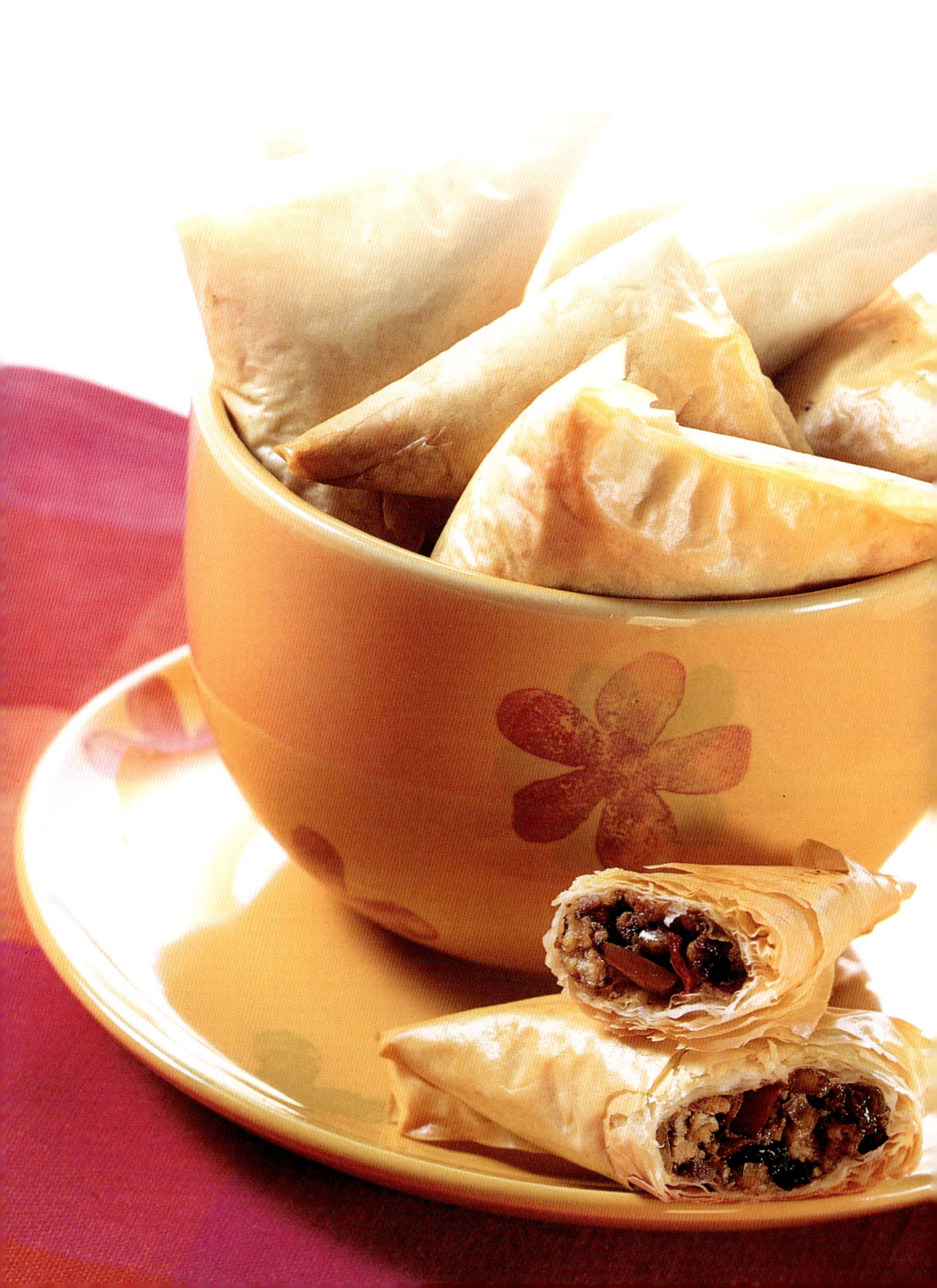

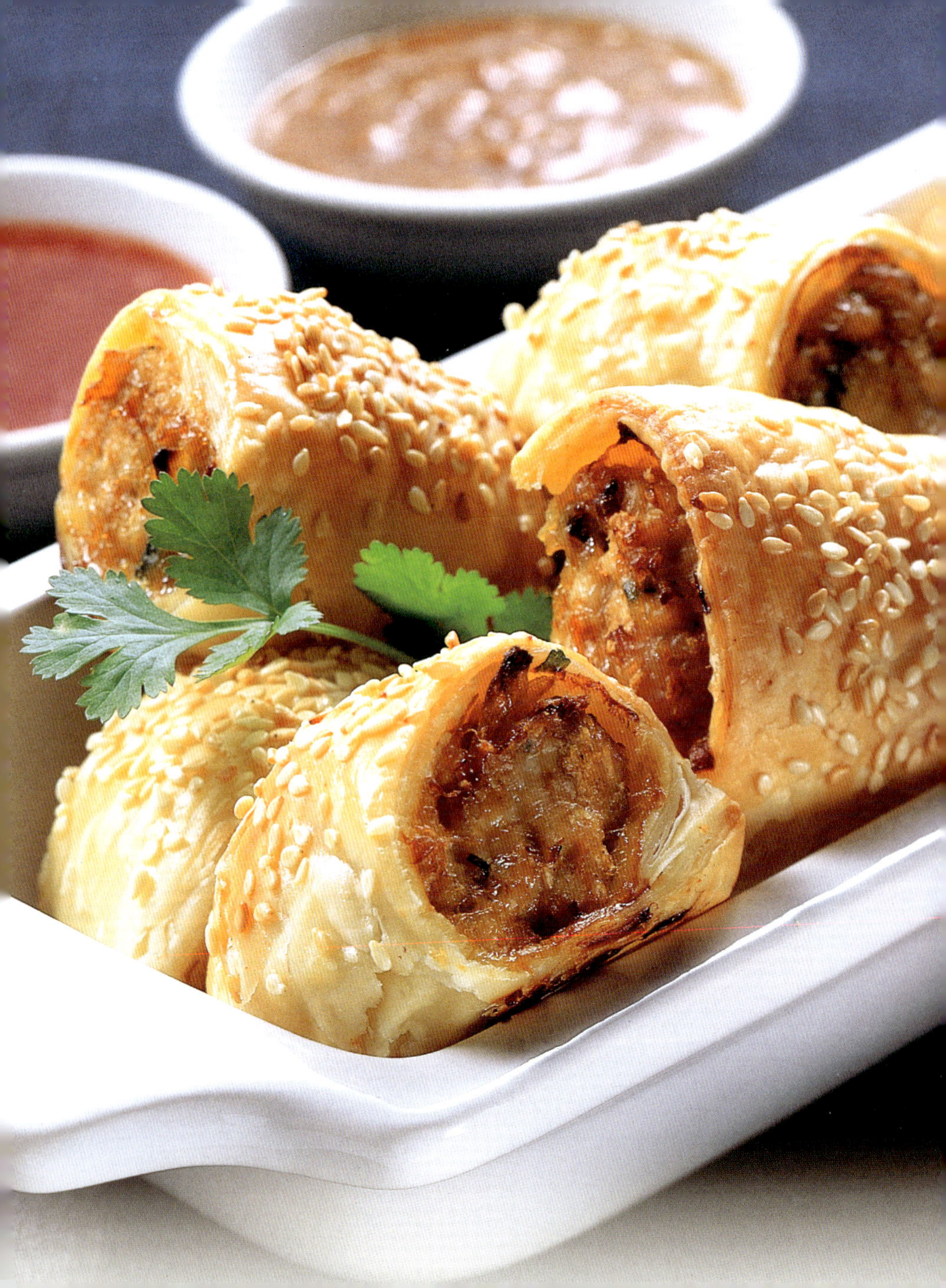

Curried chicken rolls

MAKES 16

1 lb/500g chicken mince
2 teaspoons canola oil
1 medium onion, finely chopped
1 small clove garlic, crushed
2 teaspoons mild curry paste
1½ tablespoons lemon juice
3 tablespoons dried breadcrumbs

½ teaspoon salt
½ teaspoon pepper
¼ cup fresh cilantro/coriander, chopped
2 sheets frozen puff pastry
1 tablespoon milk
1 tablespoon sesame seeds

1. Remove chicken from the refrigerator and bring to room temperature. Heat oil in a small pan, add onion and garlic and fry until onion is soft. Stir in curry paste and cook a little. Add lemon juice and stir to mix. Set aside. Combine the mince, breadcrumbs, salt, pepper and cilantro with the onion mixture. Mix well.
2. Place a thawed sheet of puff pastry on the bench and cut in half across the centre. Take one of these halves and pile a quarter of the mince mixture in a ½ ins/1cm wide strip along the centre. Brush the exposed pastry at the back with water, lift the front strip of pastry over the filling and roll up. Press lightly to seal. Cut the roll into 4 equal portions. Repeat with second half and then with second sheet. Glaze with milk and sprinkle with sesame seeds. Place on a flat baking tray.
3. Preheat the oven to 375°F/190°C. Cook for 10 minutes, reduce heat to 360°F/180°C and continue cooking for 15 minutes until golden brown. Serve hot as finger food.

Chicken balls with coconut and cilantro sauce

SERVES 4

1 lb/500g chicken mince
1 teaspoon salt
¼ cup dried breadcrumbs
1 medium onion, finely chopped
¼ cup cilantro/coriander, chopped
1 tablespoon mild curry paste
1 egg
1 cup all-purpose/plain flour

½ teaspoon pepper
¼ cup canola oil
Sauce
2 tablespoons mild curry paste
2 tablespoons lemon juice
½ cup coconut milk
½ cup cilantro/coriander, chopped

1. Place mince in a bowl and add half the salt, the breadcrumbs, onion, cilantro, curry paste and egg. Mix together very well. Rest 10–20 minutes to absorb juices before shaping.
2. Take a heaped teaspoon of mixture and with wet hands roll into a ball. Repeat with remainder, placing in a single layer on a flat tray. Refrigerate until ready to fry.
3. Mix flour, remaining salt and pepper together and place on a flat plate. Heat oil in a wide heavy-based frying pan. Roll each ball in the flour mixture, shake off excess and place in pan. Do not crowd the pan, and adjust heat when necessary to fry at a steady pace. Turn frequently and roll around to keep a good shape. Remove as they cook and drain on absorbent paper.
4. Pour oil from pan and wipe clean with absorbent paper. Return pan to medium heat, add curry paste and stir to heat through, then mix in the lemon juice. Lower heat and stir in the coconut milk and cilantro, simmer 2 minutes. Place the chicken balls on a serving dish and pour the sauce over. Serve with boiled rice and sambal. If serving as finger food, place chicken balls on a platter and serve sauce in a bowl for dipping.

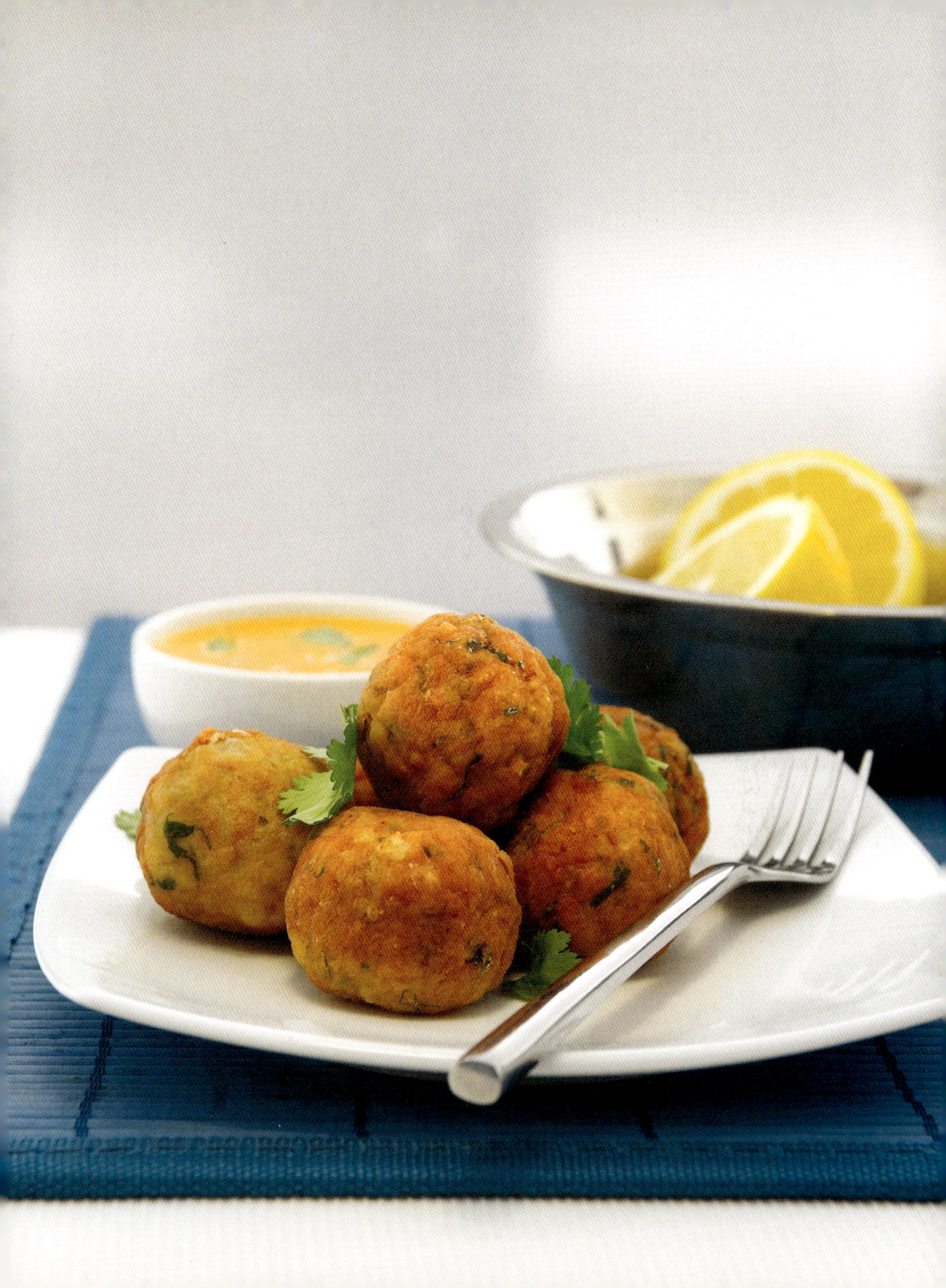

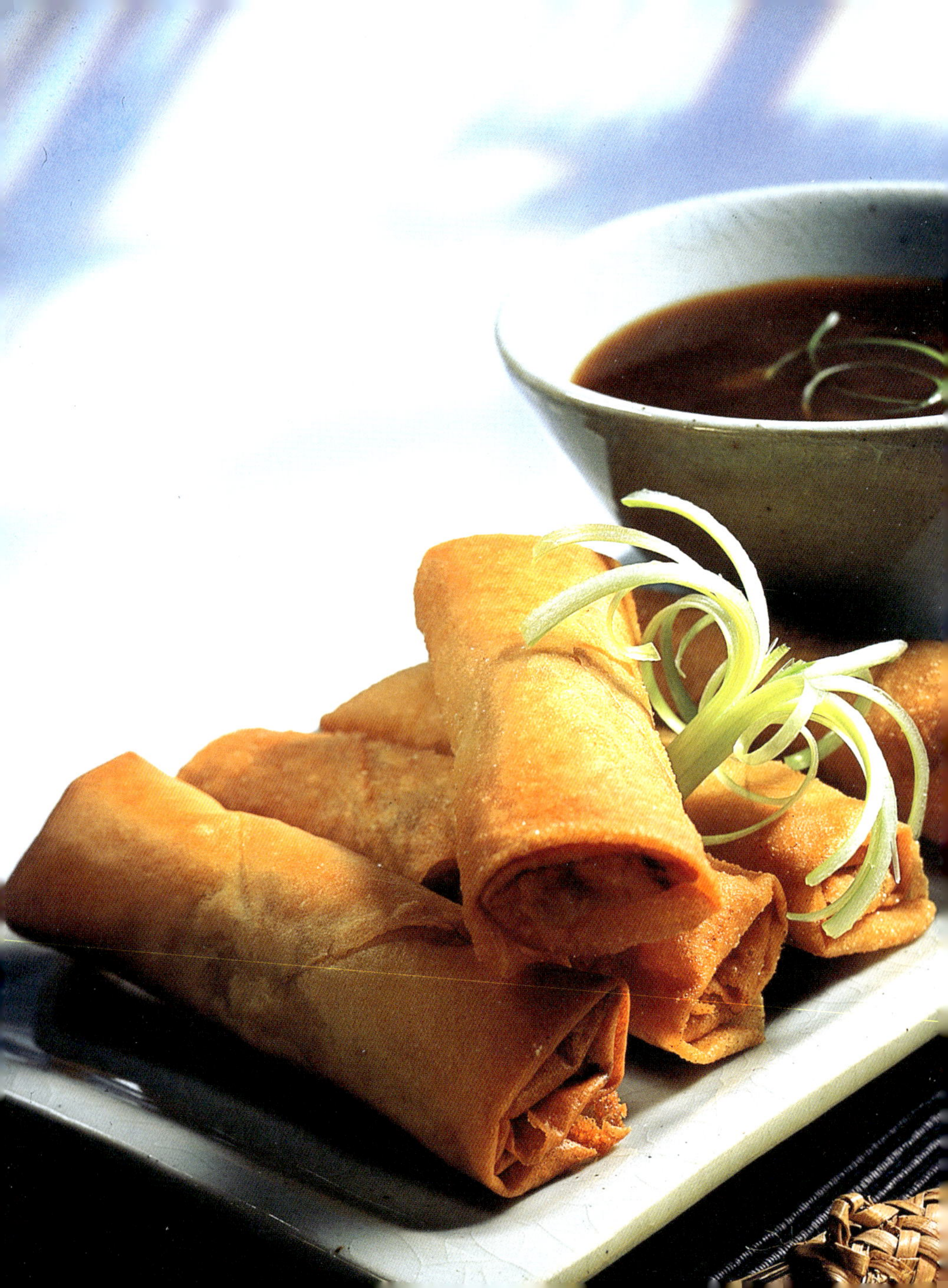

Spring rolls (egg rolls)

MAKES ABOUT 32

1 lb/500g chicken strips
2 tablespoons oil
¾ ins/2cm piece fresh ginger, finely chopped
1 small onion, finely chopped
¼ Chinese cabbage, finely chopped
½ red capsicum, thinly sliced
4 mushrooms, thinly sliced
1 tablespoon soy sauce
2 tablespoons dipping sauce

2 teaspoons cornflour
1 tablespoon water
1 packet frozen spring roll wrappers
oil for deep frying

Dipping sauce
½ cup apricot jam
1 tablespoon soy sauce
1 tablespoon lemon juice
2 tablespoons white vinegar
1 tablespoon water

1. Chop the chicken strips into smaller pieces. Heat the oil in a wok. Add ginger and onion and stir-fry until onion is pale gold. Add chicken and stir-fry until white all over, about 2 minutes. Add the vegetables and mushrooms and stir-fry one minute, mixing chicken through the vegetables.
2. Combine the soy and dipping sauces (see method), and in another bowl mix the cornflour and water together. Add the combined sauces to the wok and mix through the chicken and vegetables. Push the mixture to one side and add blended cornflour to the juices in the base of the wok. As juices thicken, stir and toss through the chicken and vegetables. Spread mixture out onto a flat tray to cool.
3. Wrap one heaped tablespoon of chicken mixture in each spring roll wrapper, according to packet directions. Wipe out the wok, heat and add fresh oil to approximately 2 ins/5cm deep. Heat oil and fry rolls a few at a time until gold and crisp. Drain on absorbent paper.
4. To make dipping sauce, mix all ingredients together and heat gently while stirring. Serve with hot chicken.

Chicken, spinach and cheese pastries

SERVES 4

½ cup brown rice
2 teaspoons oil
4½ oz/125g chicken mince
1 clove garlic, crushed
1 rasher bacon, chopped
1 cup fresh baby spinach
2 spring onions/shallots, sliced
2²/₃ oz/75g Greek fetta cheese, crumbled

¾ oz/20g parmesan cheese, grated
1 egg, beaten
freshly ground black pepper
½ teaspoon ground nutmeg
¼ cup parsley, chopped
4 sheets puff pastry

1. Combine the rice with 1 cup water in a saucepan. Bring to the boil, reduce heat to low, cover and cook for 10 minutes. Remove pan from heat, allow to stand covered for 10 minutes.
2. Heat oil in a pan, add chicken, garlic, bacon and spinach. Cook gently for 2–3 minutes or until onion has softened. Remove from heat, add spring onions and cooked rice. Allow to cool, then drain off excess juice. Combine with cheeses, egg, pepper, nutmeg and parsley.
3. Preheat oven to 390°F/200°C.
4. Using a pastry cutter 4¾ ins/12cm in diameter, cut 4 rounds out of each sheet of pastry. Place a tablespoon of mixture on one half of each pastry round. Fold over and press the edges together. Bake for 10 minutes or until puffed and golden.

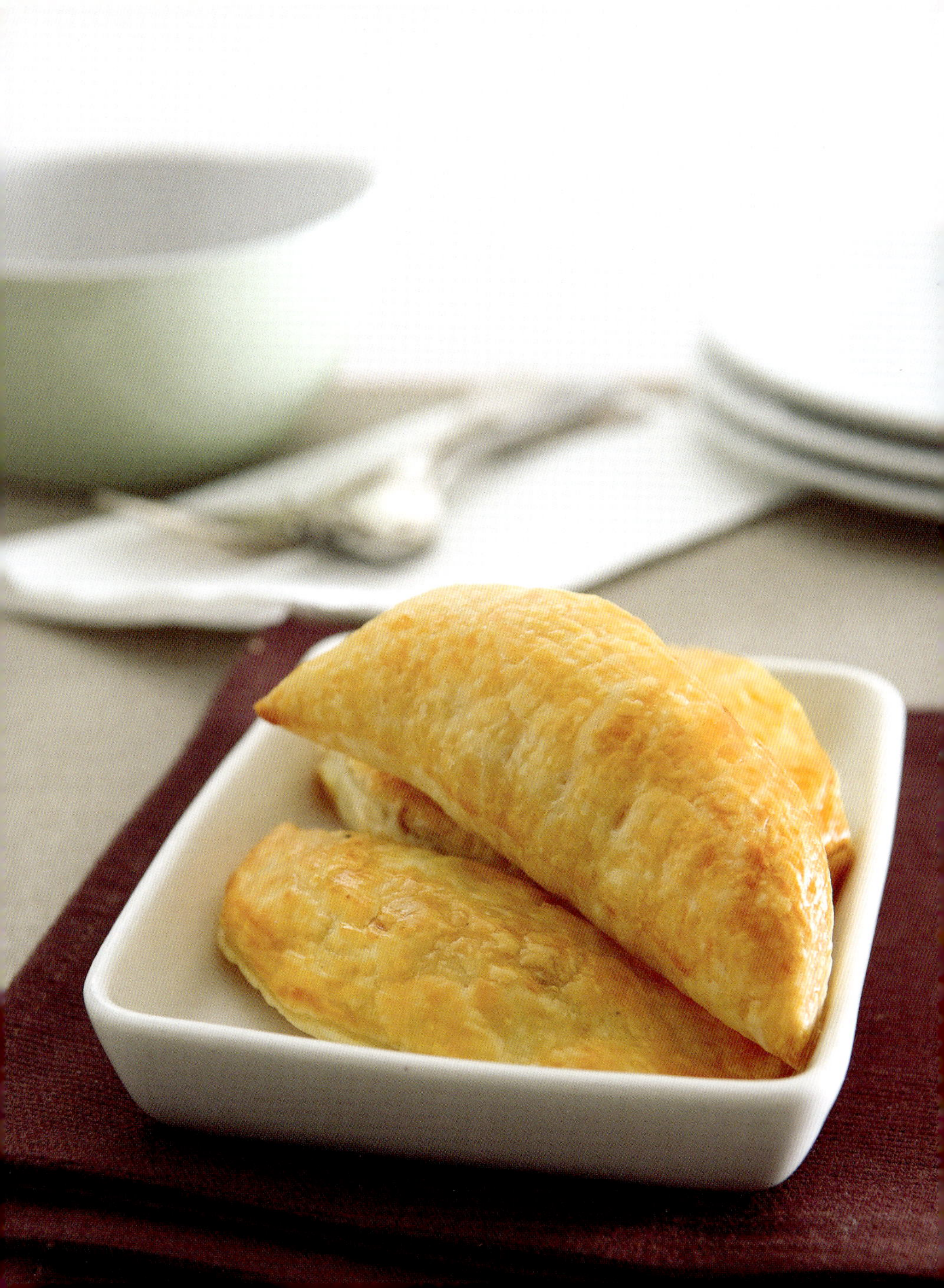

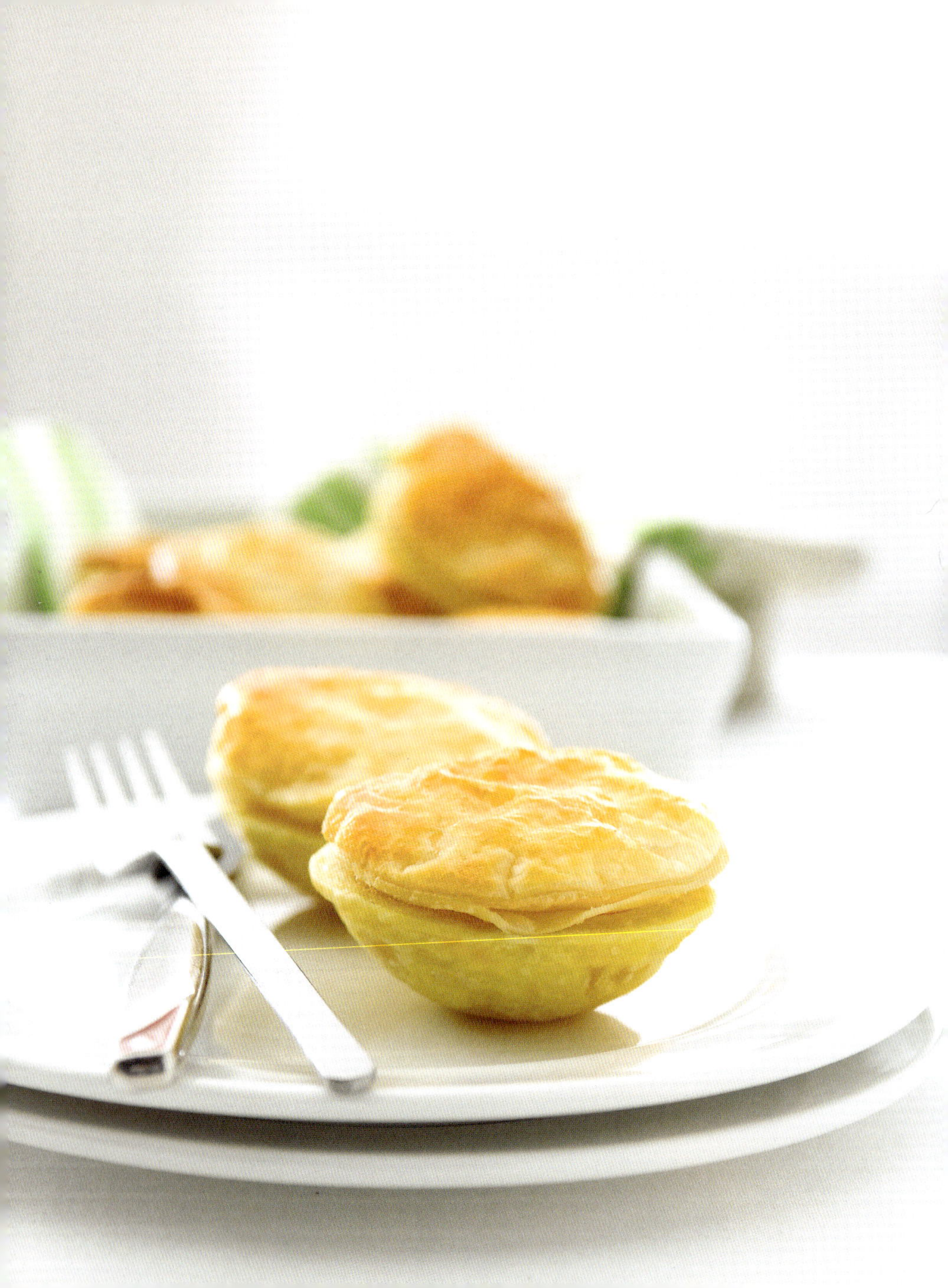

Mini chicken pies

MAKES 24

2 tablespoons olive oil
1 lb/500g chicken mince
4 cloves garlic, crushed
1 teaspoon dill seeds
½ cup parsley, very finely chopped

⅓ cup sour cream
salt and freshly ground black pepper
6 sheets shortcrust pastry
6 sheets puff pastry
1 egg, lightly beaten with dash of milk

1. Preheat oven to 430°F/220°C. Lightly spray 24 paper muffin cases, 2⅓ ins/6cm in diameter, with olive oil spray.
2. Heat the oil in a frying pan. Add chicken mince and cook for 3 minutes. Add garlic and cook for a further minute, add the dill seeds and cook for a further 2 minutes. Transfer to a bowl to cool. Stir in parsley and sour cream, and season with salt and pepper.
3. Cut shortcrust pastry and puff pastry into 2¾ ins/7cm rounds (4 rounds from each sheet). Line paper muffin cases with shortcrust pastry. Divide chicken mixture evenly between cases. Lightly brush edges with water and place puff pastry rounds on top.
4. Using a fork, gently press edges together. Make a slit in the top and brush with egg wash. Bake for 20 minutes or until puffed and golden.

Chicken sausage sticks

SERVES 4

1 lb/500g chicken mince
½ cup dried breadcrumbs
1 medium onion, very finely chopped
¼ cup parsley, chopped
½ teaspoon salt
½ teaspoon pepper

1 clove garlic, crushed
½ teaspoon ground cummin
⅛ teaspoon ground nutmeg
⅛ teaspoon ground cilantro/coriander
oil for cooking
lime wedges

1. Soak 8 bamboo skewers in cold water for at least 30 minutes. Place the mince in a bowl and add all the ingredients except oil and lime wedges. Mix well to combine, then knead, making sure the mince is broken up.
2. With wet hands, take a handful of mince and mould around each skewer.
3. Heat barbecue to medium and lightly oil the grill bars. Place the sausage sticks on the grill and cook for 15 minutes, turning frequently until cooked through. Serve with lime wedges.

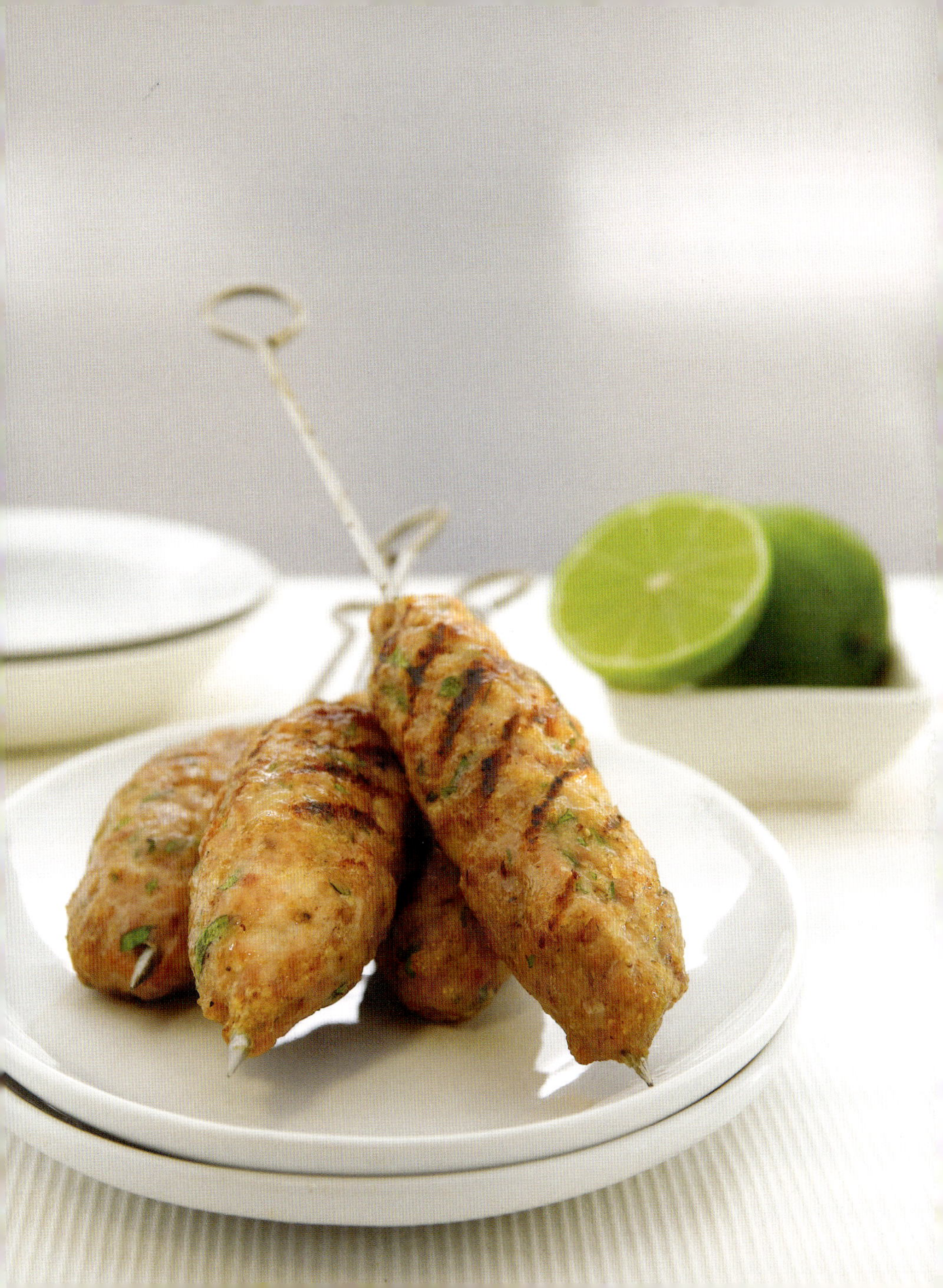

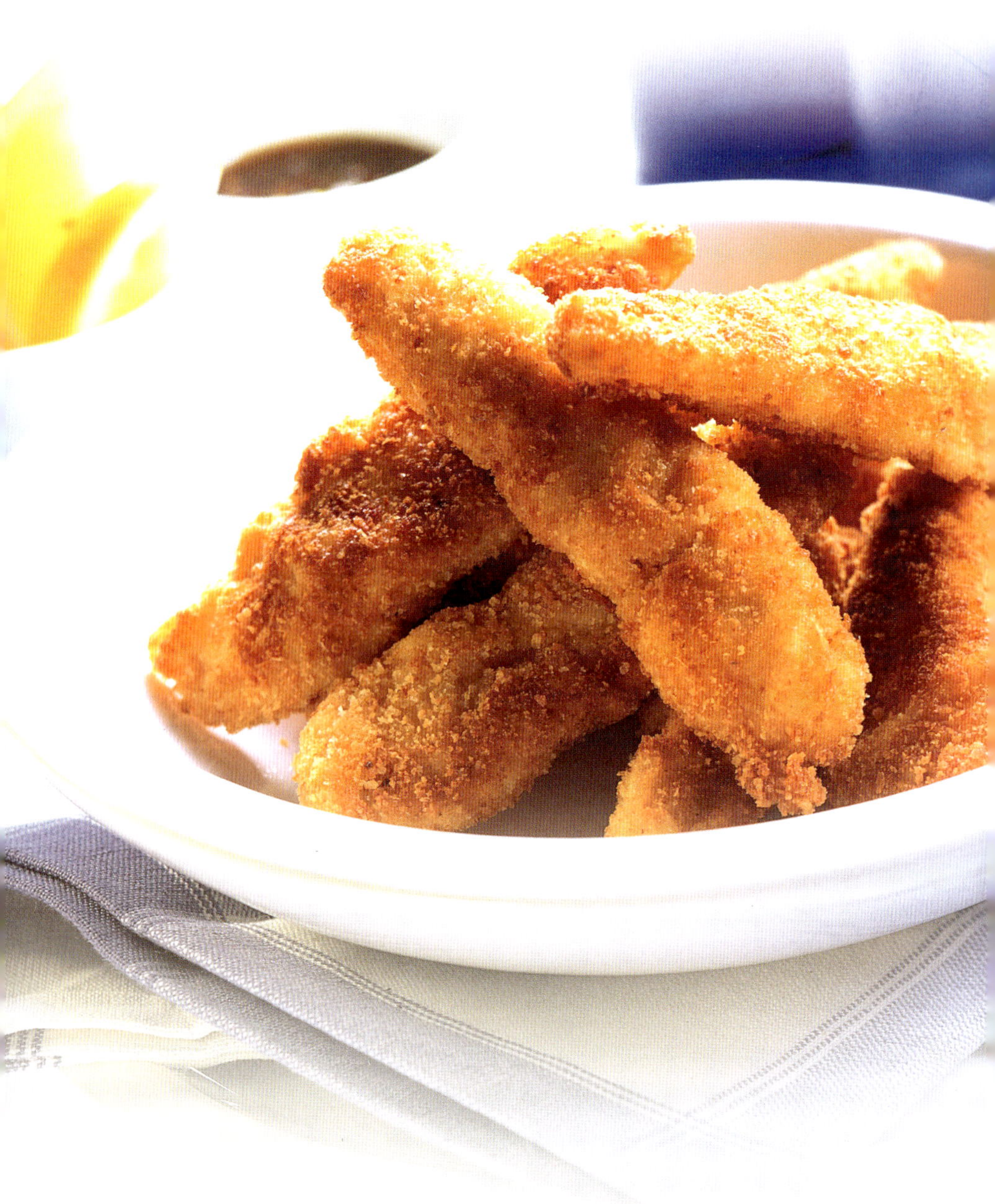

Chicken fingers

SERVES 4

2 lbs/1kg chicken tenderloins
1 clove garlic, crushed
2 tablespoons lemon juice
½ teaspoon salt
¼ teaspoon pepper
1 cup all-purpose/plain flour
2 eggs, beaten with 1 tablespoon water

1½ cups dried breadcrumbs
½ cup canola oil
Dipping sauce
½ cup sweet chili sauce
1 teaspoon soy sauce
1 tablespoon honey

1. Place tenderloins in a large non-metallic dish. Add garlic, lemon juice, salt and pepper and marinate for one hour. Remove from marinade and coat with flour. Dip into the egg then cover with breadcrumbs, making sure to press crumbs on firmly. Place in a single layer on a flat tray. Refrigerate until ready for use.
2. Add enough oil to cover the base of a large frying pan and heat. Test with a piece of chicken – if it sizzles, the oil is ready. Add one layer of tenderloins and fry about two minutes each side until golden. Remove and drain on absorbent paper. Add more oil if necessary and cook the remainder. Place chicken on a large platter.
3. To make dipping sauce, combine the sweet chili sauce, soy sauce and honey together. Serve chicken with dipping sauce on the side.

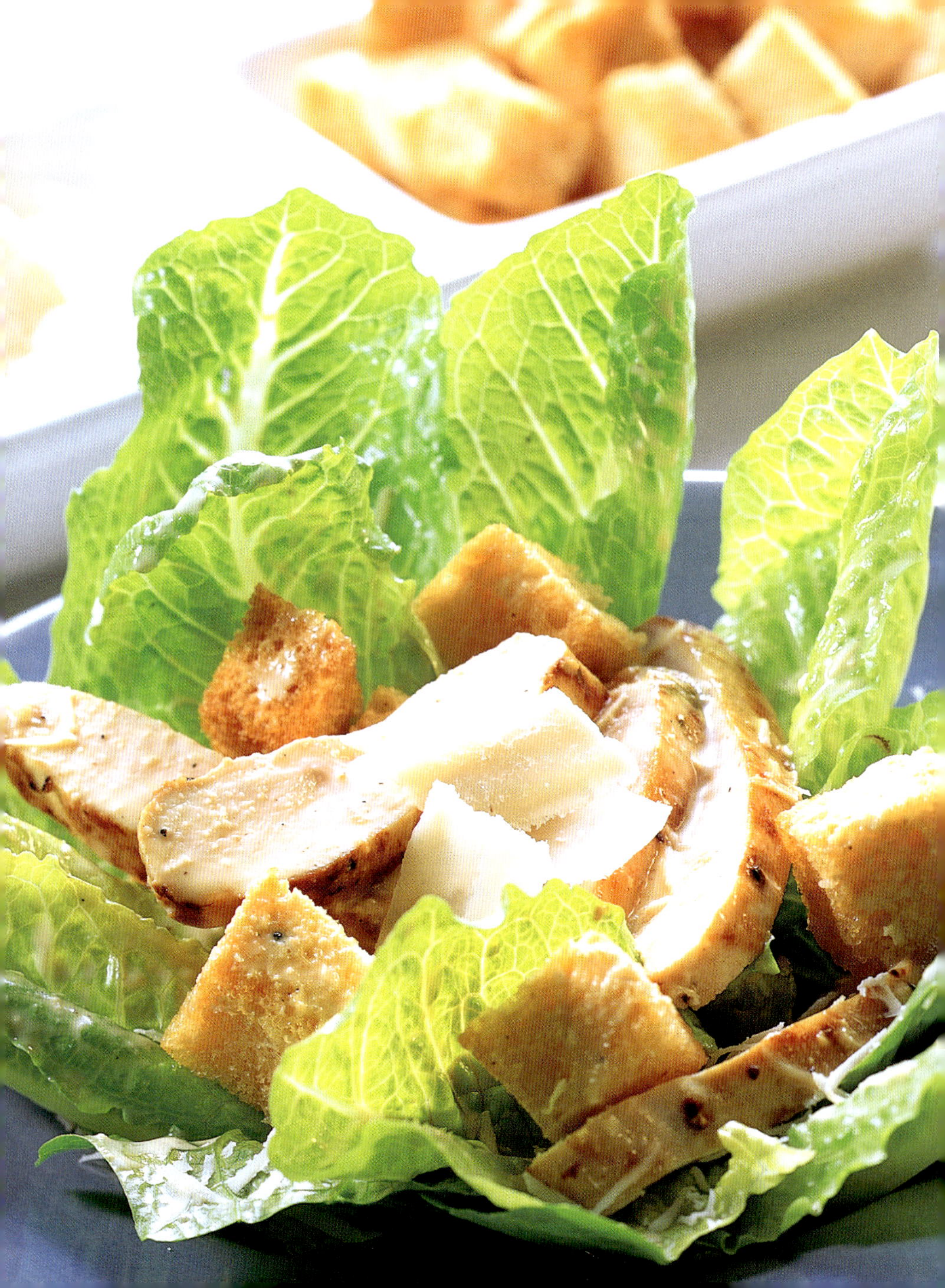

salads

Marinated chicken salad

SERVES 4

1 lb/500g chicken strips
1½ cups seasoned flour
2 cups vegetable oil
¼ cup orange juice
¼ cup olive oil
¼ cup mint, chopped

½ teaspoon salt
freshly ground black pepper
1 avocado
15 oz/425g canned apricots
3½ oz/100g snowpea sprouts

1. Dip the chicken strips in the flour a few at a time. Heat oil in a deep frying pan and deep-fry the chicken until cooked and golden. Drain on absorbent paper, then place in a glass bowl.
2. Combine orange juice, oil, mint, salt and pepper in a screw-top jar and shake well. Pour over chicken strips and refrigerate for a minimum of 30 minutes.
3. Slice avocado and drain apricot halves, reserving two tablespoons of juice from the can. Arrange sprouts on individual plates. Top with chicken strips, avocado pieces and apricot halves. Add about 1–2 teaspoons juice to remaining marinade and drizzle over salad. Serve with crusty bread.

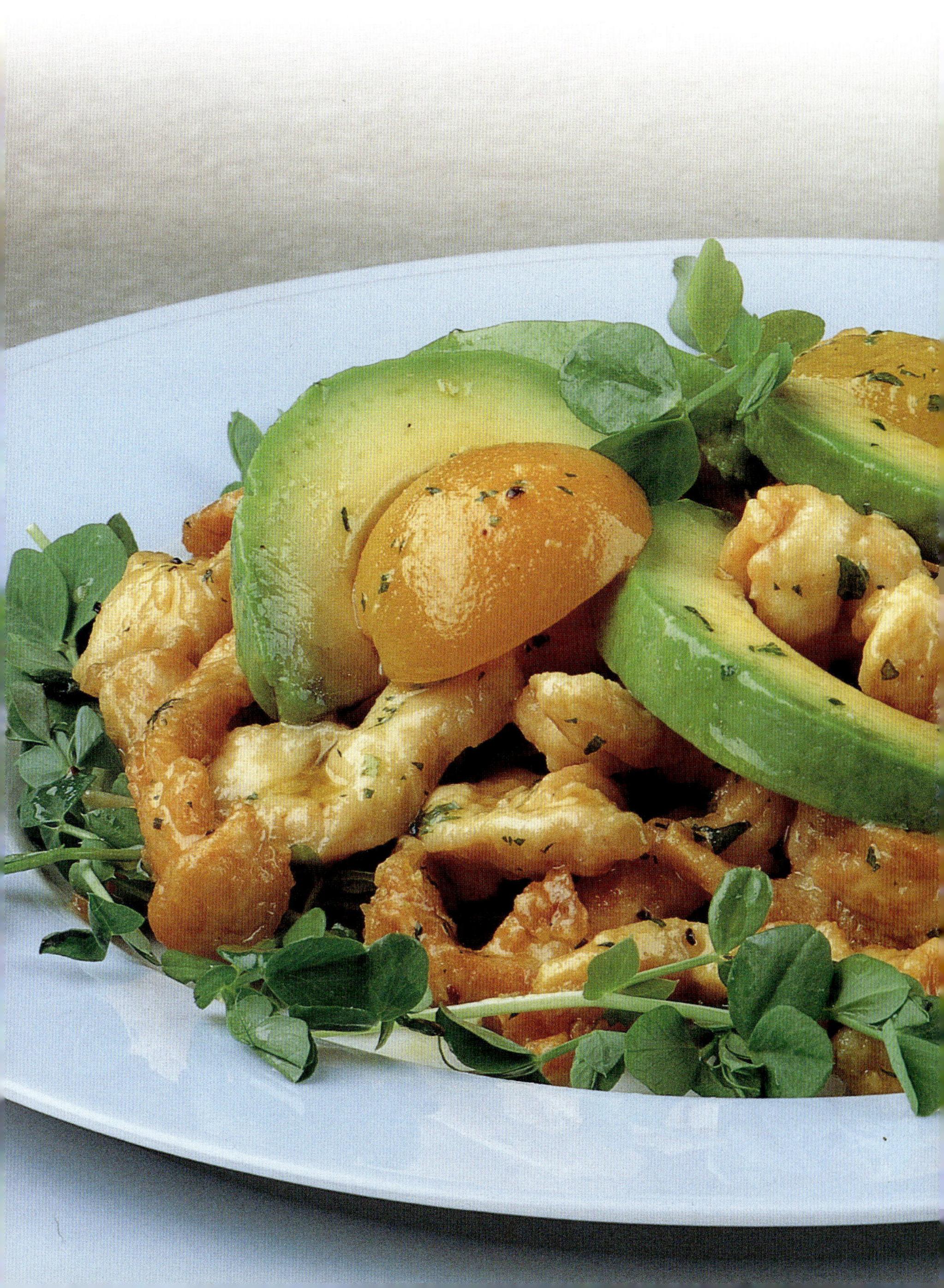

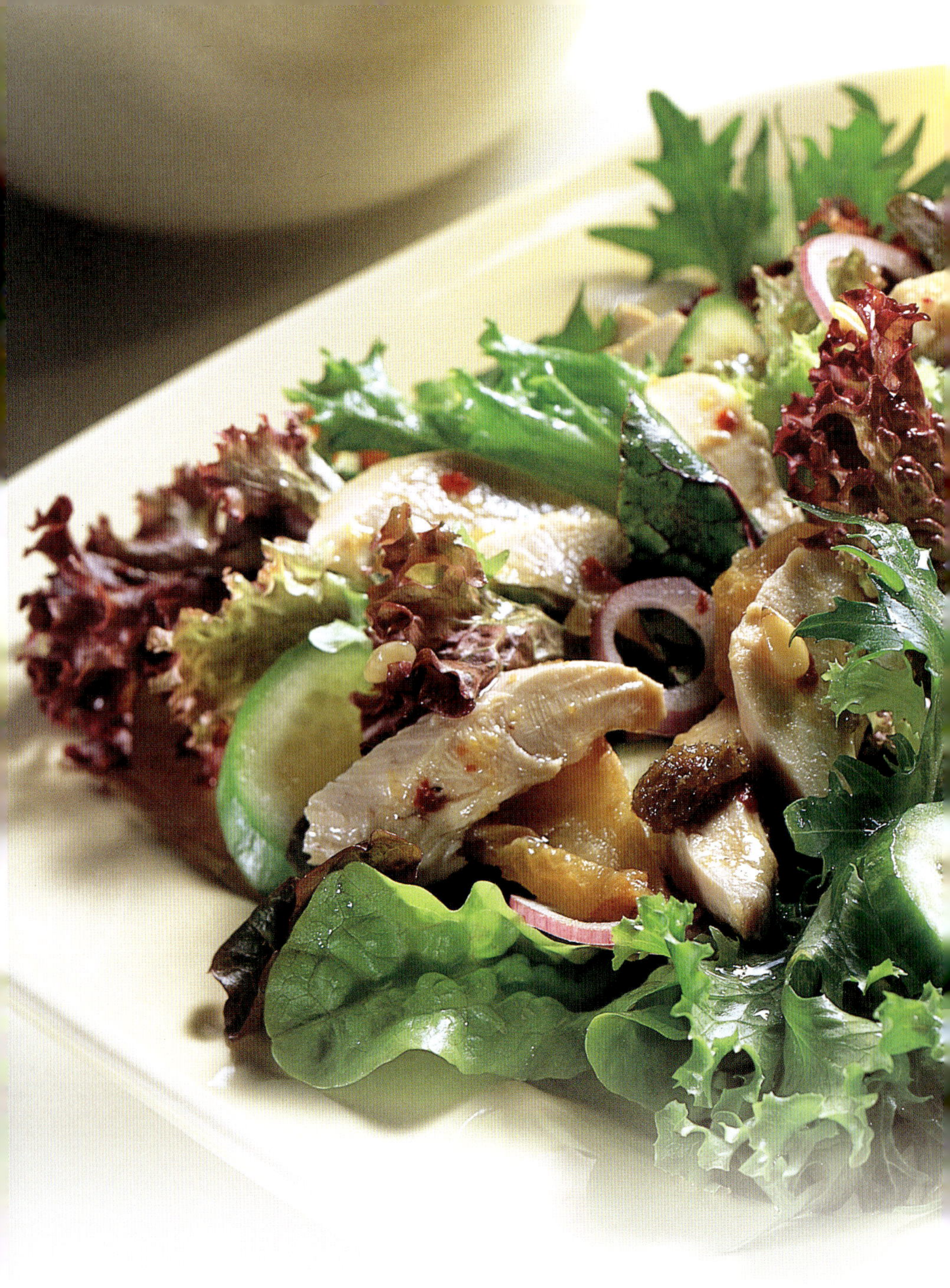

Chicken and pear salad

SERVES 4

1 cooked chicken
7 oz/200g dried pears
12 oz/300g mixed salad greens
1 Lebanese cucumber, thinly sliced
½ red onion, sliced

Marinade
½ cup olive oil
½ cup orange juice
2 tablespoons red wine vinegar
3 whole cloves
3 small bay leaves
2 tablespoons pine nuts
¼ cup raisins
1 teaspoon sweet chili sauce

1. Remove the flesh from the chicken, slice into bite-size pieces. Place in a wide, non-metallic dish and place dried pears on top.
2. Mix marinade ingredients together, pour over chicken and pears and refrigerate for 2 hours.
3. Place salad greens, cucumber and onion on serving plate, arrange the chicken and pears on the salad. Whisk the remaining marinade with a little extra oil and spoon over the salad.

Chicken caesar salad

SERVES 4

2 chicken breast fillets
1 clove garlic, crushed
salt and pepper
2 teaspoons olive oil
1 tablespoon lemon juice
1 cos lettuce
Dressing
2 anchovy fillets
4 tablespoons olive oil

2½ tablespoons lemon juice
½ teaspoon salt
¼ teaspoon pepper
1 lightly boiled/coddled egg
¼ teaspoon mustard
1 teaspoon Worcestershire sauce
1½ oz/40g parmesan cheese, grated, plus 1½ oz/40g shaved
1 cup garlic croutons

1. Trim the chicken fillets. Mix together the garlic, salt, pepper, oil and lemon juice, pour over the chicken, cover and marinate for 30 minutes in the refrigerator. Heat grill or chargrill until hot. Sear the fillets one minute on each side, then cook 3 minutes each side. Remove and rest for 5 minutes before cutting into ¼ ins/5mm slices on the diagonal.
2. Separate the leaves of the lettuce, discard outer leaves and wash well. Drain and shake dry in a clean tea towel. Cut greener leaves into bite-size pieces and leave the pale inner leaves whole. Cover and place in refrigerator until ready for use.
3. Place the anchovy in the base of a salad bowl and mash while adding the oil. Gradually add the lemon juice while whisking, and sprinkle in the salt and pepper. Break in the egg, scraping the set white from inside the shell, and lightly stir. Add the mustard and Worcestershire sauce.
4. Add the lettuce leaves and toss to coat lightly with dressing while sprinkling over the grated parmesan cheese. Toss in the chicken and croutons. Rearrange the whole leaves to stand upright and garnish with shaved parmesan cheese. Serve immediately.

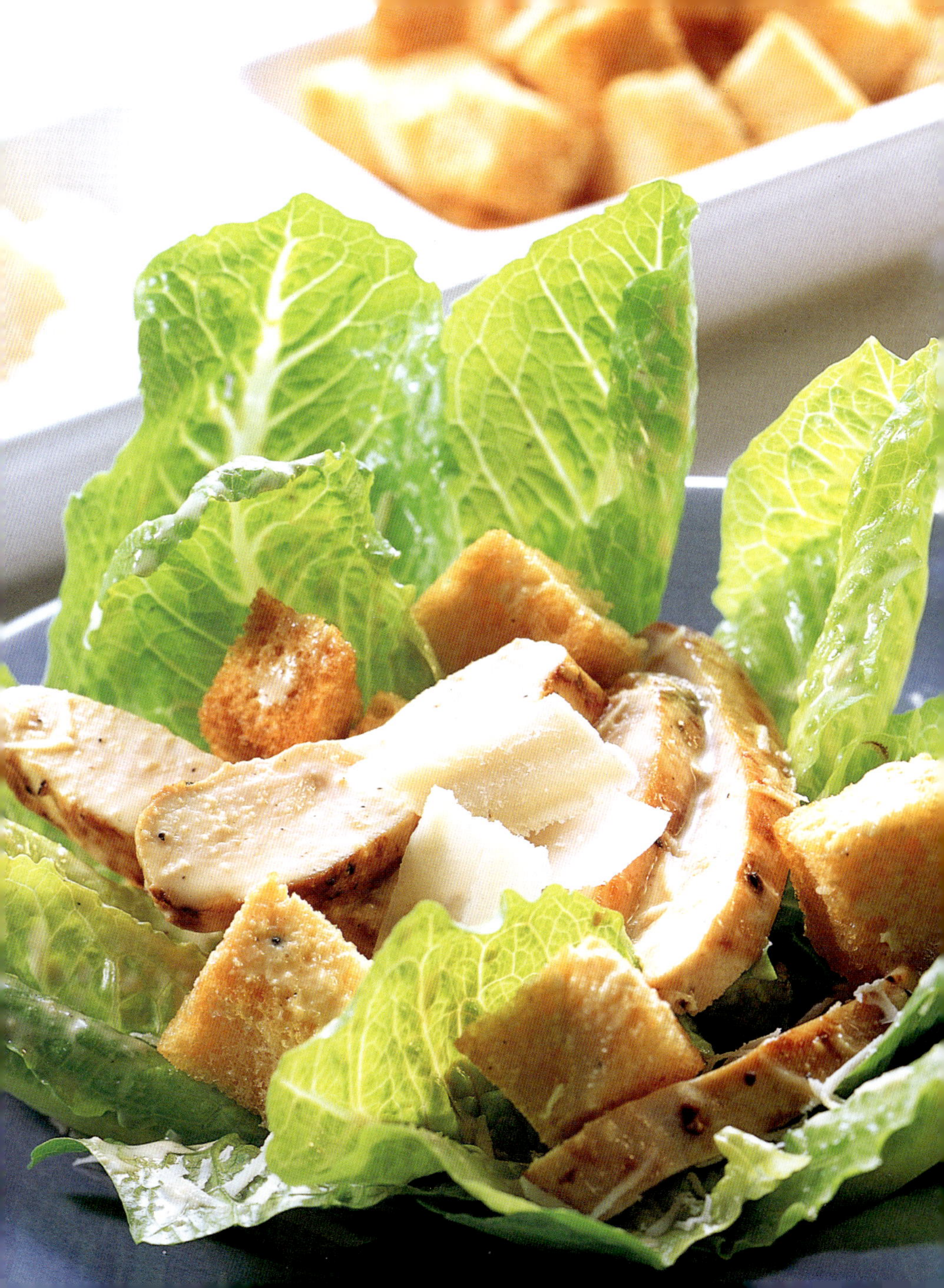

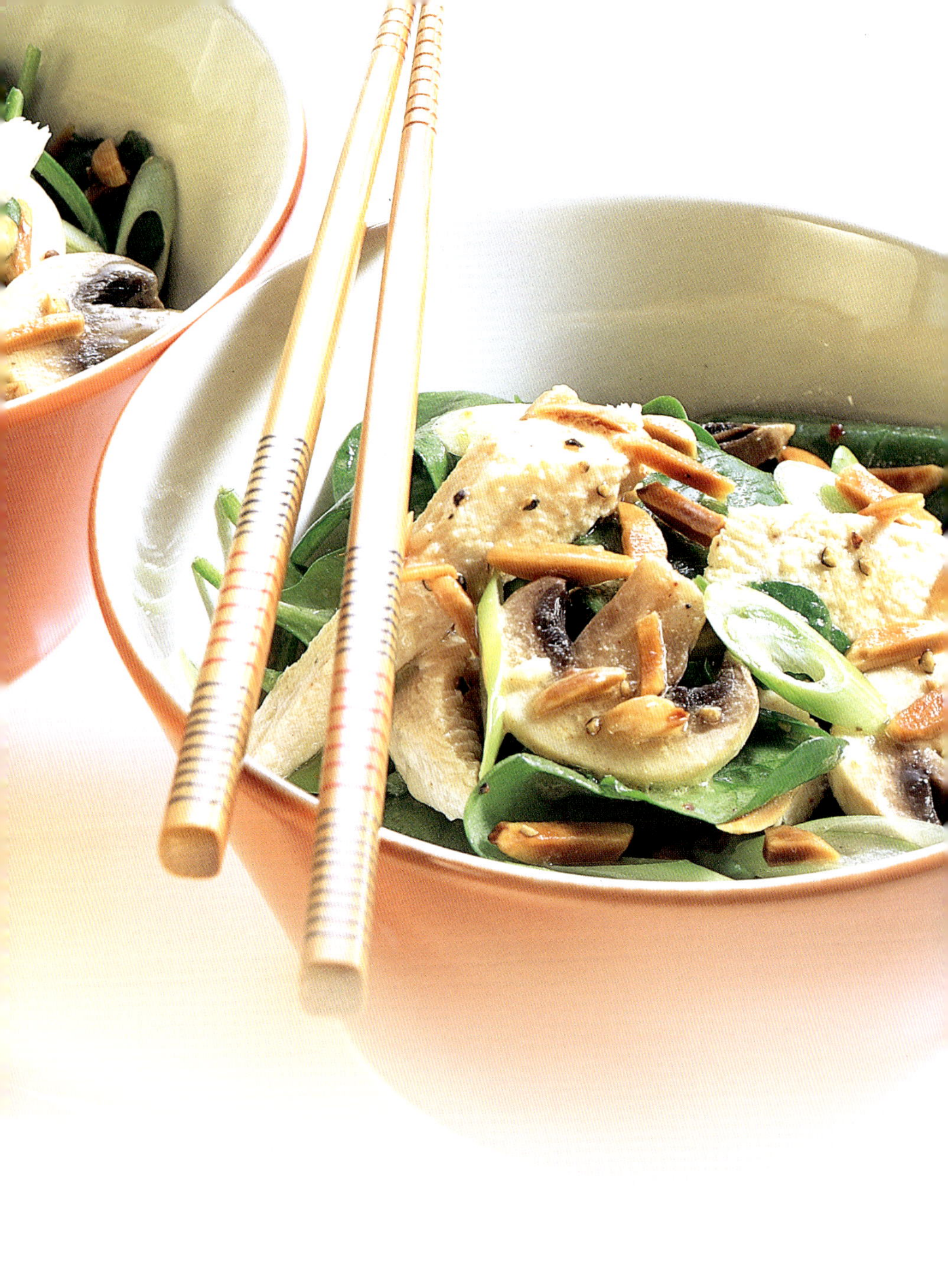

Spinach and almond chicken salad

SERVES 4

2 chicken breast fillets, poached
5¼ oz/150g button mushrooms, sliced
14 oz/400g baby spinach leaves
6 spring onions/shallots, sliced
3½oz/100g slivered almonds, toasted
Dressing
½ cup olive oil

2 tablespoons lemon juice
1 tablespoon white wine vinegar
1 clove garlic, crushed
2 teaspoons Dijon mustard
½ teaspoon brown sugar
salt and pepper
⅛ teaspoon nutmeg

1. Poach the chicken breasts (see note below), cool a little so they can be handled, then slice into long strips.
2. Mix together the mushrooms, spinach and spring onions. Add the chicken and toss with the vegetables.
3. Whisk all the dressing ingredients together and pour over salad. Add half the almonds and toss through.
   Scatter remaining almonds over top of salad. Serve immediately with crusty bread.

To poach chicken, cover breast fillets with hot water, add a little salt, a small chopped onion, a piece of celery and a carrot. Bring to a simmer and cook gently for 20–25 minutes until tender. Remove chicken to cool. Strain stock and reserve for future use. Discard the vegetables.

Chicken waldorf salad

SERVES 4

1 chicken breast fillet, poached
2 red apples
1 tablespoon lemon juice
2 stalks celery, diced

2 oz/60g walnuts, coarsely chopped
½ cup mayonnaise
1 lettuce, separated into cups

1. Poach chicken breasts (see Spinach and almond chicken salad), and cool. Cut into ½ ins/1cm cubes. Wash apples well, leave skin on and cut into ½ ins/1cm cubes. Sprinkle with lemon juice.
2. Toss chicken, apples, celery and walnuts together. Add mayonnaise and gently mix through.
3. Spoon into the lettuce cups and serve, or line a salad bowl with lettuce leaves and pile salad into the centre.

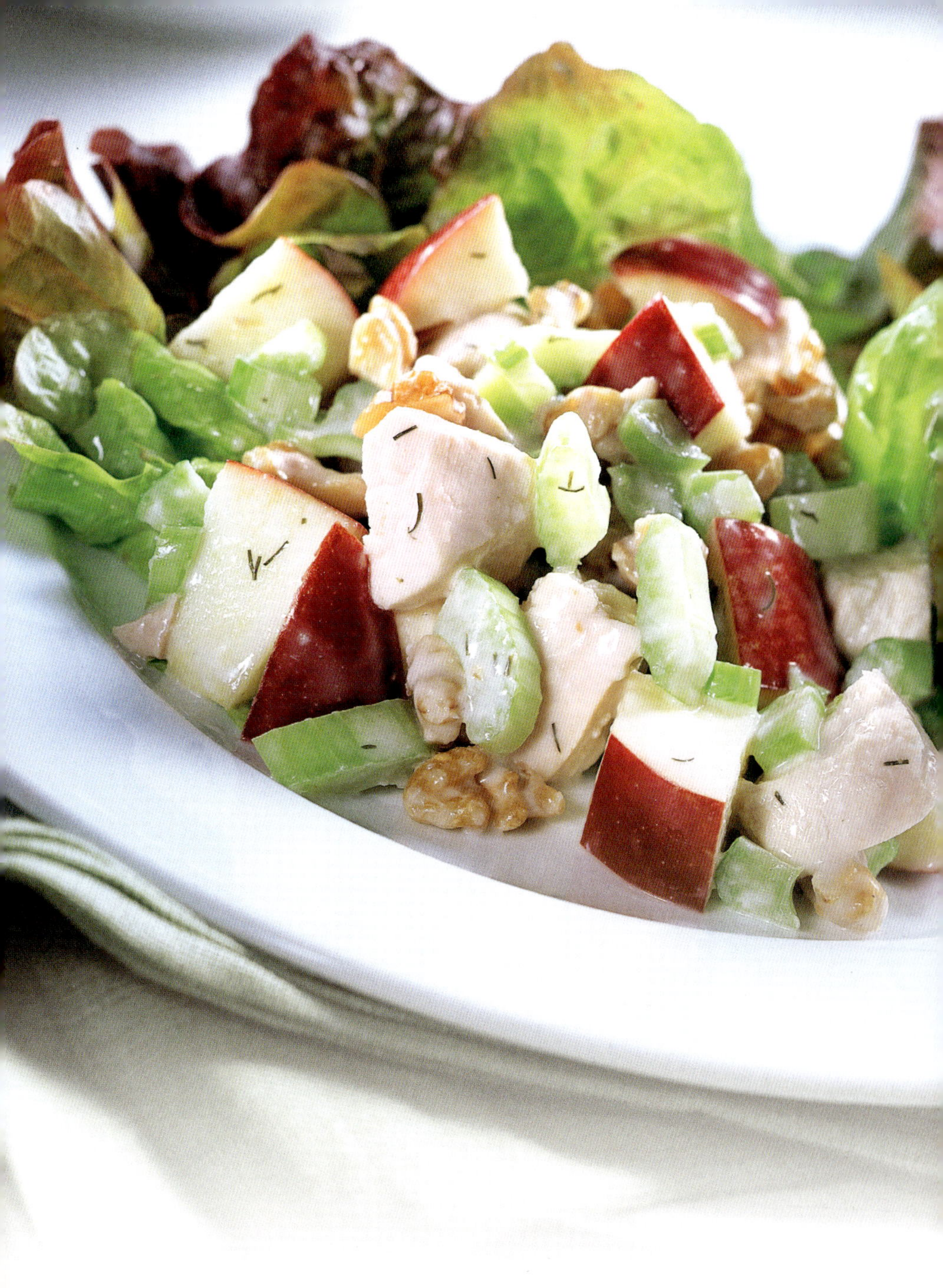

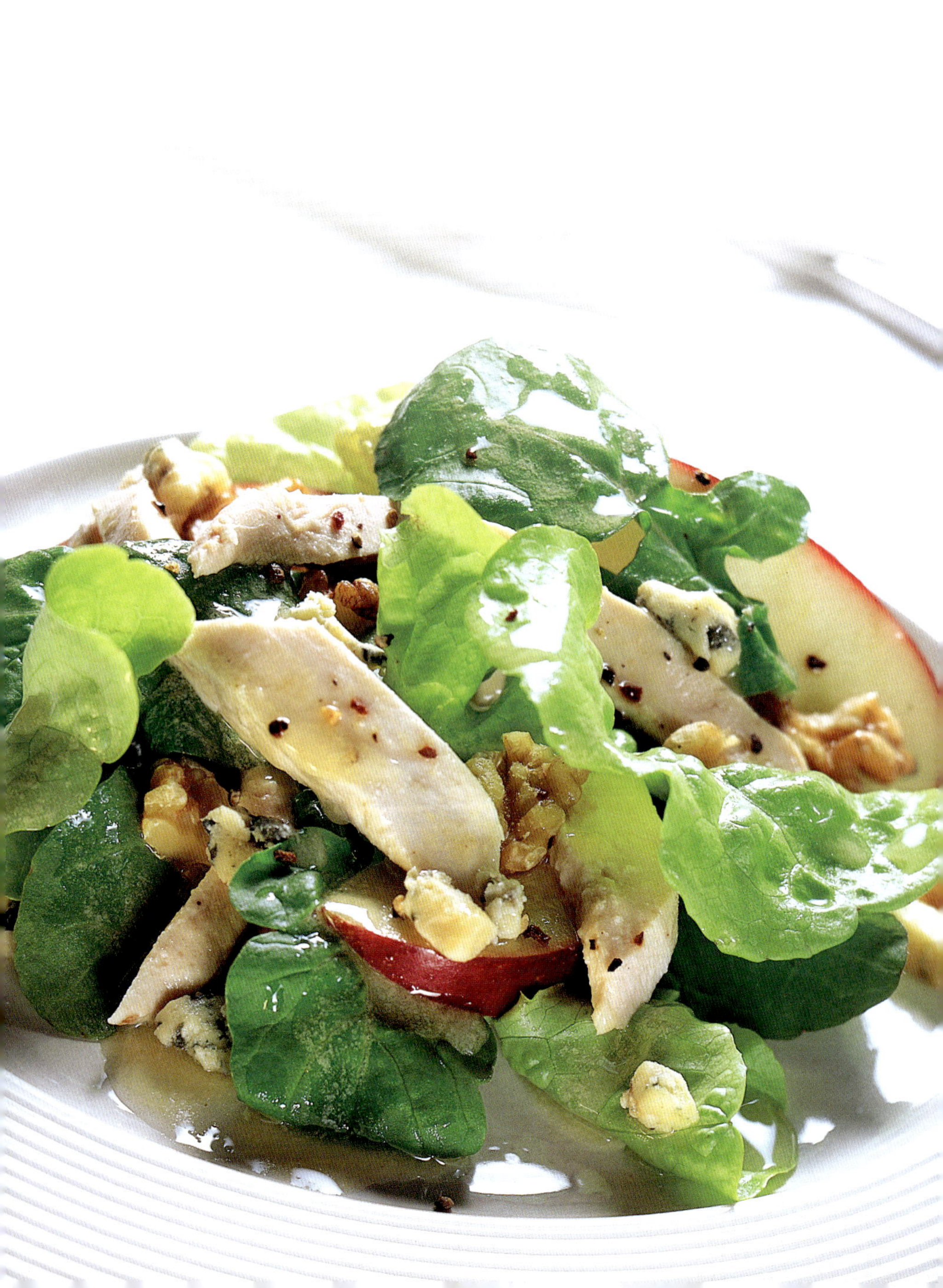

Warm chicken and blue cheese salad

SERVES 4

2 skinless chicken breast fillets, poached
1 bunch arugula/rocket
1 coral lettuce
1 mignonette lettuce
1 red apple, cored, thinly sliced, splashed with lemon juice
2 oz/60g walnut pieces

Dressing
⅓ cup olive oil
2 tablespoons white wine vinegar
1 tablespoon lemon juice
¼ teaspoon sugar
1 tablespoon Dijon mustard
pinch of cayenne pepper
3½ oz/100g blue cheese, crumbled

1. Poach the chicken breasts (see Spinach and almond chicken salad), cool a little so they can be handled, and cut into slices.
2. Wash greens, drain and shake in a tea towel to dry. Arrange on 4 individual plates with apple slices and half the walnuts.
3. Arrange the chicken with salad greens. Whisk the oil, vinegar, lemon juice, sugar, mustard, cayenne and ⅓ of the cheese together and pour over each salad. Sprinkle with remaining walnuts and blue cheese.

Crunchy chicken and potato salad

SERVES 4

7 oz/200g chicken mince
1 lb/500g potatoes
1 teaspoon salt
1 tablespoon olive oil
1 large onion, finely chopped
1 clove garlic, crushed

1 tablespoon lemon juice
salt and pepper
1 cup mayonnaise
1 small red chili, deseeded and finely chopped
dill and lettuce leaves to serve (optional)

1. Remove the chicken from refrigerator and bring to room temperature. Wash and peel potatoes and cut into wedges. Place in boiling water to cover, add salt and cook for 20 minutes. Drain and cool.
2. Heat oil in a large frying pan, add onion and garlic and fry until onion is soft. Stir in chicken mince and brown, stirring continuously. This will take about 15 minutes. Add lemon juice and stir up cooked pan juices. When mince is brown and crumbly, season with a little salt and pepper, remove from heat and cool.
3. Mix cooled potatoes, ⅔ of the crumbly mince and the mayonnaise together gently, tossing in the chopped chili. Pile into a salad bowl or platter and place remaining chicken mince in a pile on the top. Garnish with dill and surround with small lettuce leaves if desired.

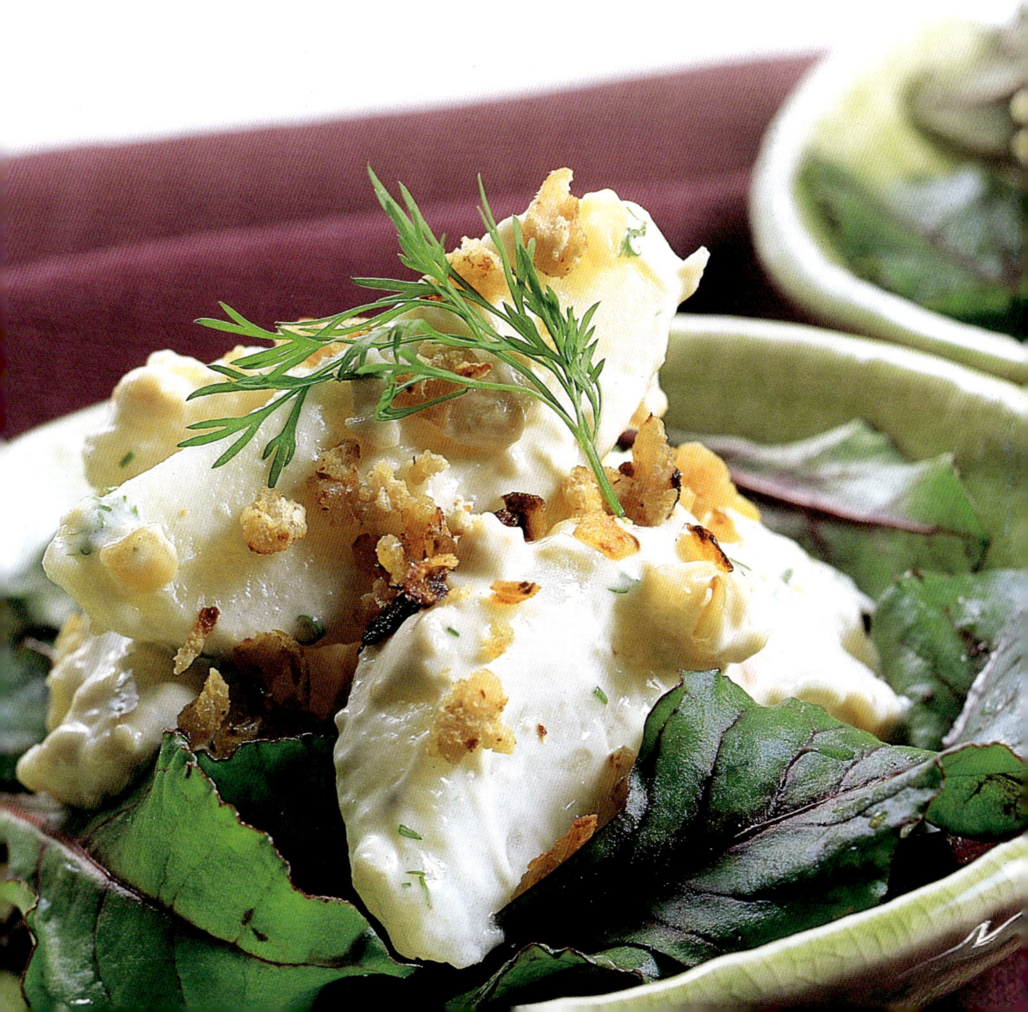

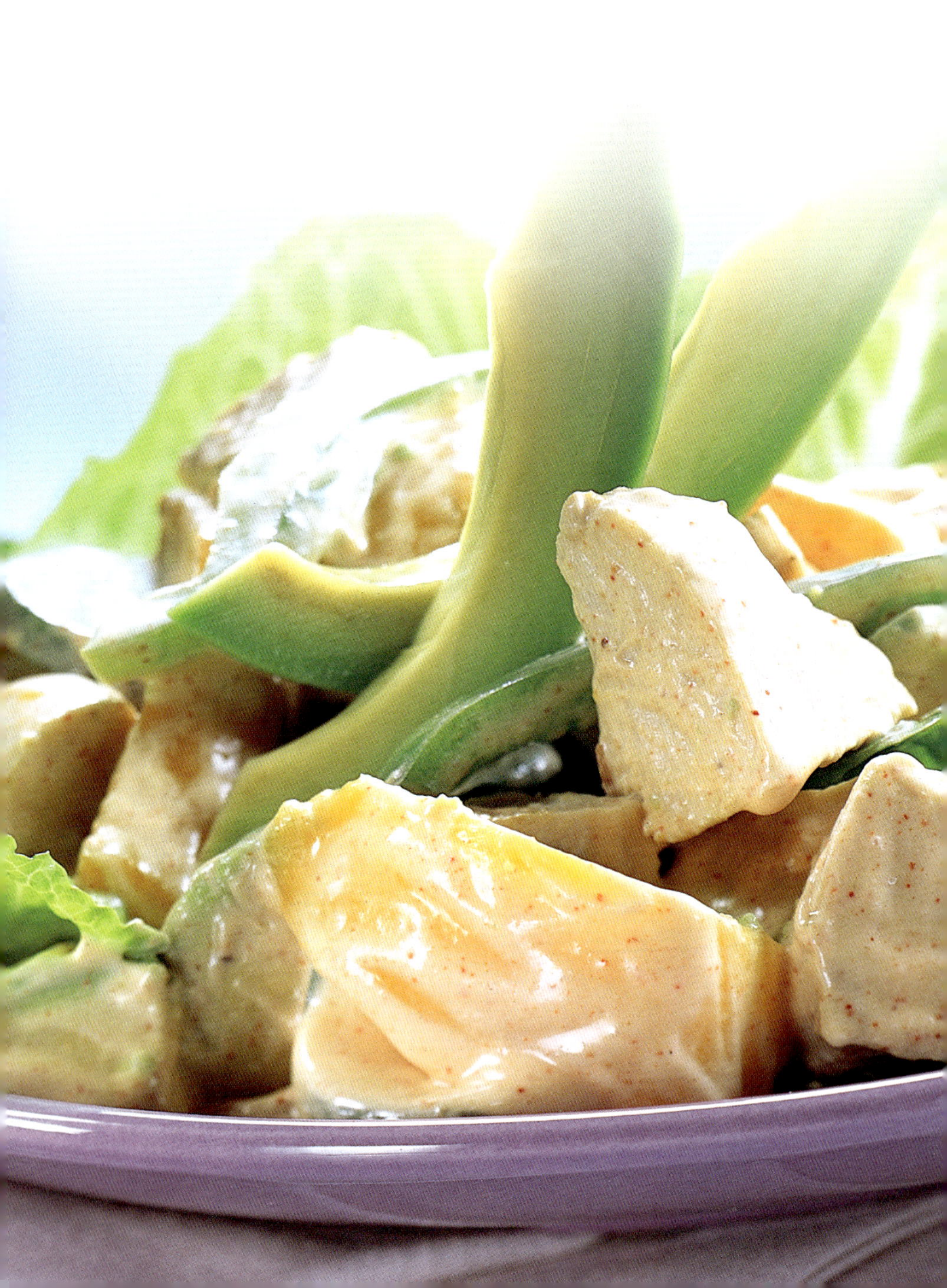

Avocado and chicken salad

SERVES 4

1 lb/500g chicken breast fillets
1 avocado
1 tablespoon lemon juice
1 stalk celery, thinly sliced
1 oz/30g slivered almonds, toasted
½ green bell pepper/capsicum, cut into slices
½ fresh mango, sliced

1 Lebanese cucumber, sliced
1 small lettuce

Dressing
½ cup thickened cream, whipped
¼ cup mayonnaise
¼ teaspoon grated nutmeg
½ teaspoon paprika
salt and pepper

1. Poach chicken breasts (see Spinach and almond chicken salad), cool a little so they can be handled, then cut into ¾ ins/2cm cubes. Peel and slice avocado, sprinkle with lemon juice. Combine the chicken, celery, almonds, bell pepper and most of the avocado, mango and cucumber.
2. Mix the cream, mayonnaise, spices and seasoning together, pour over the salad and toss gently. Arrange lettuce leaves on a shallow platter and pile on the chicken mixture. Garnish with reserved avocado, mango and cucumber.

Curried chicken salad

SERVES 4

1 cooked chicken
2 stalks celery, finely chopped
6 spring onions/shallots, sliced
1/3 cup raisins, soaked
2 oz/60g slivered almonds, toasted
7 oz/200g mixed salad greens

Dressing
½ cup mayonnaise
½ cup low-fat yoghurt

3 tablespoons sweet mango chutney
1 tablespoon mild curry paste
2 tablespoons lemon juice
zest of 2 lemons, grated
fresh fruit and toasted shredded coconut, to serve (optional)

1. Remove the chicken meat from the bones and cut into bite-size pieces. Toss with the celery, spring onions, raisins and almonds. Place all dressing ingredients in a bowl and whisk until smooth.
2. Pour dressing over chicken, toss to mix through. Cover and chill 2 hours or more. Line platter or individual plates with salad greens and pile on the chicken mixture.
3. Garnish with fresh fruits of your choice (we used mango). Sprinkle top of salad with toasted shredded coconut.

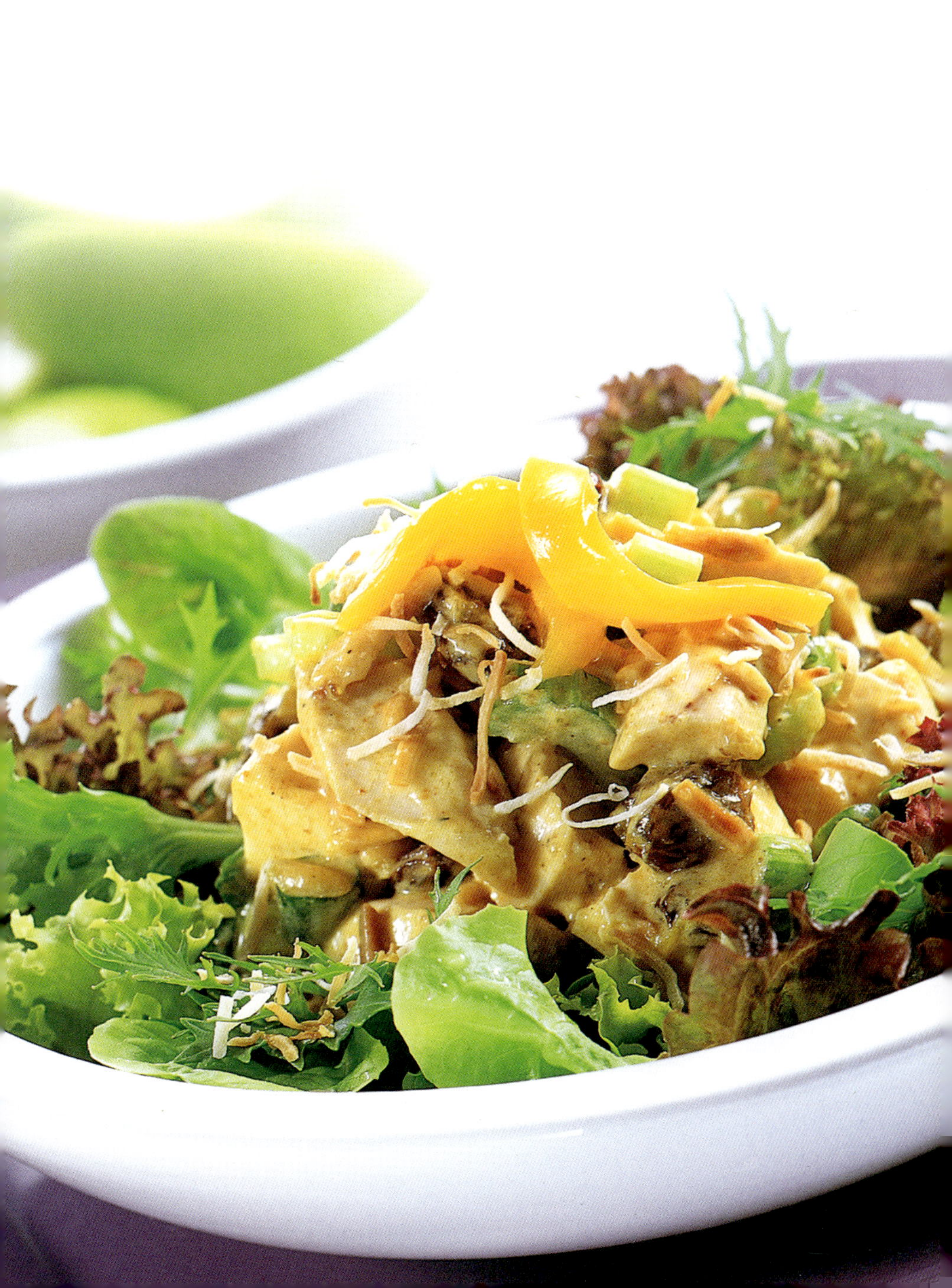

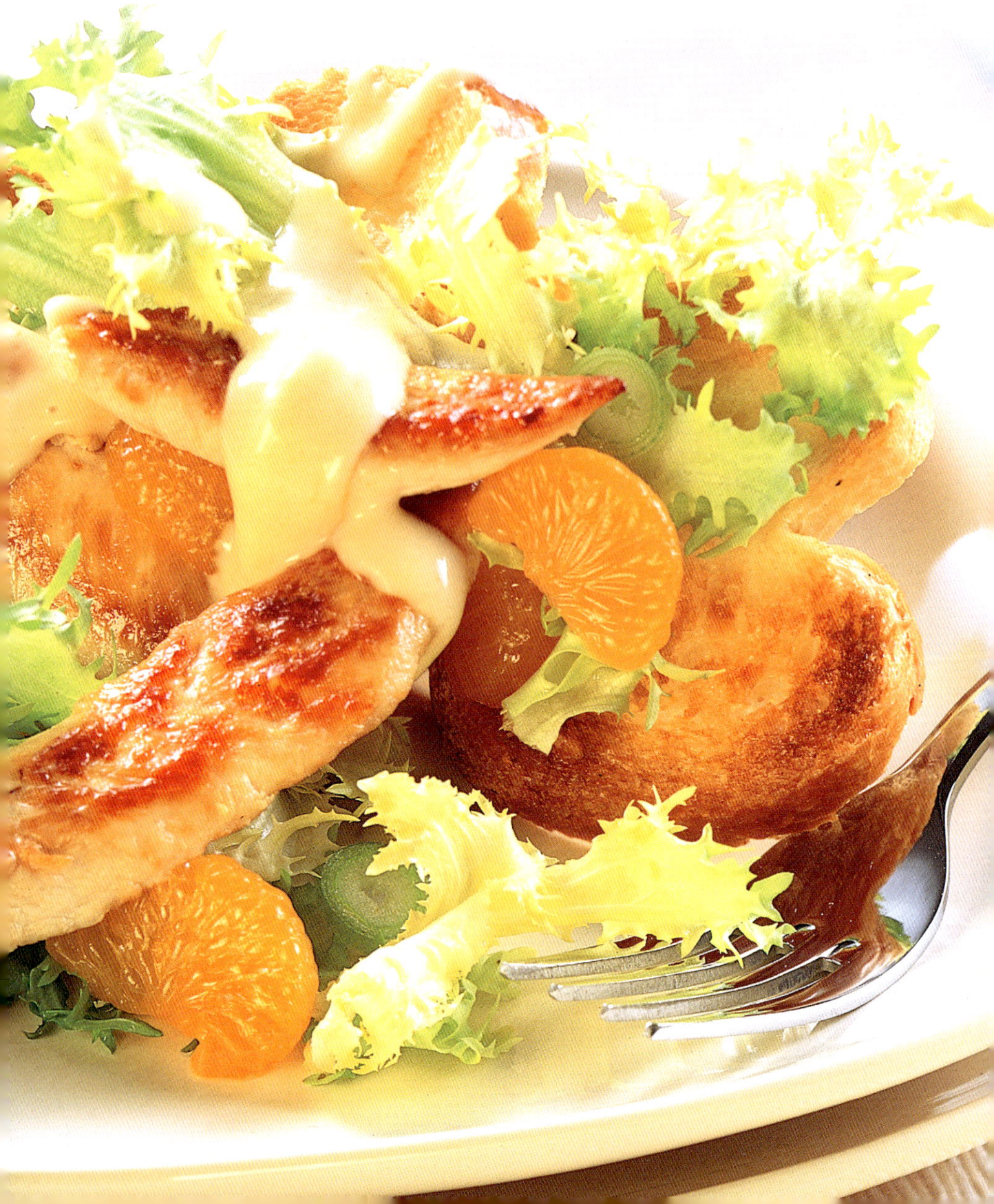

Chicken and endive salad with creamy dressing

SERVES 4

9 oz/250g chicken tenderloins
1 baguette
1 clove garlic, crushed
2 tablespoons oil
8½ oz/240g canned mandarin segments
1 bunch curly endive

4 spring onions/shallots, sliced
Dressing
1 cup coleslaw dressing
1 teaspoon Dijon mustard

1. Cook tenderloins in a lightly oiled non-stick pan for 2 minutes on each side.
2. Cut baguette into ¼ ins/5mm slices. Mix garlic and oil together and brush onto bread slices. Place on a tray in a moderate oven at 340°F/170°C and cook until crisp and golden. Drain the mandarins, reserving the juice. Break endive into 2 ins/5cm pieces, mix with spring onions and mandarin segments.
3. Mound the croutons and endive salad onto individual serving plates and arrange chicken on top. Mix dressing ingredients together and pour on top, allowing it to run down the sides.

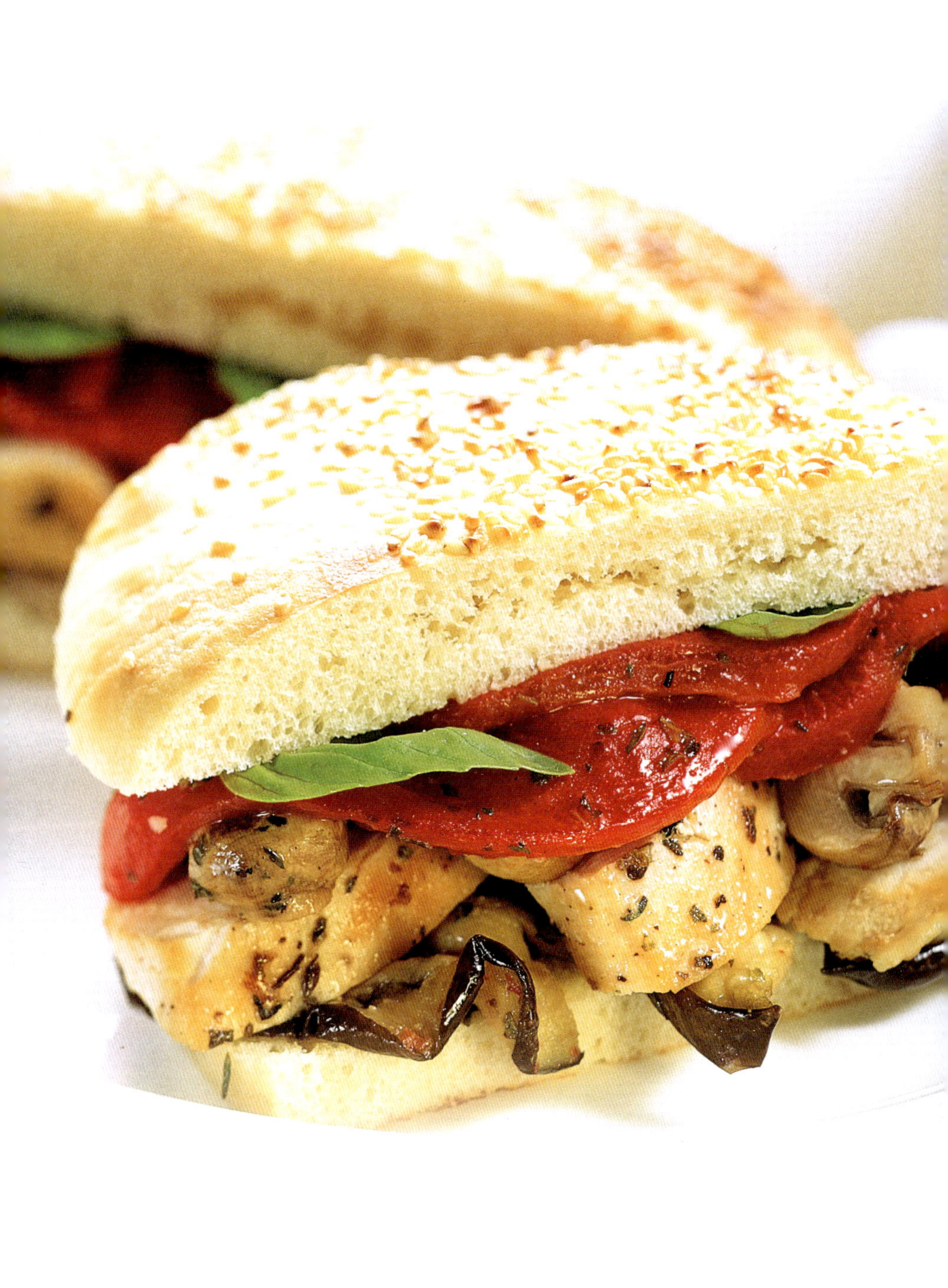

sandwiches and wraps

Lavash rolls

SERVES 4

*1 lb/500g chicken tenderloins
canola oil spray
4 pieces lavash bread
1 cup mayonnaise
1 small lettuce, shredded
½ bunch spring onions/shallots, chopped*

*2 tomatoes, sliced
1 Lebanese cucumber, sliced
½ cup hummus
2 tablespoons lemon juice
salt and pepper*

1. Trim any excess fat from the chicken. Spray a heated non-stick pan with oil spray and cook tenderloins for 2 minutes on each side.
2. Place each lavash sheet on the bench and spread lightly with mayonnaise. Sprinkle with lettuce, leaving the bottom 1½ ins/4cm uncovered. Sprinkle spring onions over the lettuce and add sliced tomato and cucumber. Place 3 or 4 tenderloin pieces down the middle and drizzle with a little hummus thinned down with lemon juice.
3. Turn up bottom edge to hold in the filling and roll from the side into a tight roll. Wrap bottom half in baking paper or foil and serve.

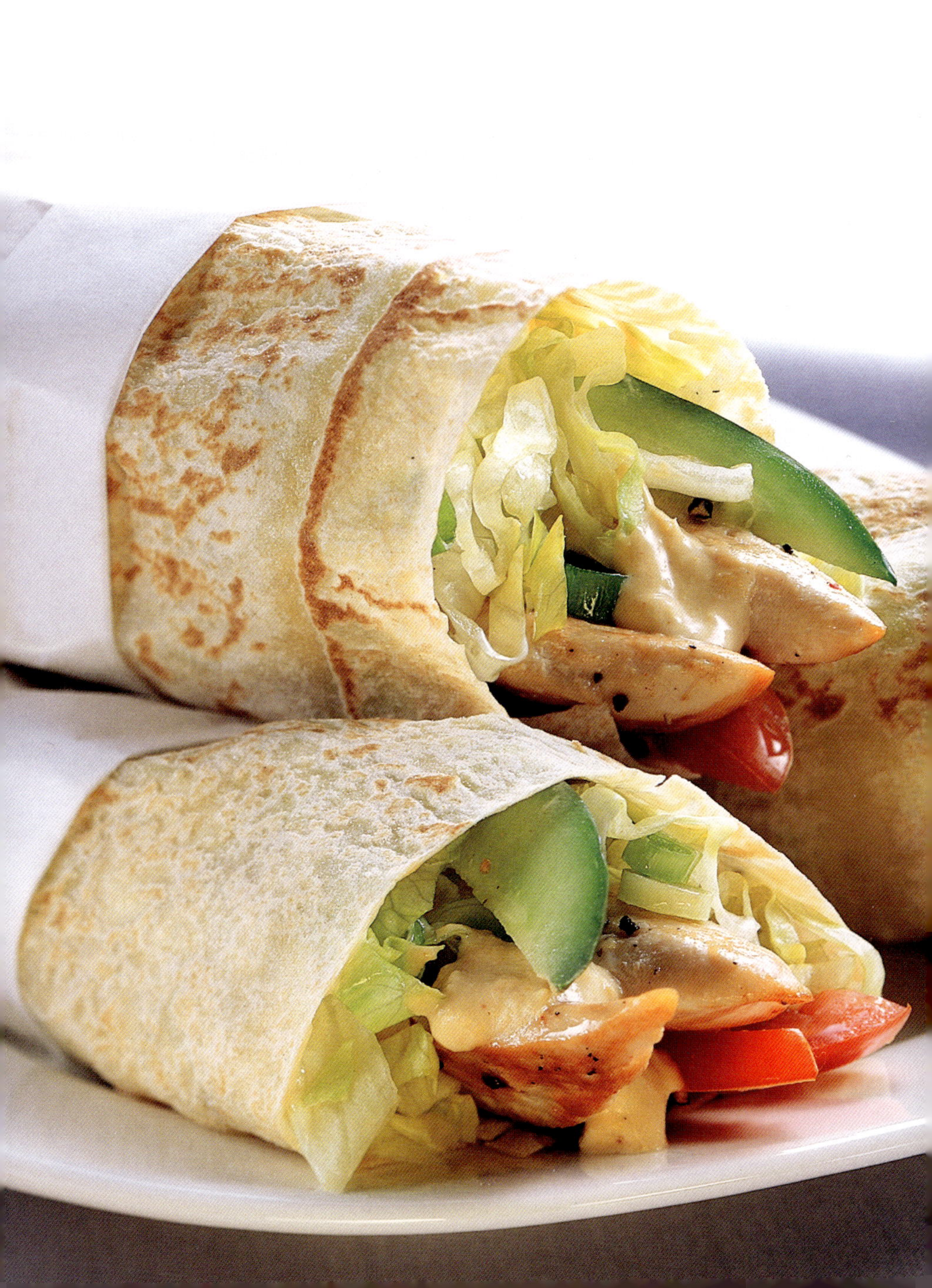

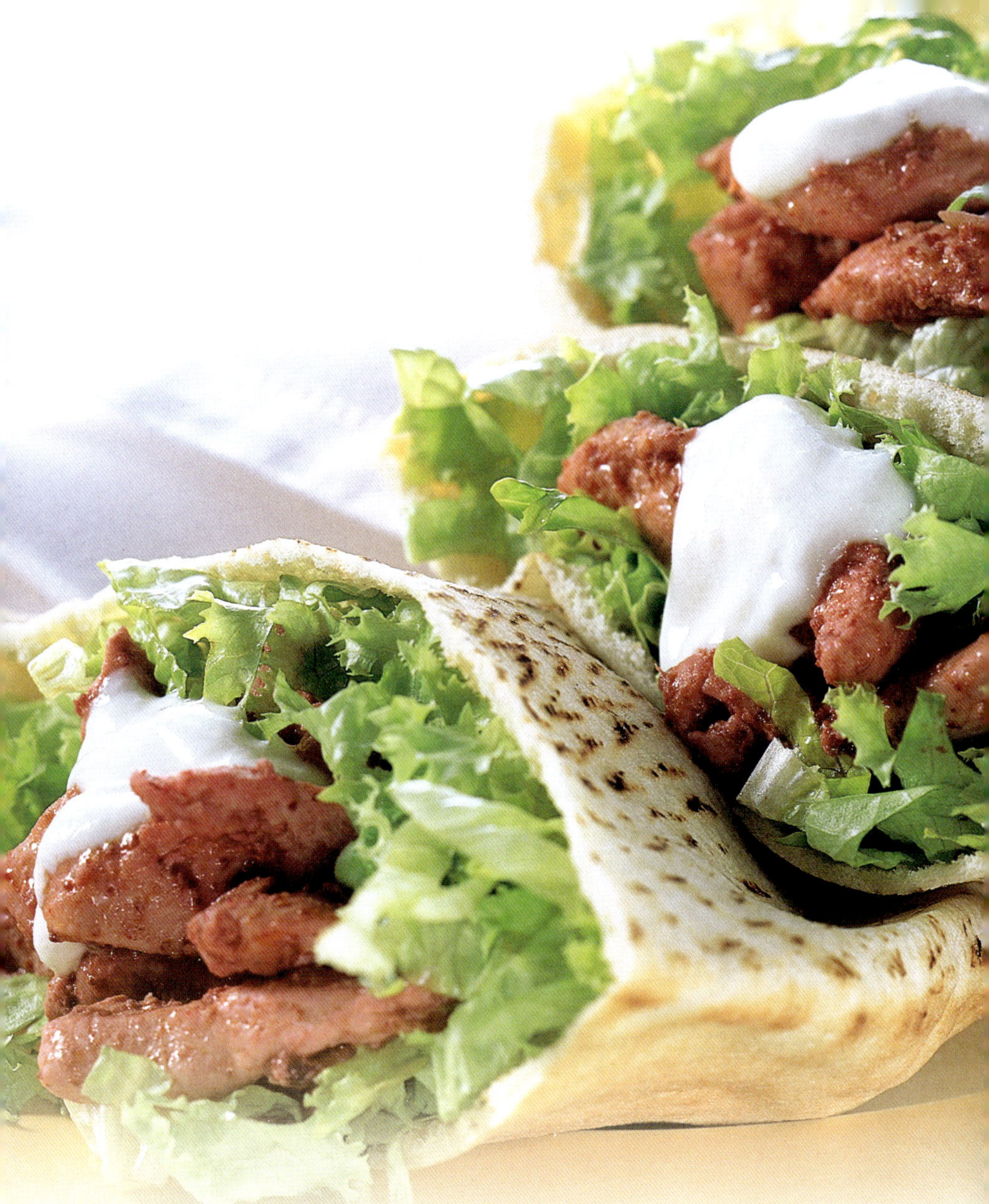

Tandoori chicken pockets

SERVES 4

14 oz/400g chicken strips
½ teaspoon salt
2 teaspoons canola oil
1 small onion, finely chopped
2 teaspoons tandoori curry paste

1 tablespoon lemon juice
1 tablespoon water
8 pieces pita bread
3 cups shredded lettuce
½ cup natural yoghurt

1. Cut chicken into small pieces, sprinkle with salt and set aside. Heat the oil in a small pan, add onion and fry until soft. Add the chicken and fry until almost cooked. Stir in the curry paste, cook a little, then add the lemon juice and water. Allow to simmer until most of the liquid has evaporated. Stir occasionally.
2. Cut the pita bread in half and open the pocket. Place lettuce in the base of the pocket and fill with the curried chicken. Add a tablespoon of yoghurt on top. Serve immediately.

Spicy chicken burritos

SERVES 4

1 lb/500g chicken strips
1 tablespoon olive oil
1 large onion, finely chopped
1 clove garlic, crushed
12 oz/300g jar tomato salsa
½ teaspoon chili powder
12 tortillas
Toppings
1 cup guacamole

2 large onions, thinly sliced
1 cup sour cream
12^{1}/$_{3}$ oz/350g aged cheddar cheese, grated
16 oz/450g canned refried beans, heated

1. Chop the chicken strips into smaller pieces. Heat the oil in a large frying pan. Add onion and garlic and fry until soft. Add the chicken and stir to brown on all sides. Stir in half the jar of salsa and the chili powder. Simmer for 15 minutes or until chicken is cooked.
2. Prepare the toppings and place in suitable serving dishes. Heat the tortillas according to packet directions and stack in a serviette. Serve in the serviette in a basket.
3. Make each burrito by placing chicken mixture on the tortilla then adding a selection of toppings. Roll the buritto and enjoy.

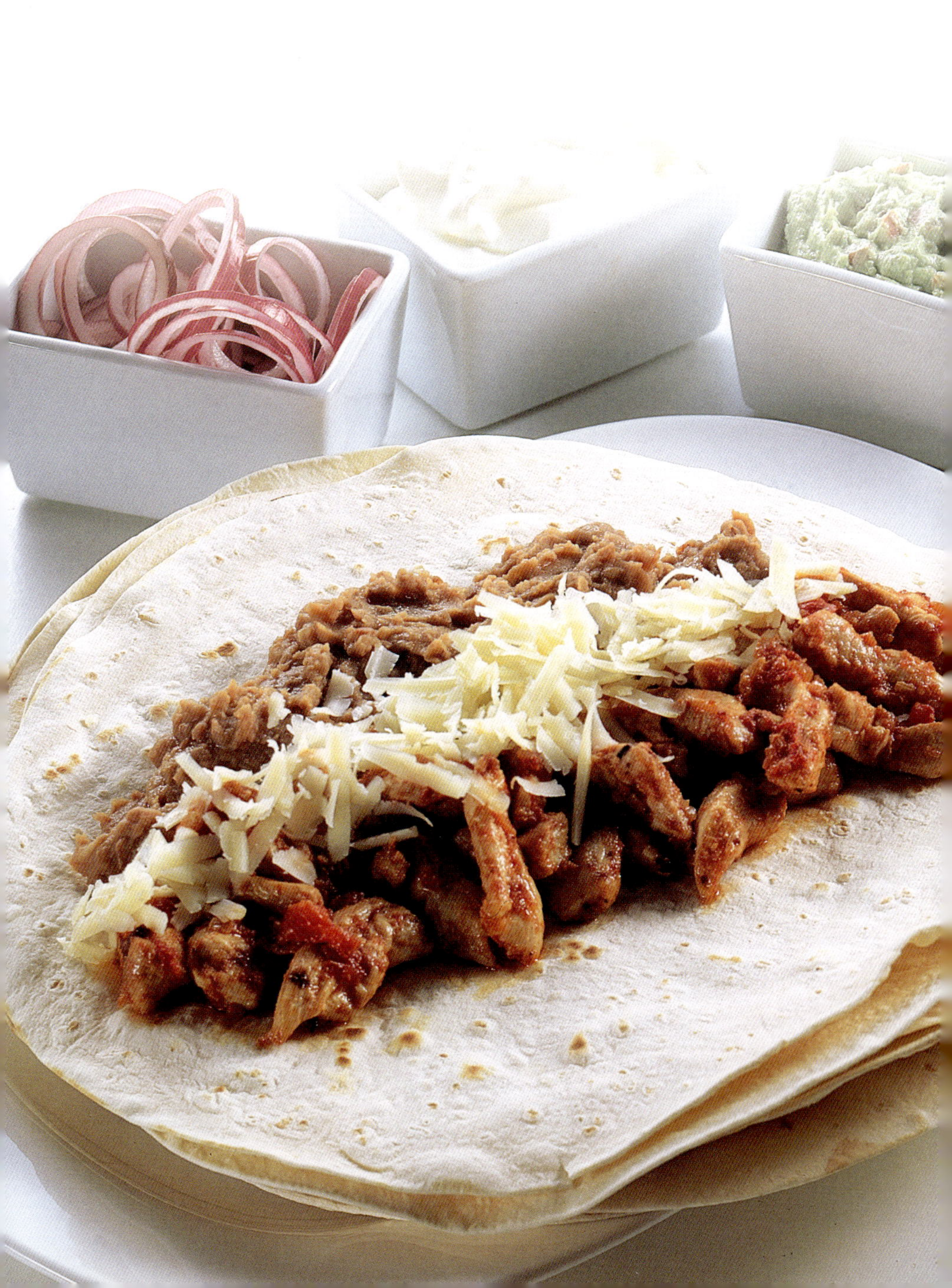

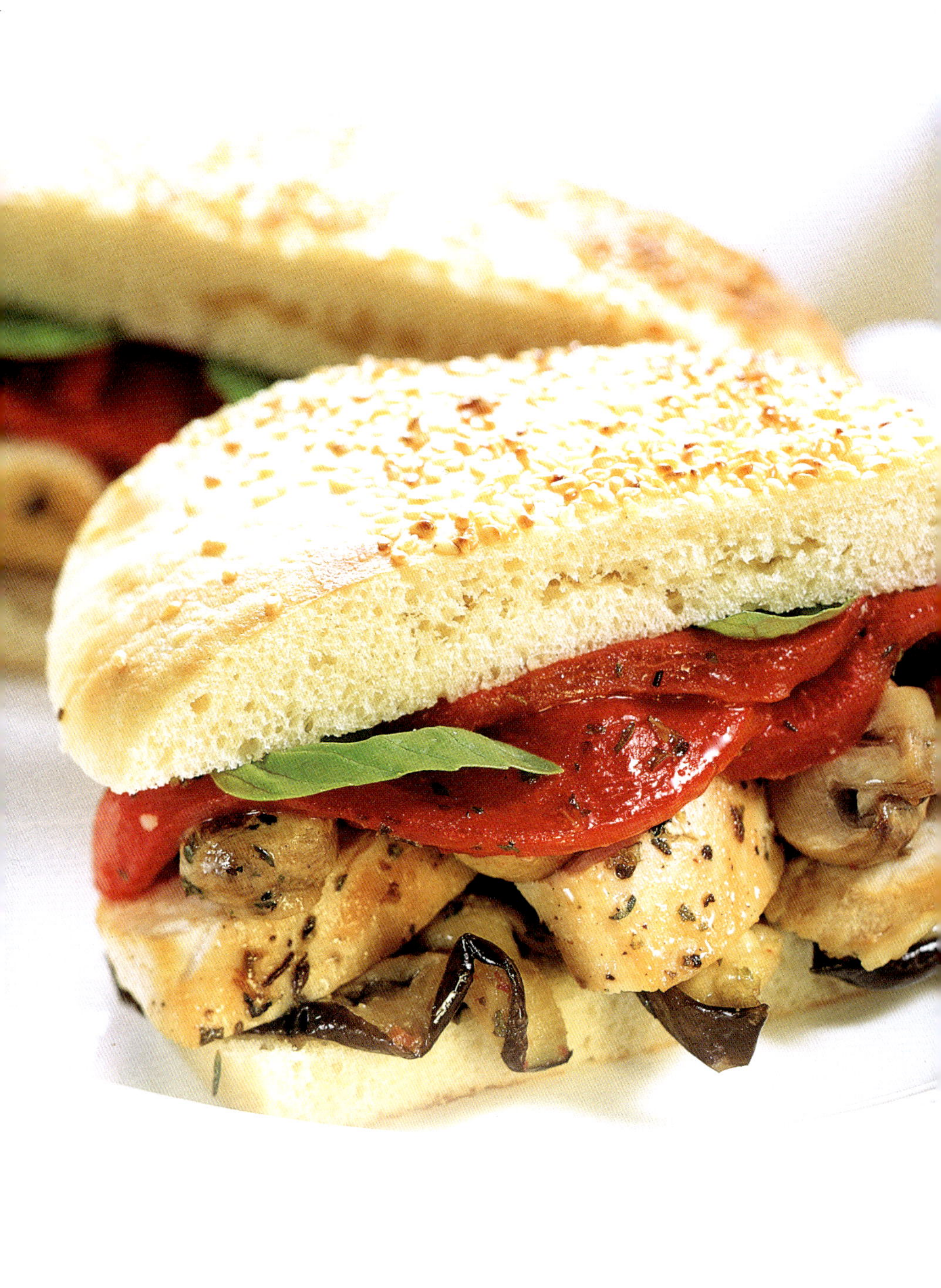

Chicken focaccia

SERVES 4

1 lb/500g skinless chicken breast fillets
1 clove garlic, crushed
salt and pepper
1 tablespoon lemon juice
3 tablespoons olive oil
4 pieces focaccia

4 slices marinated roasted aubergine/ eggplant
3½ oz/100g marinated mushrooms
4 slices marinated roasted red pepper/ capsicum

1. Trim breast fillets, take out the tenderloin. Place in a non-metallic dish and add garlic, seasonings, lemon juice and 2 tablespoons of the oil. Cover and marinate for 30 minutes in the refrigerator. Heat a non-stick pan, sear the fillets 1 minute on each side, then cook for 3 minutes on each side. Cook tenderloins 2 minutes each side. When cooked, cut into diagonal slices. Keep hot.
2. Preheat oven to 320°F/160°C. Split the focaccia in half through the centre. Use the remaining oil to brush each cut surface.
3. Place a slice of aubergine on each base, arrange chicken slices on top and cover with mushrooms and roasted pepper. Replace top slice of focaccia. Bake for 10 minutes. Serve hot with extra marinated vegetables.

Piri piri chicken burgers

SERVES 4

1 lb/500g chicken tenderloins, trimmed
¼ cup all-purpose/plain flour
2 teaspoons piri piri seasoning
¼ cup canola oil
4 pieces Turkish bread
corn relish or tomato chutney

1¾ oz/50g baby spinach leaves, washed and trimmed
1 small red onion, sliced
1 Lebanese cucumber, sliced
1 avocado, sliced

1. Flatten the chicken tenderloins with a meat mallet. Combine the flour and piri piri seasoning in a bowl. Coat each tenderloin lightly in the flour mixture.
2. Heat the oil in a large frying pan over medium heat. Cook the chicken tenderloins in batches for 1–2 minutes on each side or until cooked.
3. Slice the Turkish bread in half and lightly toast under the grill. Spread one piece of bread with corn relish or tomato chutney. Top with spinach leaves, chicken, onion, cucumber and avocado. Top with the remaining bread and serve.

To stop sliced avocado from going brown, brush with a little lemon juice.

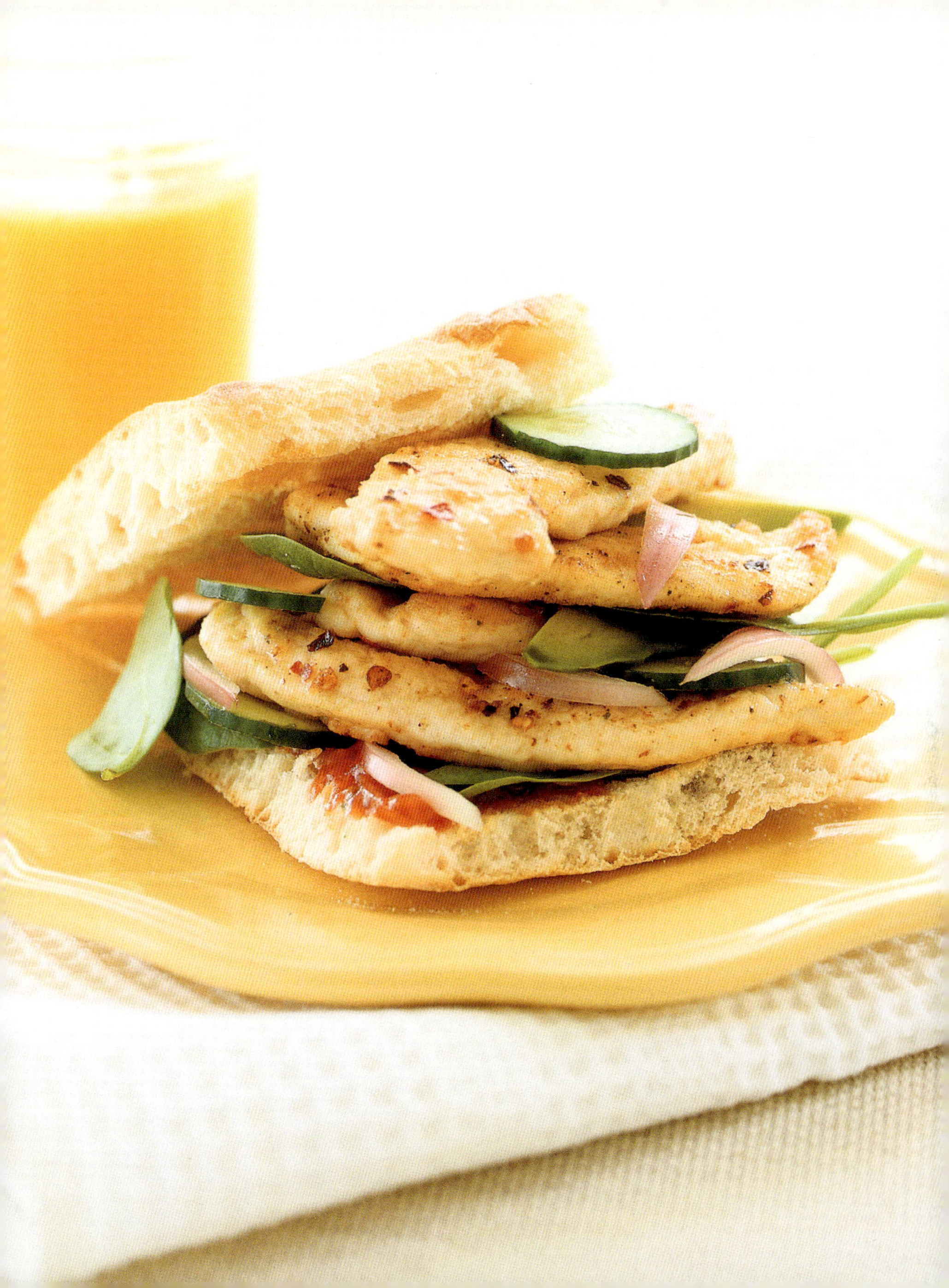

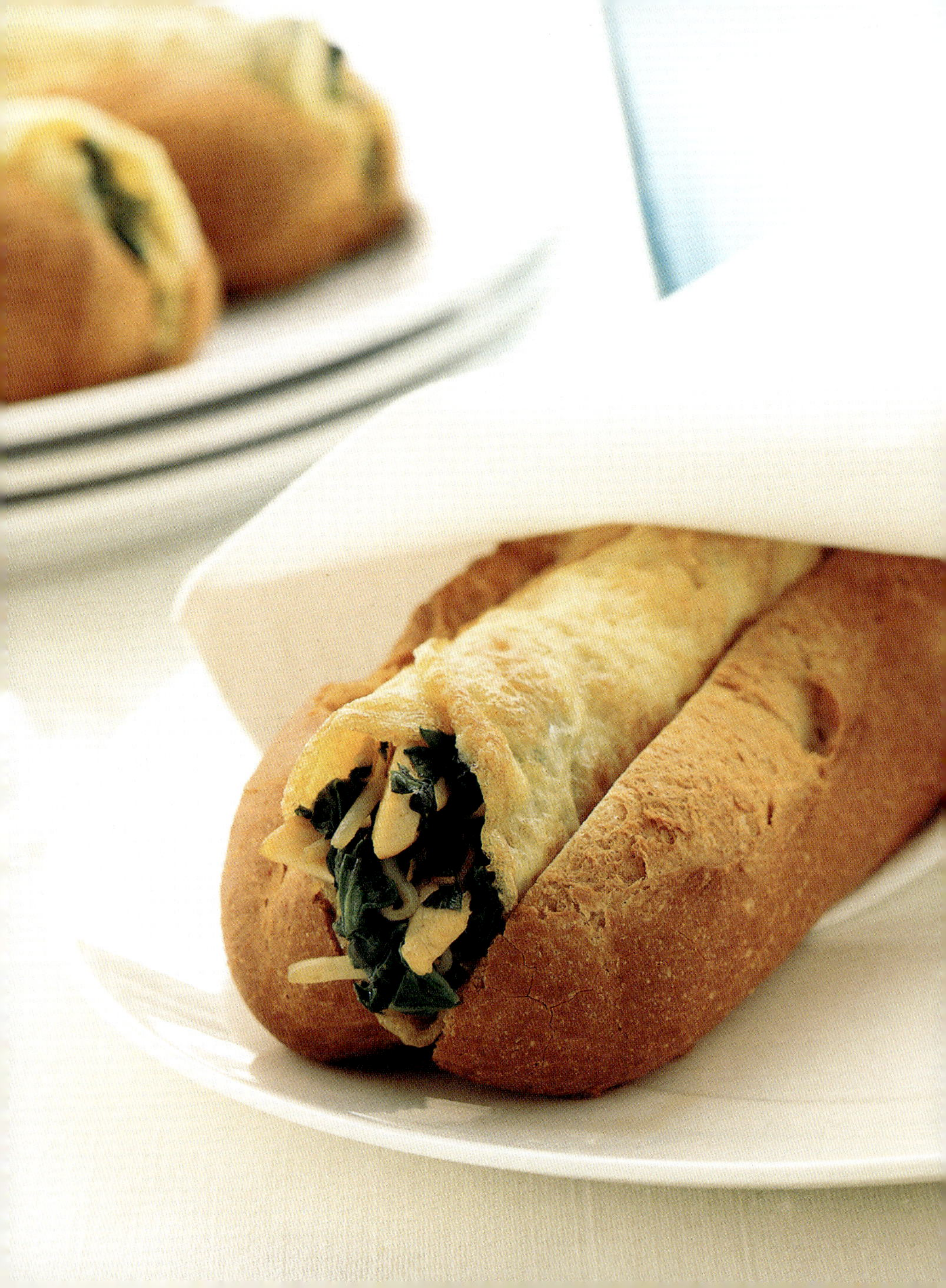

Spinach and chicken omelette baguettes

SERVES 4

4 medium eggs
½ teaspoon salt
1 teaspoon sugar
1 tablespoon vegetable oil, plus extra for brushing
1 skinless chicken breast fillet, cut into very thin strips

1 clove garlic, crushed
9 oz/250g fresh spinach, shredded
2 oz/55g bean sprouts
2 teaspoons light soy sauce
4 small baguettes, cut in half lengthwise

1. Break the eggs into a bowl, add the salt and sugar and beat lightly. Heat an 8 ins/20cm heavy-based frying pan and lightly brush with oil. Pour in a quarter of the egg mixture and swirl to coat the bottom of the pan. Cook for 1½ minutes or until the omelette is set and golden on the base, then turn over and cook for 30 seconds more or until cooked through. Remove from the pan and keep warm. Cook the remaining 3 omelettes in the same way.
2. Heat 1 tablespoon of oil in the frying pan, add the chicken strips and garlic, then cook for 3 minutes or until the chicken is cooked through. Add the spinach and bean sprouts and cook for 1–2 minutes, until the spinach starts to wilt. Sprinkle with soy sauce.
3. Top each omelette with a quarter of the chicken and spinach mixture. Roll up and place in a baguette, then serve immediately.

Chicken burger with tomato salsa

SERVES 4

2 large skinless chicken breast fillets, cut in half horizontally
1 medium egg, beaten
4 tablespoons all-purpose/plain flour
freshly ground black pepper
1 tablespoon vegetable oil
4 burger buns
4 talespoons mayonnaise
lettuce leaves to serve

Salsa
2 tomatoes
1 spring onion/shallot, finely chopped
2 tablespoons chopped fresh cilantro/ coriander
1 teaspoon fresh lemon juice
salt and freshly ground black pepper

1. First make the salsa. Place the tomatoes in a bowl, cover with boiling water and leave for 30 seconds. Peel, deseed, then chop the flesh. Combine with the spring onion, cilantro and lemon juice. Season and set aside.
2. Place each chicken piece between 2 sheets of cling film and beat with a rolling pin to an even thickness. Put the beaten egg into a shallow dish. Mix together the flour and seasoning in another dish.
3. Dip both sides of each chicken piece into the egg, then coat evenly with the seasoned flour. Heat the oil in a non-stick frying pan and cook the coated chicken for 5–6 minutes on each side, until golden and cooked through.
4. Split the buns. Spread the mayonnaise over the bases and arrange the lettuce leaves, chicken and salsa on top. Replace the bun tops.

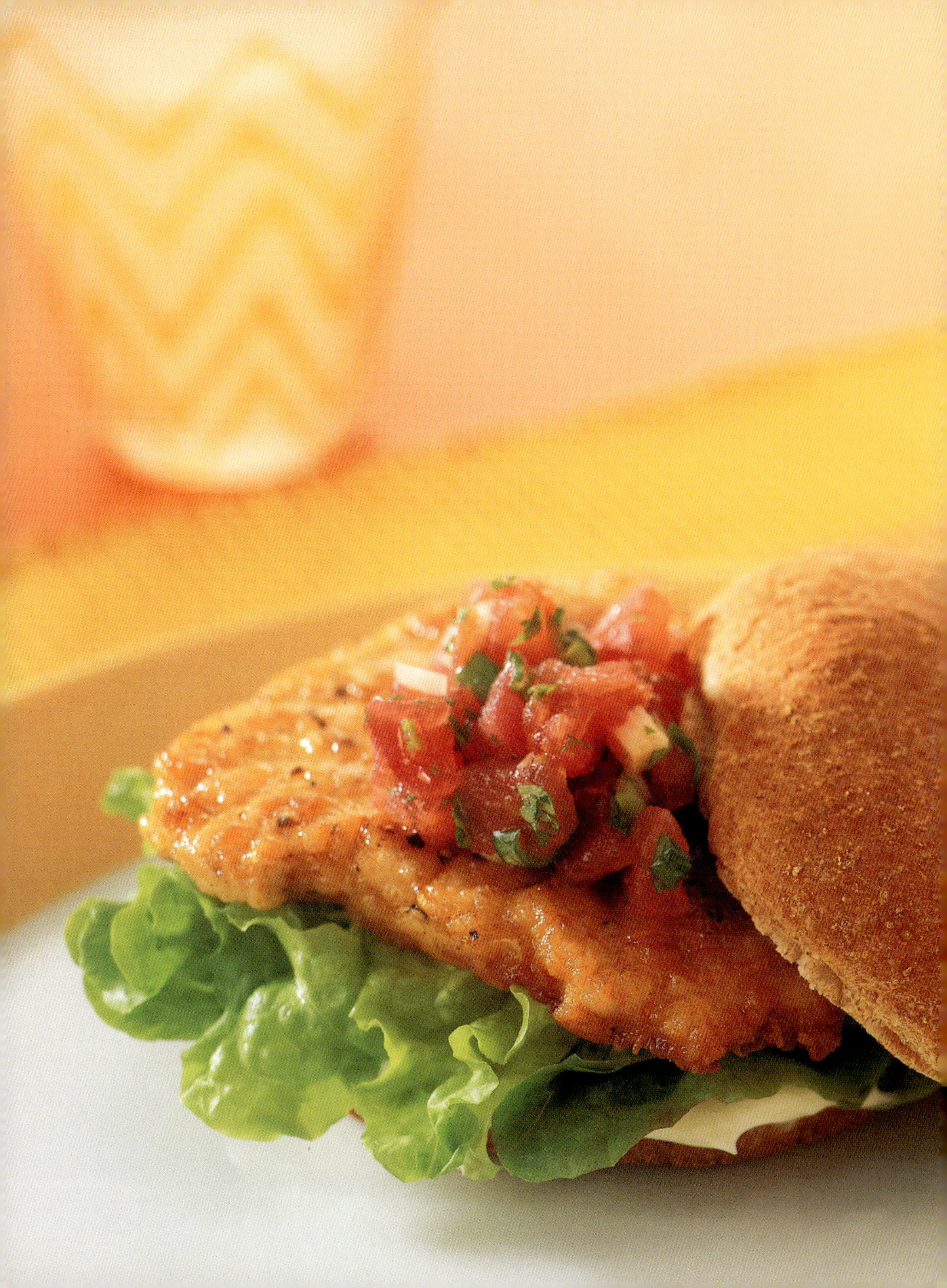

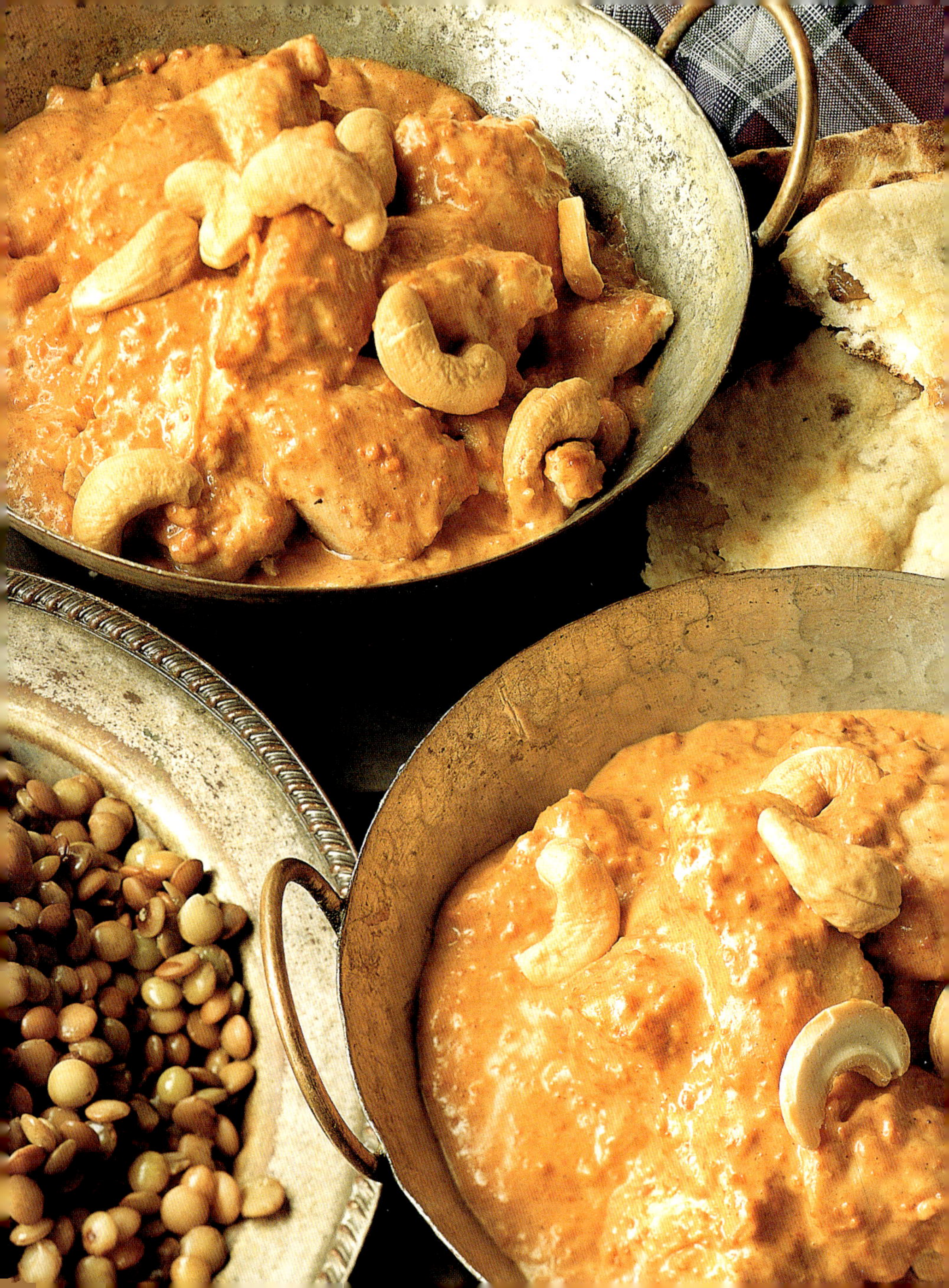

curry chicken

Chicken rogan josh

SERVES 4

8 skinless chicken thigh fillets
1 tablespoon vegetable oil
1 small red pepper/capsicum, thinly sliced
1 small green bell pepper/capsicum, thinly sliced
1 onion, thinly sliced
2 ins/5cm piece fresh ginger, finely chopped
2 cloves garlic, crushed

2 tablespoons garam masala
1 teaspoon paprika
1 teaspoon turmeric
1 teaspoon chili powder
4 cardamom pods, crushed salt
7 oz/200g Greek yoghurt
14 oz/400g canned chopped tomatoes
fresh cilantro/coriander to garnish
rice, yoghurt and chutney, to serve

1. Cut each chicken thigh into 4 pieces. Heat the oil in a large heavy-based frying pan and add the peppers, onion, ginger, garlic, spices and a good pinch of salt. Fry over a low heat for 5 minutes or until the capsicum and onion have softened.
2. Add the chicken and 2 tablespoons of the yoghurt. Increase the heat to medium and cook for 4 minutes or until the yoghurt is absorbed. Repeat with the rest of the yoghurt.
3. Increase the heat to high, stir in the tomatoes and ¾ cup of water and bring to the boil. Reduce the heat, cover, and simmer for 30 minutes or until the chicken is tender, stirring occasionally and adding more water if the sauce becomes too dry.
4. Uncover the pan, increase the heat to high and cook, stirring constantly, for 5 minutes or until the sauce thickens. Garnish with cilantro and serve with rice, yoghurt and chutney.

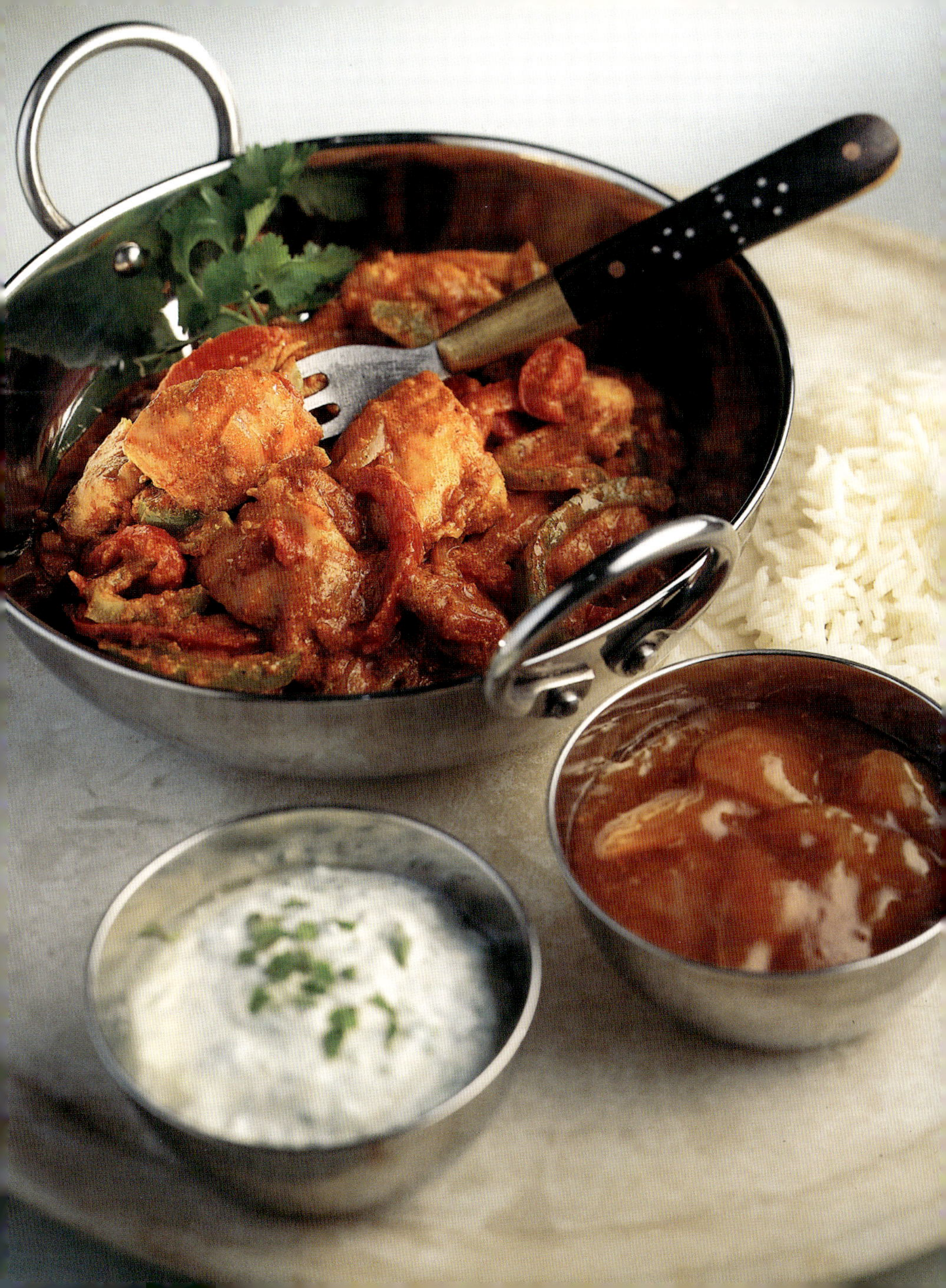

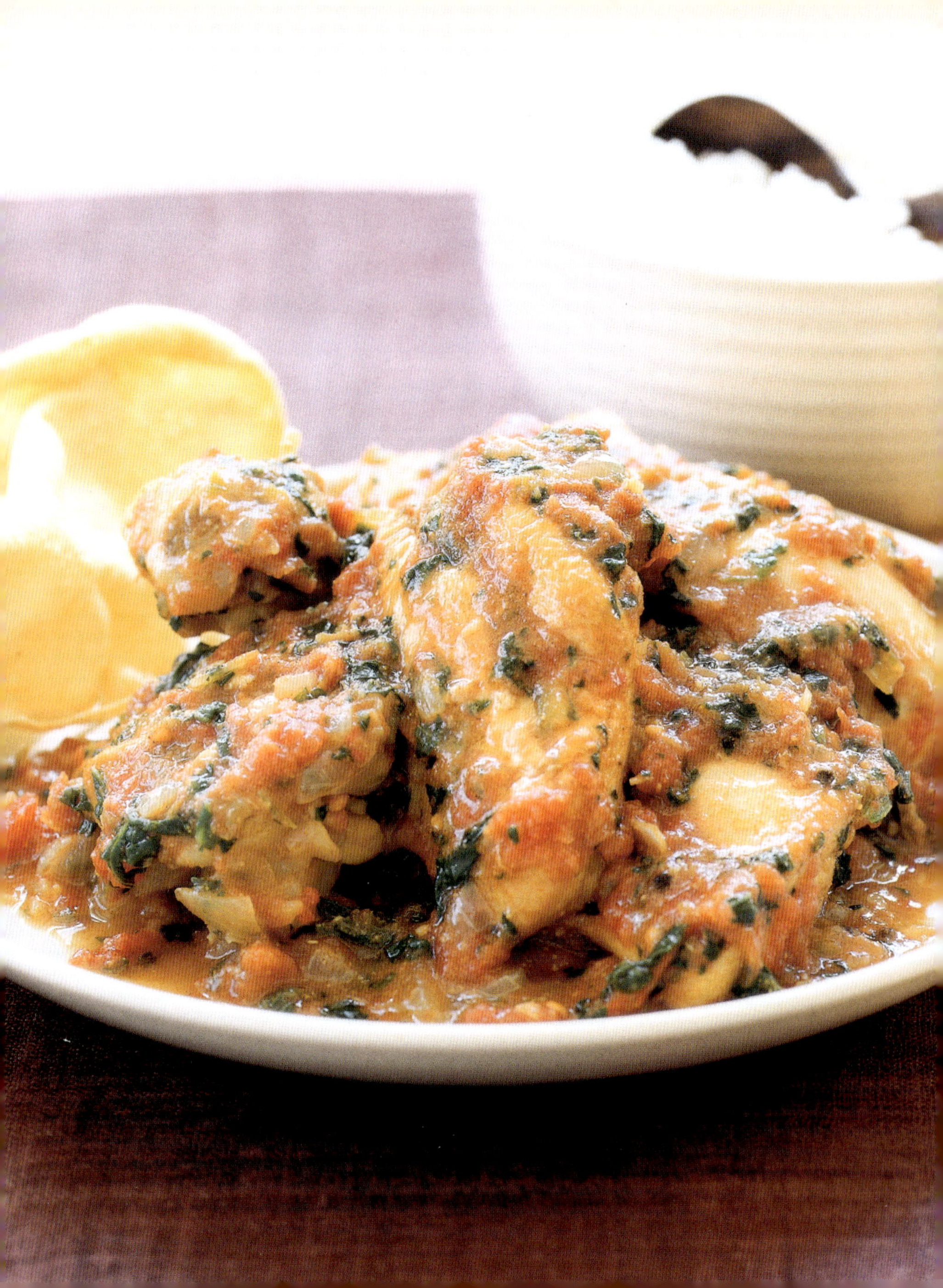

Chicken curry with spinach

SERVES 4

8 chicken pieces
salt
1 bunch spinach, washed and trimmed
2 tablespoons canola oil
2 onions, chopped
1¾ lbs/800g canned chopped tomatoes
2 bay leaves
rice and pappadums to serve (optional)

Paste
2 tablespoons canola oil
3 long green chilies, deseeded and sliced
3 cloves garlic, crushed
1 ins/3cm piece ginger, grated
1 tablespoon ground cummin
1 tablespoon ground coriander
½ teaspoon cardamom seeds
½ teaspoon ground cloves

1. Season the chicken with salt and set aside. To make the paste, crush the ingredients in a mortar and pestle or process in a food processor until smooth.
2. Cook the spinach in a bowl of boiling water for 2 minutes. Drain and rinse under cold water. Place in a food processor and process until finely chopped.
3. Heat the oil in a large saucepan over medium-high heat. Brown the chicken in batches for 4–5 minutes. Remove and set aside.
4. Add the onion and cook for 3 minutes. Add the paste and cook for a further 2 minutes.
5. Stir in the tomatoes and the bay leaves and return the chicken to the pan. Bring to the boil, cover and simmer over low heat for 30 minutes, stirring from time to time. Stir in the spinach, remove the lid and cook for a further 15 minutes or until the chicken is tender. Season with salt.
6. Serve the chicken with rice and pappadums.

When handling chilies, use rubber gloves or wash your hands straight after as the juice from the chili can irritate skin and eyes.

Asian chicken curry

SERVES 4

1 lb/500g chicken thigh fillets
2 tablespoons oil
1 large onion, finely chopped
1 cup Madras curry sauce

2 tablespoons sultanas
2 bananas, sliced
1 green apple, peeled and cut into large dice

1. Cut chicken thighs into 3 pieces. Heat half the oil in a large saucepan, add 1/3 of the chicken and quickly brown on both sides. Remove to a plate and brown remaining chicken in 2 batches, adding remaining oil when necessary. Remove last batch of chicken.
2. Add onion and cook a little then stir in the curry sauce. Quarter-fill the can with water to rinse down remaining sauce and then pour into saucepan.
3. Bring to the boil, turn down heat and return the chicken to the saucepan. Cover and simmer for 20 minutes. Add sultanas, banana and apple and simmer 15–20 minutes more. Serve immediately with boiled rice.

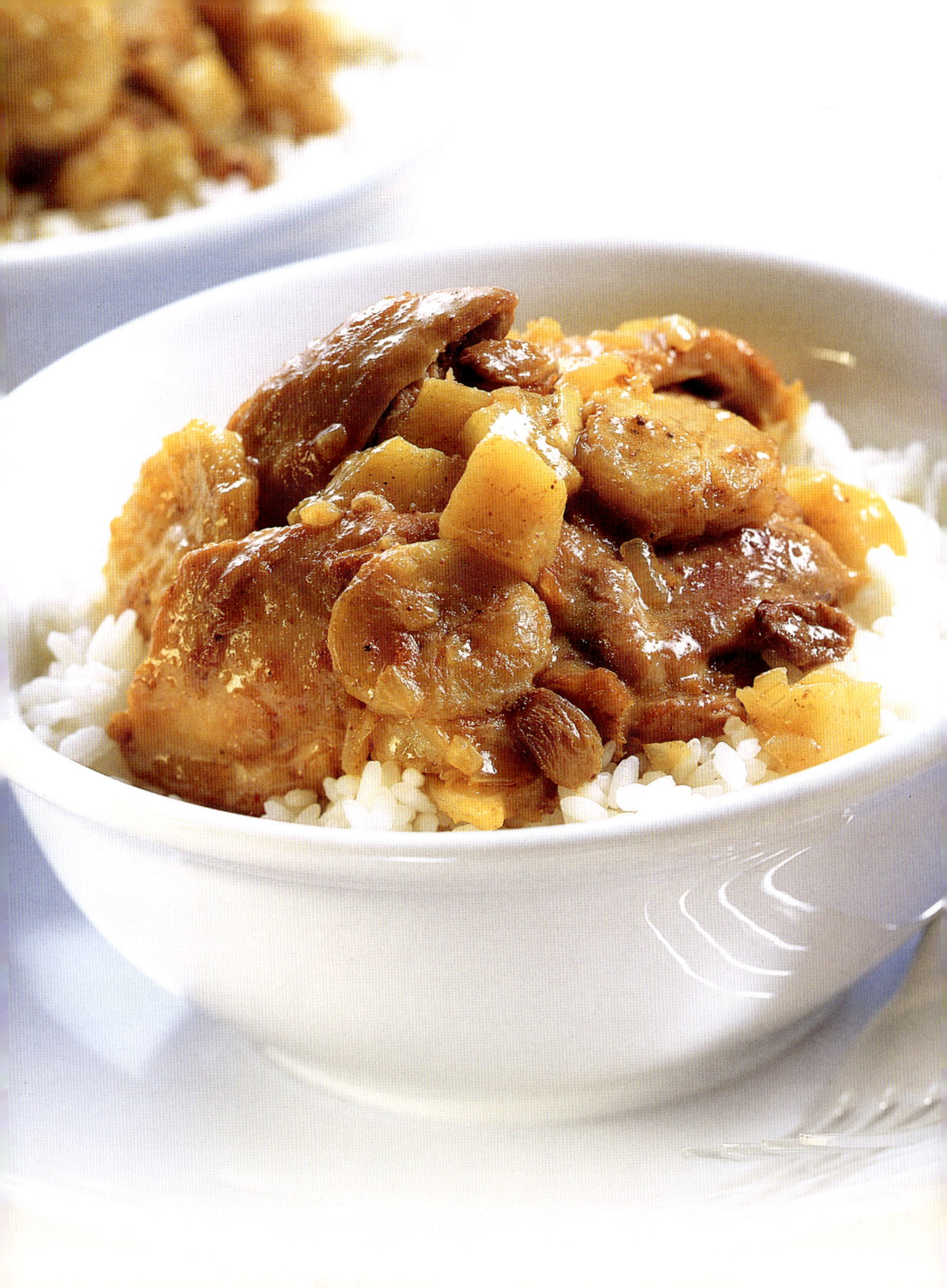

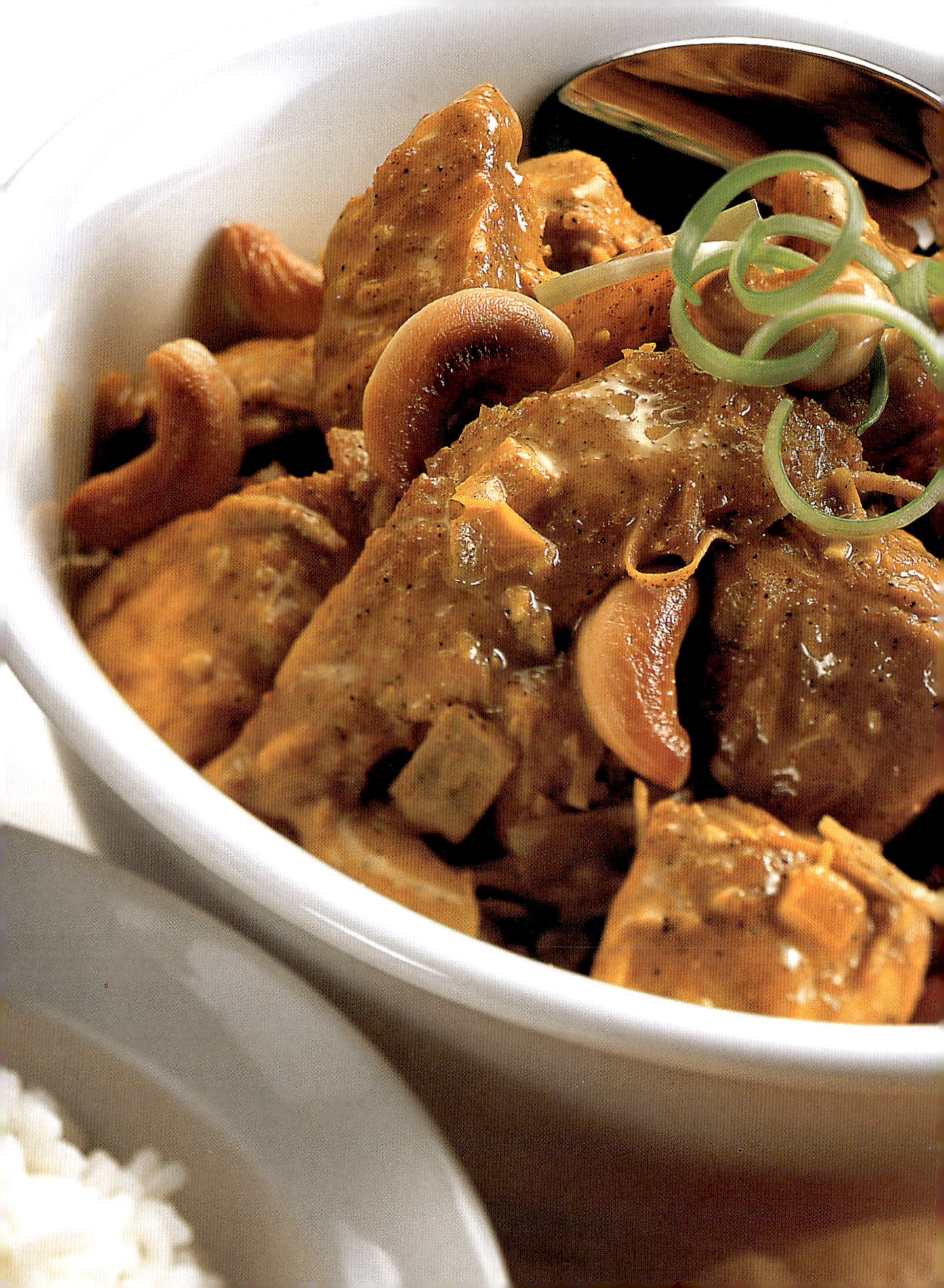

Chicken and pear curry

SERVES 4

1 lb/500g chicken tenderloins
5 large dried pears
1 tablespoon butter
1 tablespoon oil
1 medium onion, finely chopped
1 tablespoon Madras curry powder

1 teaspoon sugar
½ cup thickened cream
½ cup white wine
2 tablespoons shredded coconut
2 tablespoons toasted cashew nuts

1. Cut tenderloins into bite-size pieces. Cut pears into ½ ins/1cm strips, set aside. Heat butter and oil in a large frying pan, add chicken and brown over a high heat. Remove from pan.
2. Add onion and fry gently until soft. Stir in curry powder and cook 1 minute. Reduce heat. Add sugar, cream, wine and coconut, stir well.
3. Return chicken to pan and add pears. Cover and simmer 15 minutes, taking care not to boil. Remove to a heated dish and sprinkle with toasted cashew nuts. Serve with boiled rice.

Cashew nut butter chicken

SERVES 4

1 lb/500g skinless chicken thigh fillets
1¾ oz/50g ghee (clarified butter)
2 cloves garlic, crushed
2 onions, minced
1 tablespoon Madras curry paste
1 tablespoon ground cilantro/coriander
½ teaspoon ground nutmeg
1¾ oz/50g cashew nuts, roasted and ground
1¼ cups double cream
2 tablespoons coconut milk

1. Cut chicken into ¾ ins/2cm cubes. Melt ghee in a saucepan over medium heat, add garlic and onion and cook, stirring, for 3 minutes or until onion turns golden.
2. Stir in curry paste, cilantro and nutmeg and cook for 2 minutes or until fragrant.
3. Add chicken and cook, stirring, for 5 minutes or until chicken is brown.
4. Add cashews, cream and coconut milk and simmer, stirring occasionally, for 40 minutes or until chicken is tender.

To roast cashews, spread nuts over a baking tray and bake at 360°F/180°C for 5–10 minutes or until lightly and evenly browned. Toss back and forth occasionally with a spoon to ensure even browning. Alternatively, place nuts under a medium grill and cook, tossing back and forth until roasted.

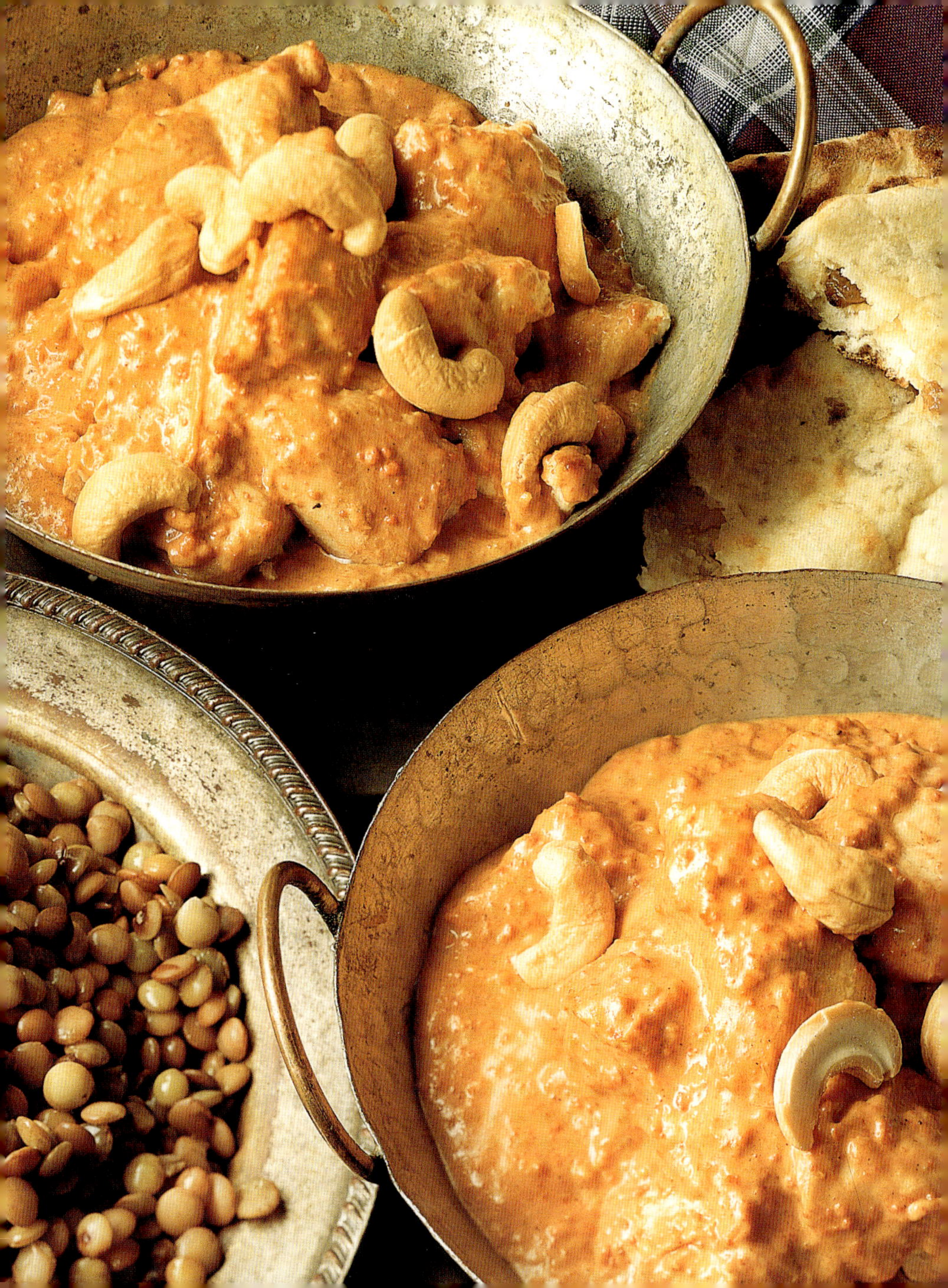

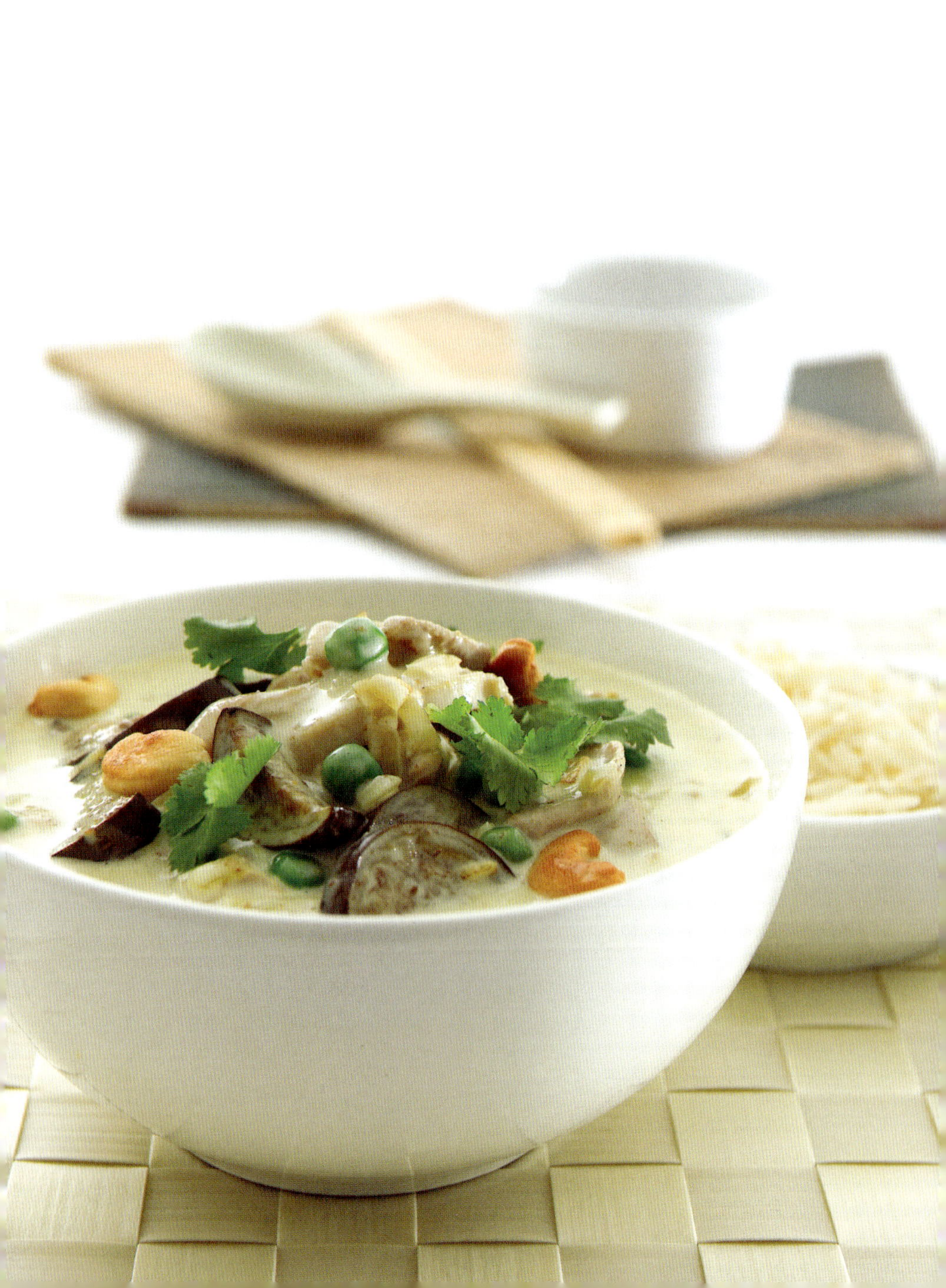

Thai chicken curry

SERVES 4

1 tablespoon canola oil
4 chicken thigh fillets, finely sliced
3 tablespoons yellow curry paste
1 onion, finely chopped
¾ oz/2cm piece of ginger, grated
1 clove garlic, finely chopped
1 aubergine/eggplant, roughly chopped

2 cups coconut cream
½ cup frozen peas
2 tablespoons oyster sauce
1 teaspoon fish sauce
½ cup cashews
½ cup fresh cilantro/coriander
rice, to serve

1. Heat oil in a wok or large frying pan, add chicken and cook for 1–2 minutes. Remove and set aside.
2. Add curry paste, fry for 1 minute or until fragrant, then add onion, ginger, garlic and aubergine. Stir-fry for 1–2 minutes. Return chicken to the wok, add coconut cream and simmer for 10 minutes. Add peas, oyster sauce and fish sauce. Cook for a further 2 minutes.
3. Serve the curry with rice, garnished with the cashews and coriander.

Sweet mango chicken

SERVES 4

1 lb/500g chicken breast fillets
2 tablespoons peanut oil
1 onion, cut into wedges
2 teaspoons mild curry powder
1 cup chicken stock
⅓ cup mango chutney
¼ cup cilantro/coriander leaves

1 teaspoon mint flakes
1 small red pepper/capsicum, sliced
3½ oz/100g baby spinach leaves, washed and trimmed
⅓ cup cashew nuts, toasted
pappadums and rice, to serve

1. Thickly slice the chicken breasts. Heat the oil in a large saucepan over high heat. Add the chicken and cook in two batches for 3 minutes. Remove and set aside.
2. Reduce the heat to medium, add the onion and cook for 2–3 minutes. Stir in the curry powder, chicken stock, mango chutney, cilantro, mint, red pepper and chicken. Cook for 5–6 minutes or until the chicken is tender.
3. Stir through the spinach and cashews. Serve with pappadums and rice.

To toast cashew nuts, place on a baking tray lined with baking paper and bake at 360°F/180°C for 4–5 minutes or until golden. Alternatively, you can stir-fry in a pan until golden.

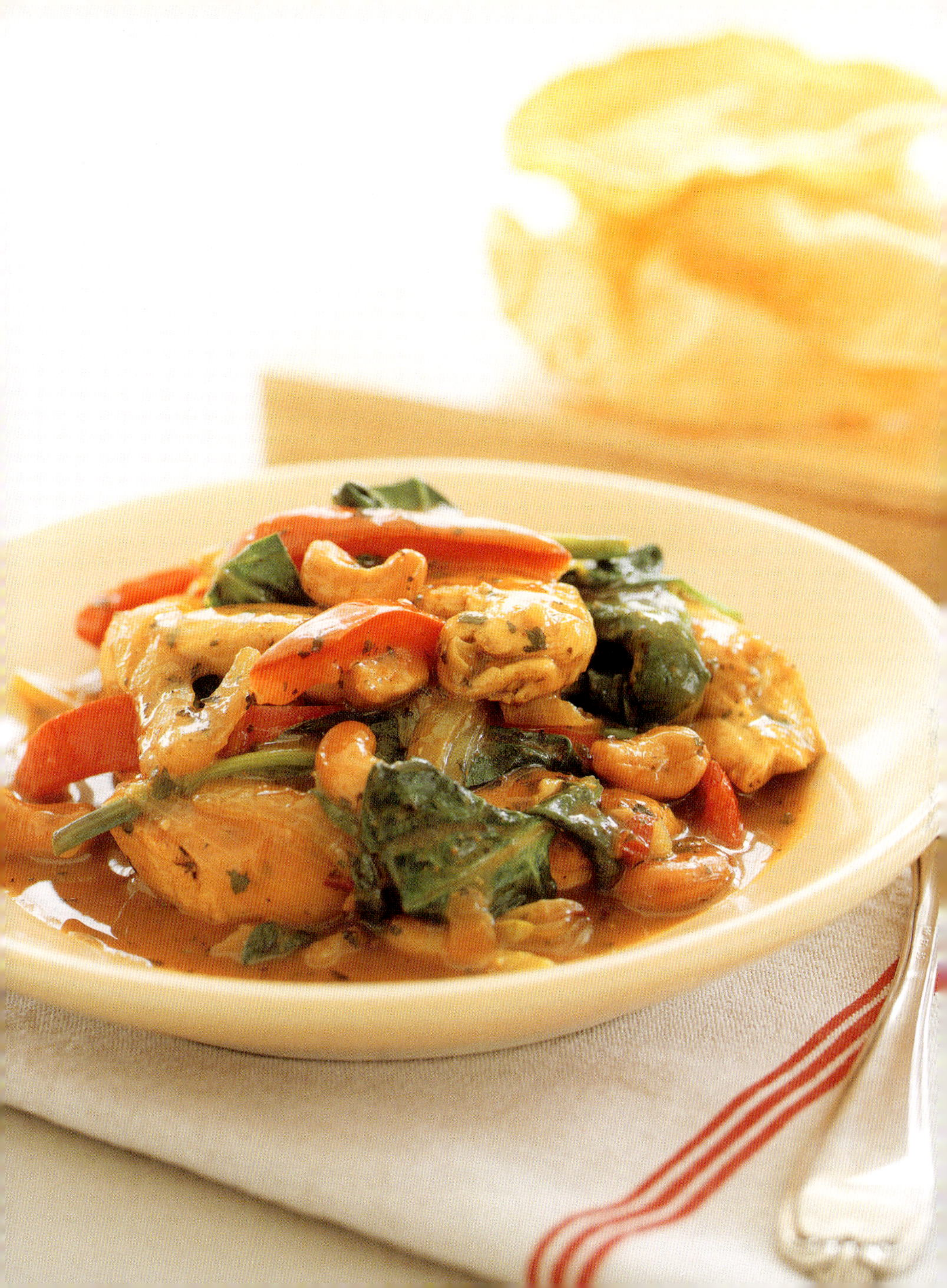

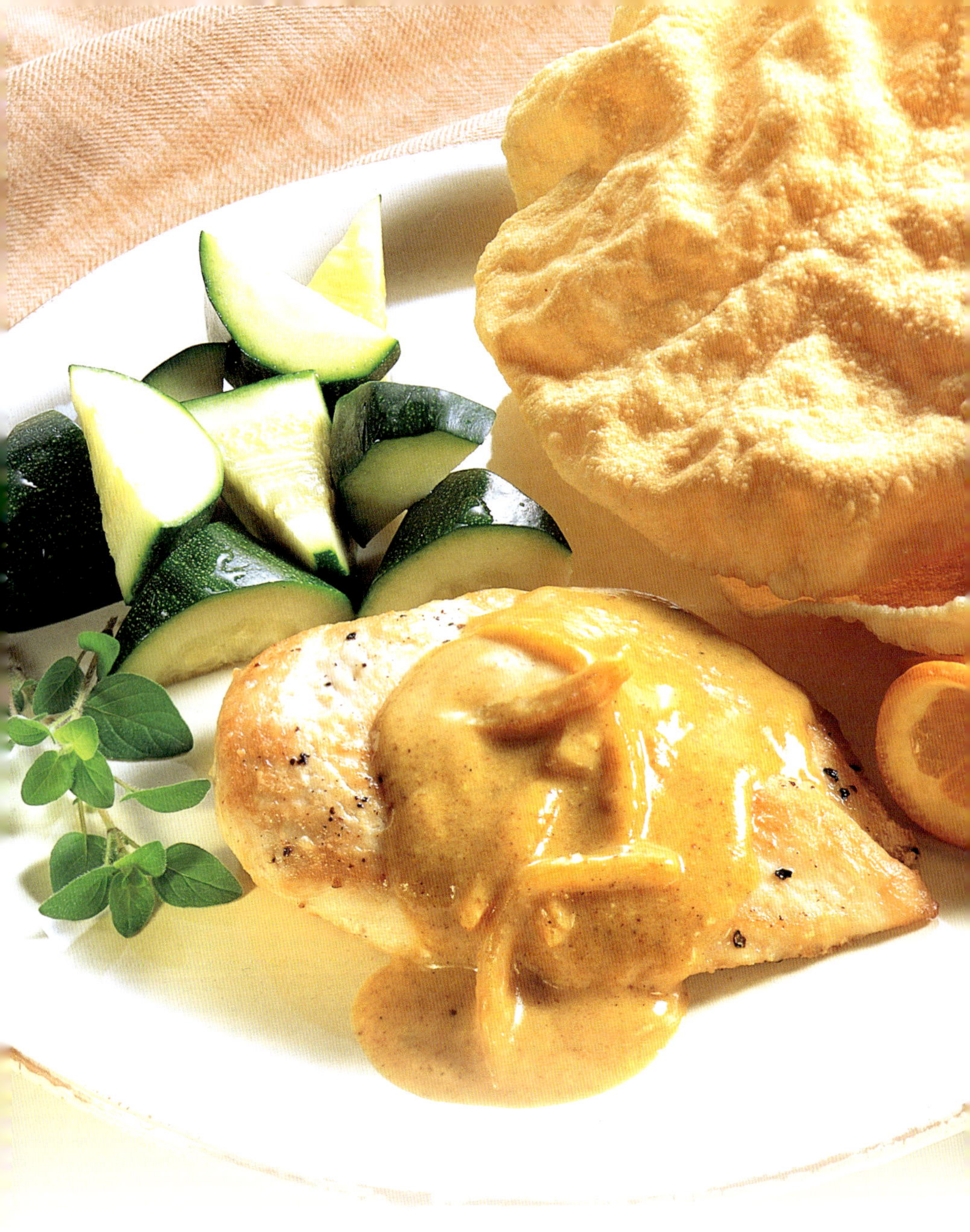

Sauté chicken with citrus and yoghurt sauce

SERVES 4

4 skinless chicken breast fillets
salt and pepper
olive oil spray
4 tablespoons mild curry paste
1 cup orange marmalade

4 tablespoons lemon juice
12 oz/300g low-fat yoghurt
pappadums and steamed courgette/ zucchini, to serve

1. Trim the breasts, flatten to even thickness and sprinkle with salt and pepper. Heat a non-stick frying pan and spray lightly with olive oil spray. Add chicken breasts and fry about 4 minutes on each side. Remove from pan and keep hot.
2. Add the curry paste and stir until it heats. Stir in the marmalade and lemon juice. Remove from heat and stir in the yoghurt until smooth, and then gently reheat. Place chicken onto heated dinner plates and drizzle with sauce. Serve immediately with pappadums and steamed courgette.

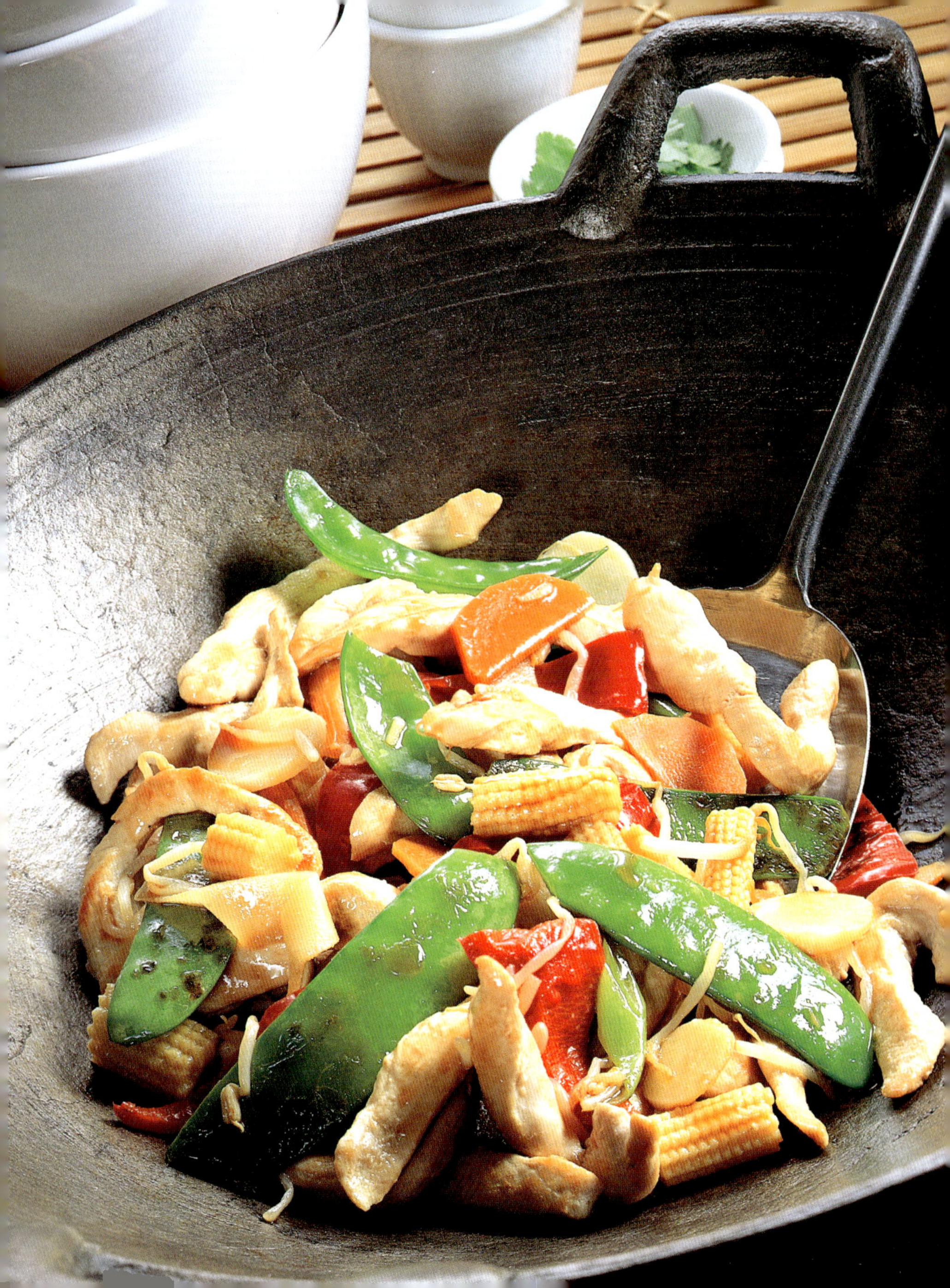

stir-fry chicken

Stir-fried chicken with almonds and broccoli

SERVES 4

1 lb/500g chicken strips
5 teaspoons cornflour
½ teaspoon Chinese five spice powder
½ teaspoon salt
oil for cooking
5¼ oz/150g blanched almonds
¾ ins/2cm piece fresh ginger, finely chopped

1 clove garlic, crushed
2 tablespoons dry sherry
1 teaspoon sugar
1 tablespoon soy sauce
2 teaspoons water
7 oz/200g broccoli florets, blanched
boiled rice, to serve

1. Place the chicken in a bowl and sprinkle over 3 teaspoons of the cornflour, the five spice powder and salt. Mix well and set aside. Heat oil in the wok and fry the almonds until golden. Remove, drain and set aside. Add the ginger and garlic and stir-fry for one minute. Add the chicken in batches and stir-fry until the chicken turns white.
2. Return all the chicken to the wok, add the sherry, sugar and soy sauce and stir a little. Combine the remaining cornflour with the water, then add to the chicken. Stir until the sauce thickens.
3. Add the broccoli and fried almonds and toss to heat through. Serve immediately with boiled rice.

To blanch broccoli, place in a saucepan of boiling water for 30 seconds or until it turns bright green. Remove immediately and plunge into a bowl of iced water. When cold, drain in a colander.

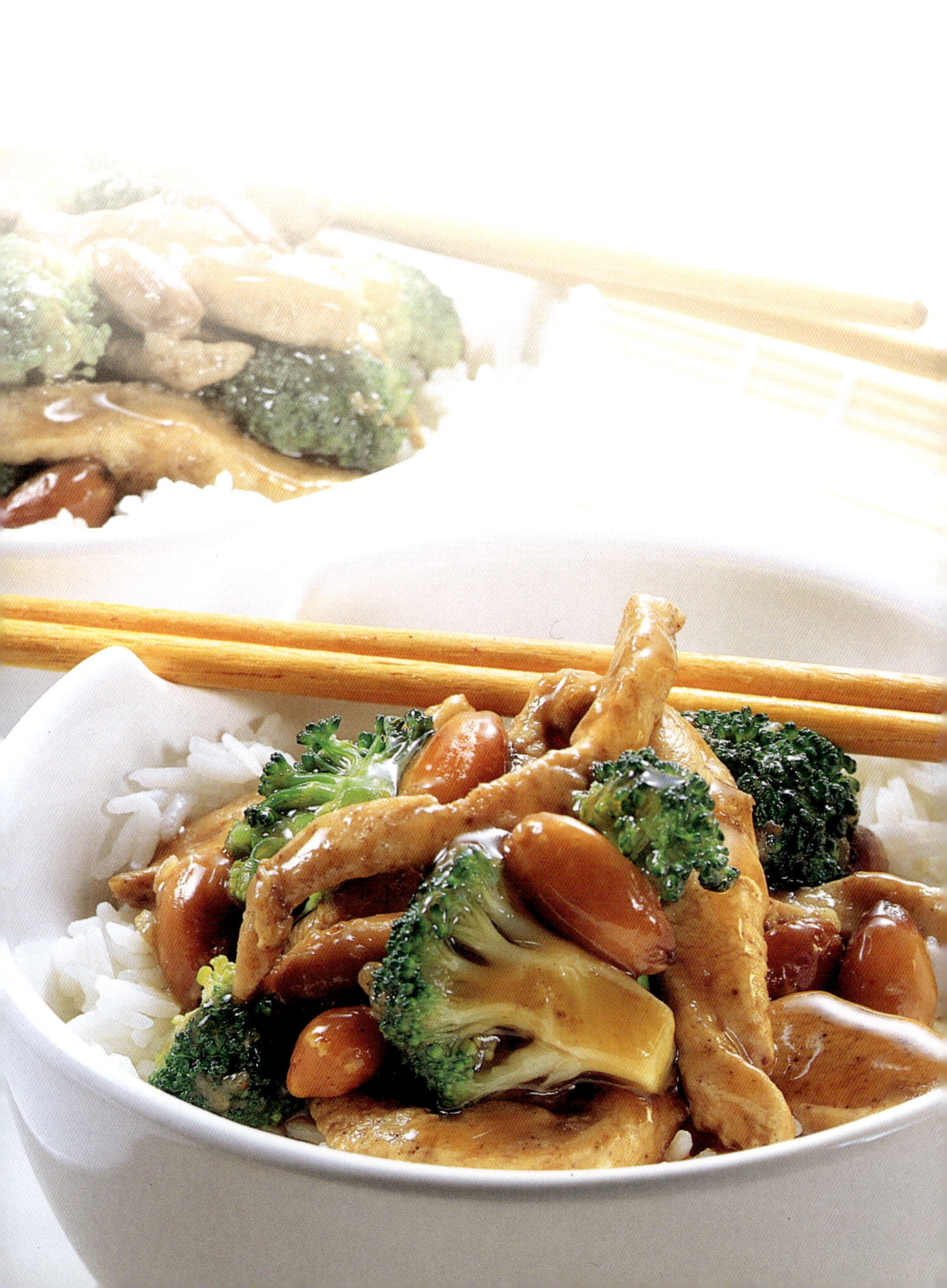

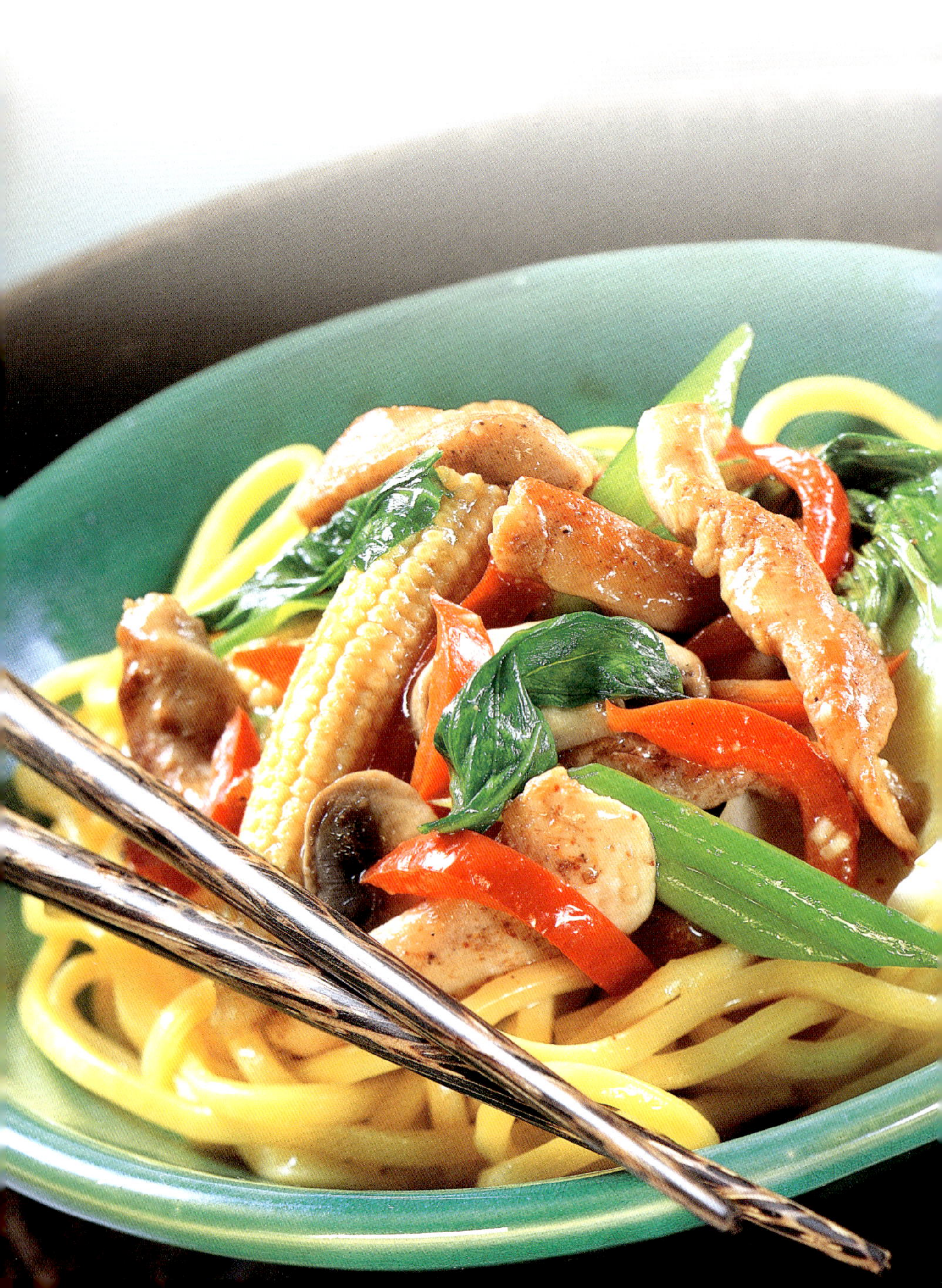

Fried noodles with chicken stir-fry

SERVES 4

1 skinless chicken breast fillet
½ teaspoon salt
½ teaspoon Chinese five spice powder
7 oz/200g wheat noodles
2 tablespoons oil
1 clove garlic, chopped
4 mushrooms, sliced

1 red pepper/capsicum, cut into strips
4 spring onions/shallots, sliced
2 baby bok choy, leaves separated
15 oz/425g canned baby corn
1 tablespoon dry sherry
2 teaspoons cornflour
1 tablespoon oyster sauce

1. Cut chicken breast into thin strips, ¼ ins/5mm wide. Sprinkle with salt and five spice powder. Soak wheat noodles in hot water for 5 minutes. Drain well. Heat wok and add 1 tablespoon of oil and heat. Stir-fry noodles until golden. Remove and keep hot.
2. Add the remaining oil, heat, and stir-fry the chicken for 2 minutes. Add the garlic, mushrooms and vegetables and continue to stir-fry. Mix the sherry and cornflour together, add the oyster sauce and pour into the wok. Toss well to distribute and thicken any juices. Stir-fry 1 minute. Pile over the noodles and serve immediately.

Sweet and sour chicken

SERVES 4

1 lb/500g chicken thigh fillets
16 oz/450g canned pineapple pieces
1 red pepper/capsicum
6 spring onions/shallots
2 teaspoons soy sauce
2 tablespoons malt vinegar
2 tablespoons brown sugar

1 tablespoon lemon juice
½ ins/1cm piece fresh ginger, finely grated
2 tablespoons tomato sauce
2 tablespoons water
1 tablespoon cornflour
2 tablespoons oil

1. Cut each thigh fillet into ½ ins/1cm-wide strips. Drain pineapple pieces and reserve the juice. Cut red pepper into strips or squares. Cut spring onions, including most of the green shoot, into ½ ins/1cm diagonal pieces. Mix together the pineapple juice, soy sauce, vinegar, sugar, lemon juice, ginger and tomato sauce. Blend water and cornflour and set aside.
2. Heat 2 tablespoons of oil in a wok, then add $1/3$ of the chicken. Stir-fry over high heat until cooked, about 1 minute. Remove and cook remaining chicken in 2 batches, adding extra oil if needed. Drain chicken well on absorbent paper. Drain all oil from the wok.
3. Pour the sauce mixture into the wok and add the blended cornflour. Cook, stirring, until mixture boils and thickens. Stir in red pepper, spring onion and pineapple pieces, cook 1 minute. Add chicken and heat through. Serve immediately with boiled rice.

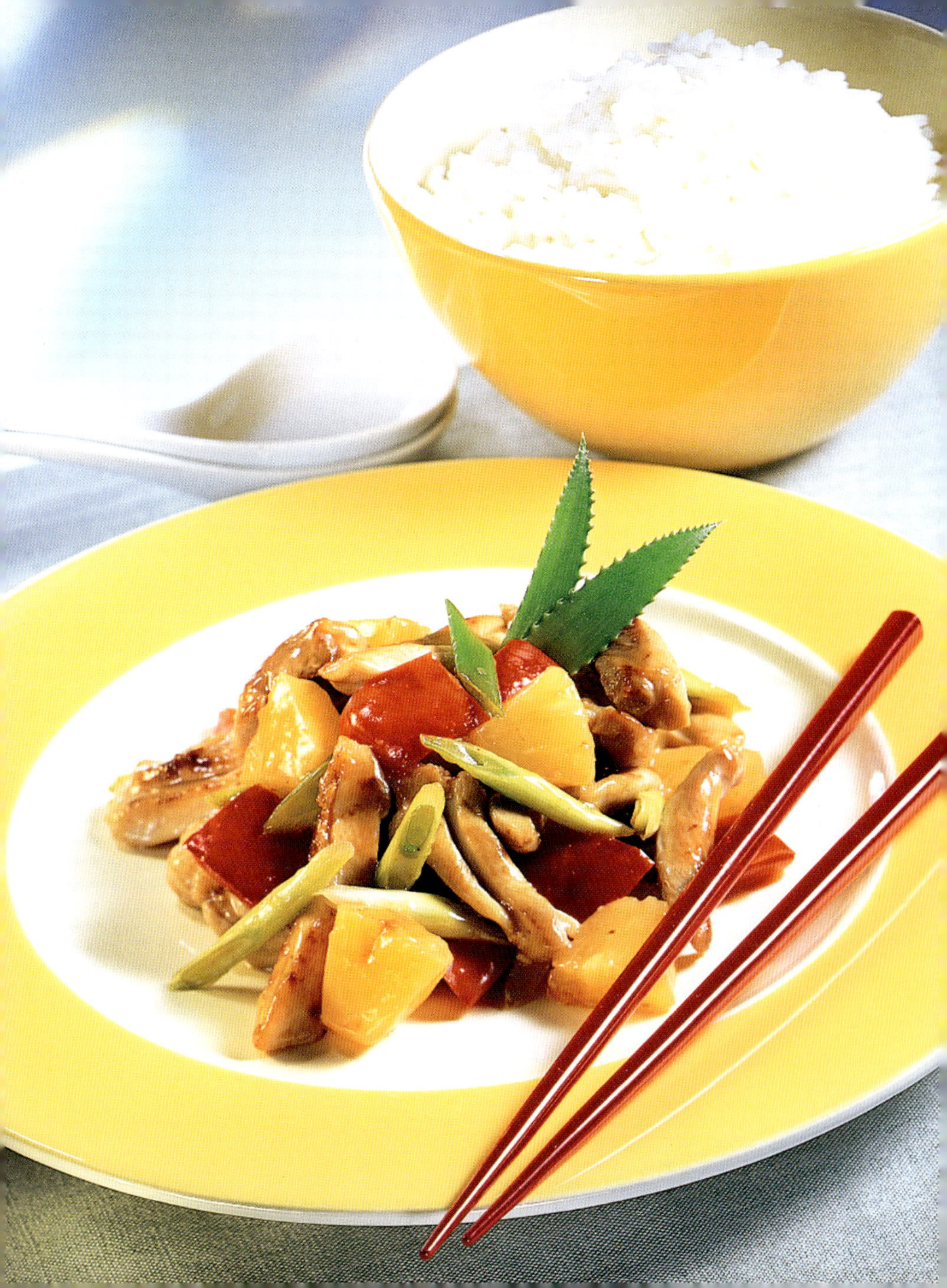

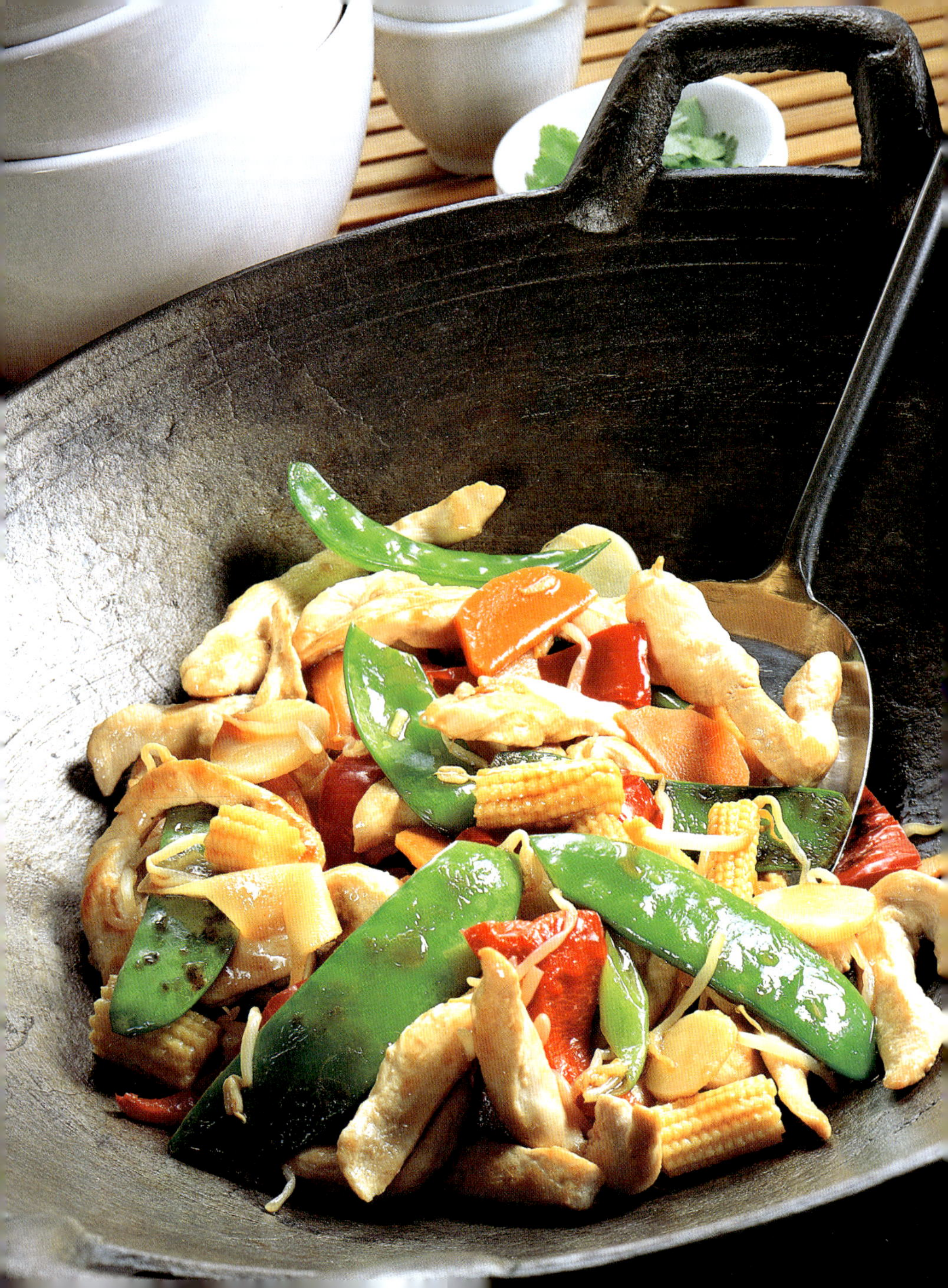

Chicken and vegetable stir-fry

SERVES 4

1 lb/500g chicken strips
2 tablespoons canola oil
1 clove garlic, crushed
½ ins/1cm piece fresh ginger, finely chopped
6 spring onions, sliced into ½ ins/1cm lengths on diagonal
2 tablespoons oyster sauce
½ teaspoon chicken stock powder
¼ cup water

1 medium carrot, chopped
1 red pepper/capsicum, cut into strips
8 oz/225g canned water chestnuts, drained
8 oz/225g canned baby corn pieces, drained
7 oz/200g mange tout/snowpeas, trimmed
½ cup bean sprouts

1. Trim any visible fat from the chicken. Heat oil in a wok, add garlic, ginger and spring onions and stir-fry for 1 minute, then add chicken and stir-fry until cooked through. Remove the chicken and spring onions from the wok.
2. Mix together the oyster sauce, stock powder and water and add to the wok. Add the carrot and red pepper and cook, lifting vegetables from the bottom and turning over continuously for 2 minutes. Add remaining vegetables and continue stirring for 2 minutes.
3. Return the chicken and spring onions to the pan and toss through vegetables for 2 minutes to reheat. Pile onto a platter and serve immediately.

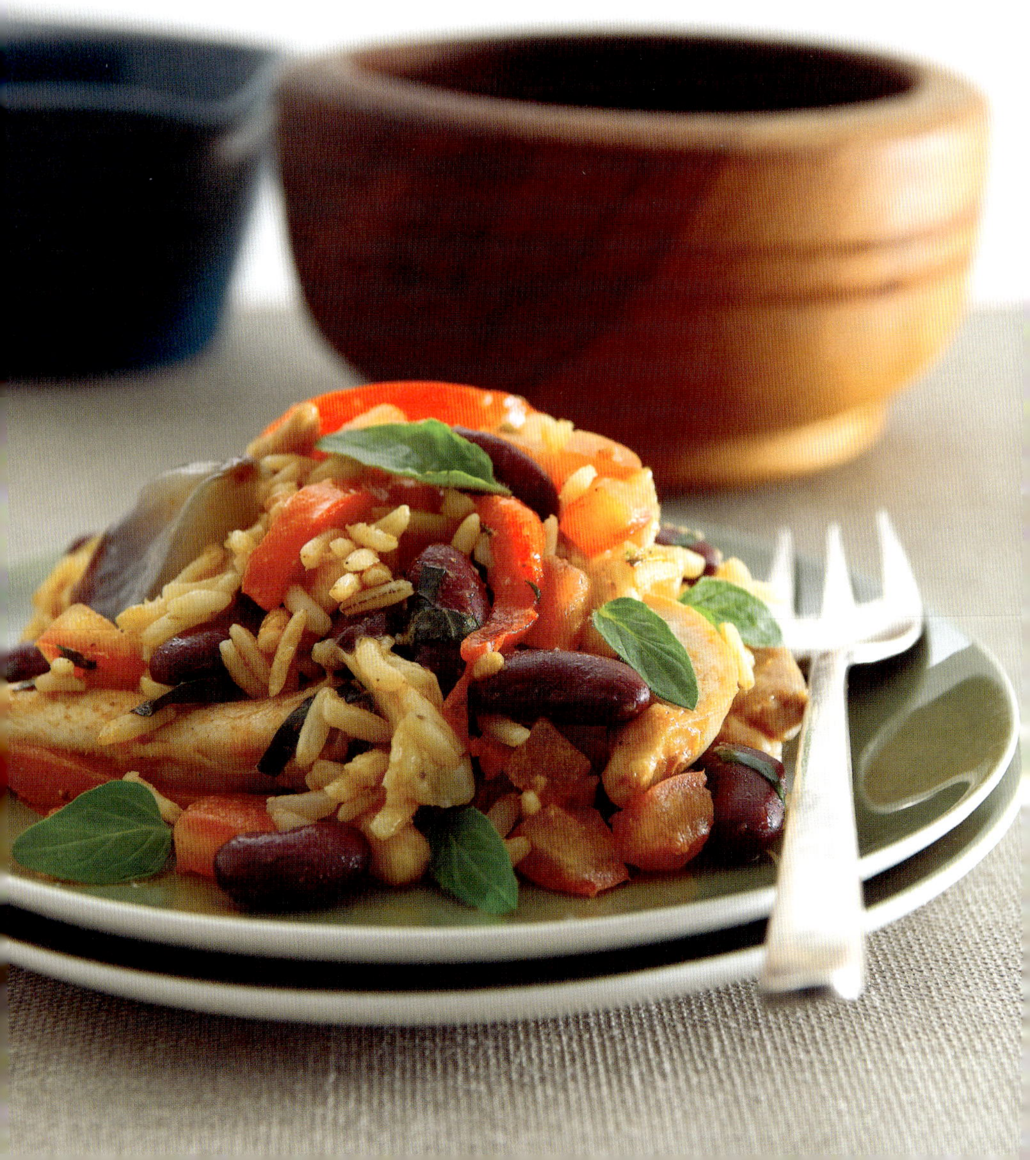

main meals

Chicken, leek and mushroom flan

SERVES 4

1 skinless chicken breast fillet
1 frozen savoury pie flan
1 tablespoon canola oil
1 leek, trimmed and thinly sliced
salt and pepper
3½ oz/100g button mushrooms, sliced
1 chicken bouillon/stock cube, crumbled
1 tablespoon lemon juice
1 cup thickened cream
1 egg, beaten
¼ teaspoon nutmeg
1¾ oz/50g flaked almonds
tossed salad, to serve

1. Slice the chicken breast into ½ ins/1cm-thick slices using a large knife, at a 45 degree angle.
2. Preheat oven to 360°F/180°C. Place the frozen pie flan on an oven tray and blind bake for 10–15 minutes, or as per packet directions. Meanwhile, heat oil in a large pan and cook leeks until soft. Push to the side of the pan, add chicken and cook 1 minute on each side. Sprinkle lightly with salt and pepper, add mushrooms, crumbled bouillon cube and lemon juice, turn down heat and simmer 3 minutes.
3. Heat cream to a simmer, remove from heat and cool slightly. Quickly stir in the beaten egg and nutmeg.
4. Fill the pie flan with the chicken, mushrooms and leek. Stir any pan juices into the cream mixture, then spoon over the chicken filling. Sprinkle with the almonds to make a dense covering. Bake for 25–30 minutes until filling is set. Serve with a tossed salad.

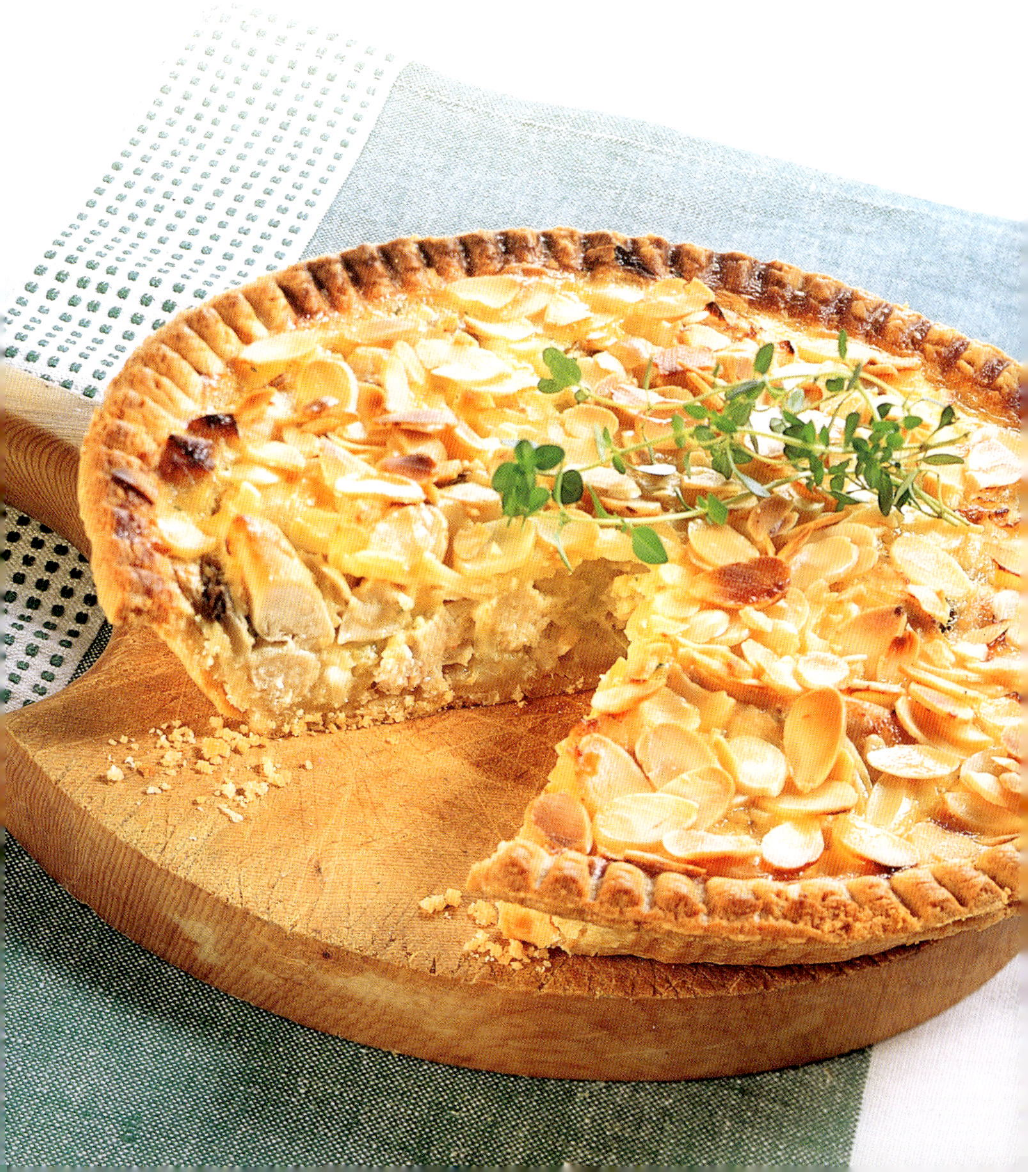

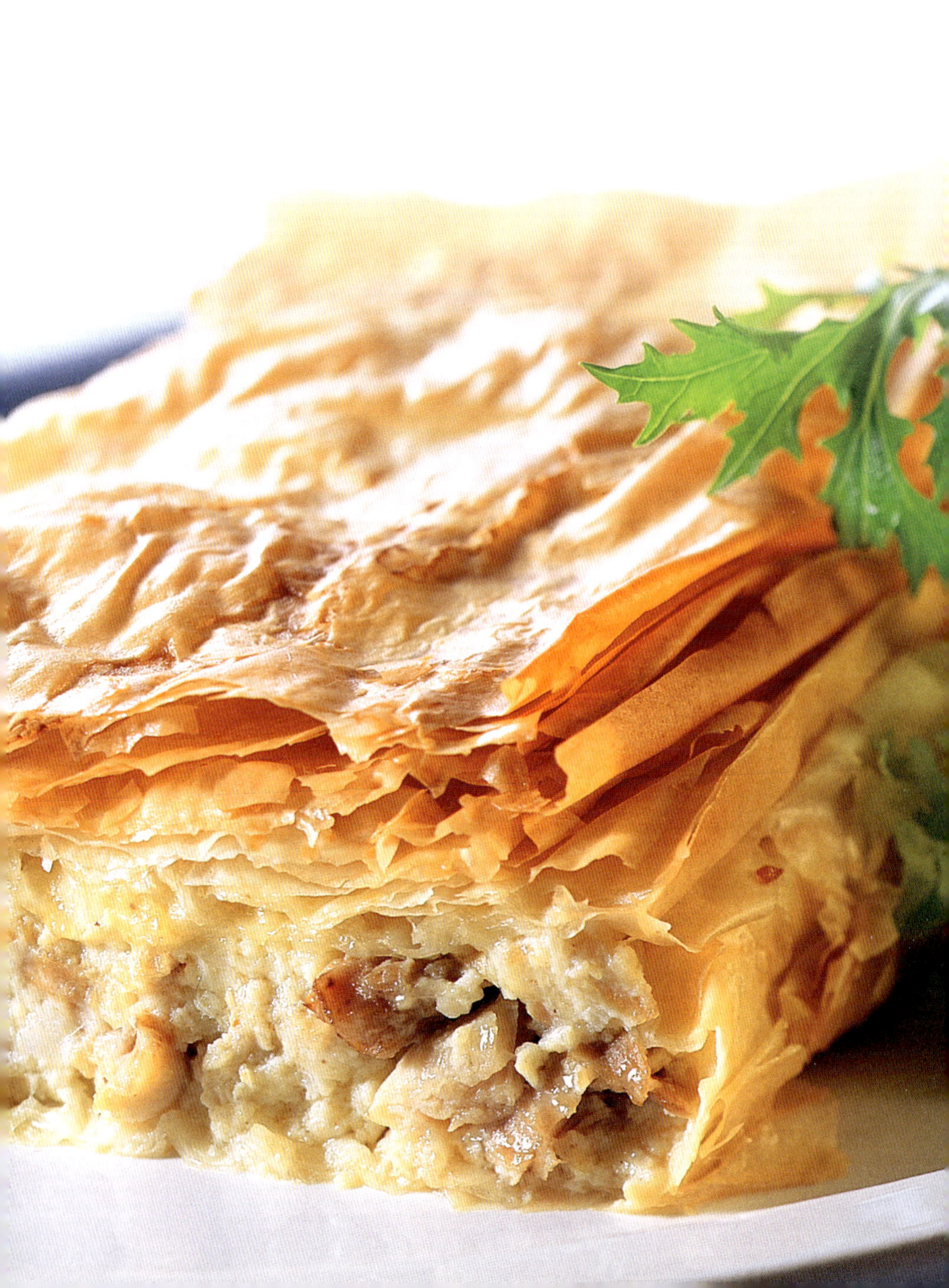

Filo chicken pie

SERVES 4

1 lb/500g chicken thigh fillets
1 cup water
½ teaspoon salt
½ teaspoon chicken bouillon powder
2 onions, chopped
1 oz/30g butter
2⅔ oz/75g Romano or parmesan cheese, grated

¼ teaspoon nutmeg
½ teaspoon freshly ground black pepper
4 eggs, beaten
canola oil spray
1 packet filo pastry

1. Place chicken in a saucepan and add the water and salt. Bring slowly to the boil, skimming off the froth as it rises. When water is clear, add the bouillon powder and onion. Cover and simmer for 30–35 minutes until chicken is tender. Remove the chicken to a plate. Continue to simmer the onion uncovered until it becomes soft and water has reduced. It should look like a pulpy, runny sauce.
2. Cut the chicken into strips and return to the saucepan. Add the butter and simmer for 2 minutes, stirring occasionally. Remove from heat and allow to cool slightly. Stir to release trapped heat. When cool, stir in the cheese, nutmeg, pepper and beaten eggs.
3. Preheat oven to 360°F/180°C. Spray the base and sides of a 2 ins/5cm-deep baking dish, approximately 7 ins x 8 ins (18cm x 20cm), with canola oil spray and line it with a sheet of filo pastry. Spray the filo with canola spray, moving in a zig-zag pattern to cover the whole surface. Place second sheet on top. Spray, then repeat until 8 sheets are placed.
4. Pour in the chicken mixture, fold overlapping pastry edges over the filling. Cover top with 8 sheets of filo, spraying with canola spray as before. Trim edges, allowing a slight overhang. With the tip of a sharp knife, lightly score the top 2 sheets into squares to make cutting easier when pie is cooked. Wet your hand and splash top of pie with water. Place in oven and bake for 45 minutes, until puffed and golden. Remove from oven and rest for 10 minutes before cutting through the score marks. Serve hot or cold.

Greek chicken meatballs

SERVES 4

1 lb/500g chicken mince
1 onion, grated
¼ cup parsley, chopped
salt and freshly ground black pepper
2 sprigs oregano, leaves removed and chopped
1 egg, beaten
1 cup dry breadcrumbs
juice and finely grated zest of 1 lemon
oil for frying
¾ oz/20g parmesan cheese, grated

Tomato sauce
1 tablespoon olive oil
1 onion, finely diced
1 clove garlic, crushed
14 oz/400g canned crushed tomatoes
1 tablespoon tomato paste
½ teaspoon dried oregano
1 teaspoon sugar
salt and freshly ground black pepper
¼ cup parsley, chopped
rice, to serve

1. Mix together the chicken, onion, parsley, salt, pepper, oregano, egg, breadcrumbs and lemon juice and zest, and work mixture well with hands until smooth. Heat about ½ ins/1cm of oil in a wide, heavy-based frying pan until hot. With wet hands, shape tablespoonfuls of the chicken mixture into balls and fry until golden and cooked through. Drain on absorbent paper.
2. To make the sauce, heat oil in a pan and cook onion and garlic for 1–2 minutes or until softened. Add tomatoes, tomato paste, oregano, sugar, salt, pepper and ½ cup water and cook for 5–6 minutes or until reduced and sauce has thickened. Remove from heat.
3. Stir parsley through sauce, then process until smooth using a stick blender. Return to heat, add meatballs and warm through. Top with the parmesan cheese and serve with rice.

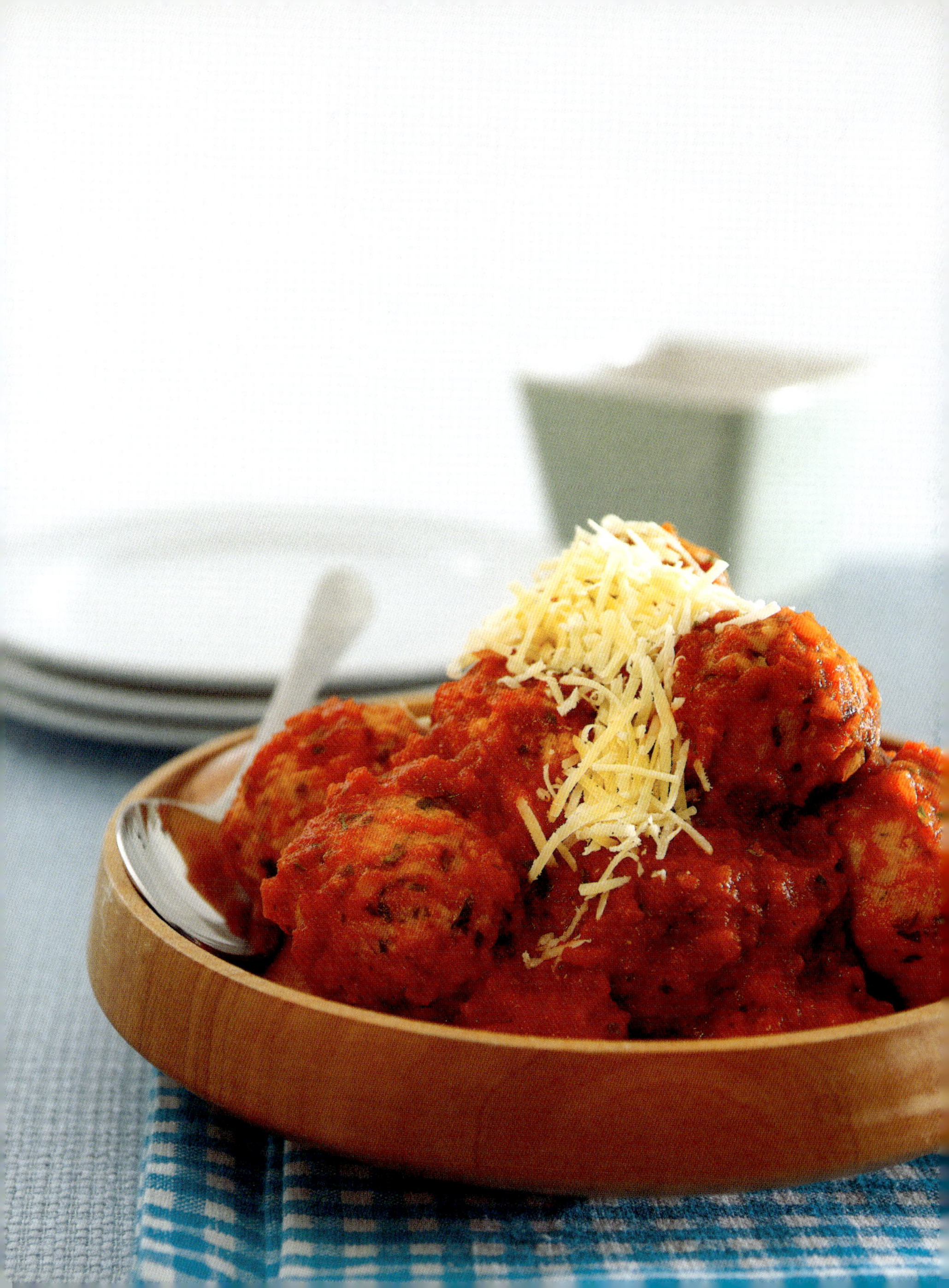

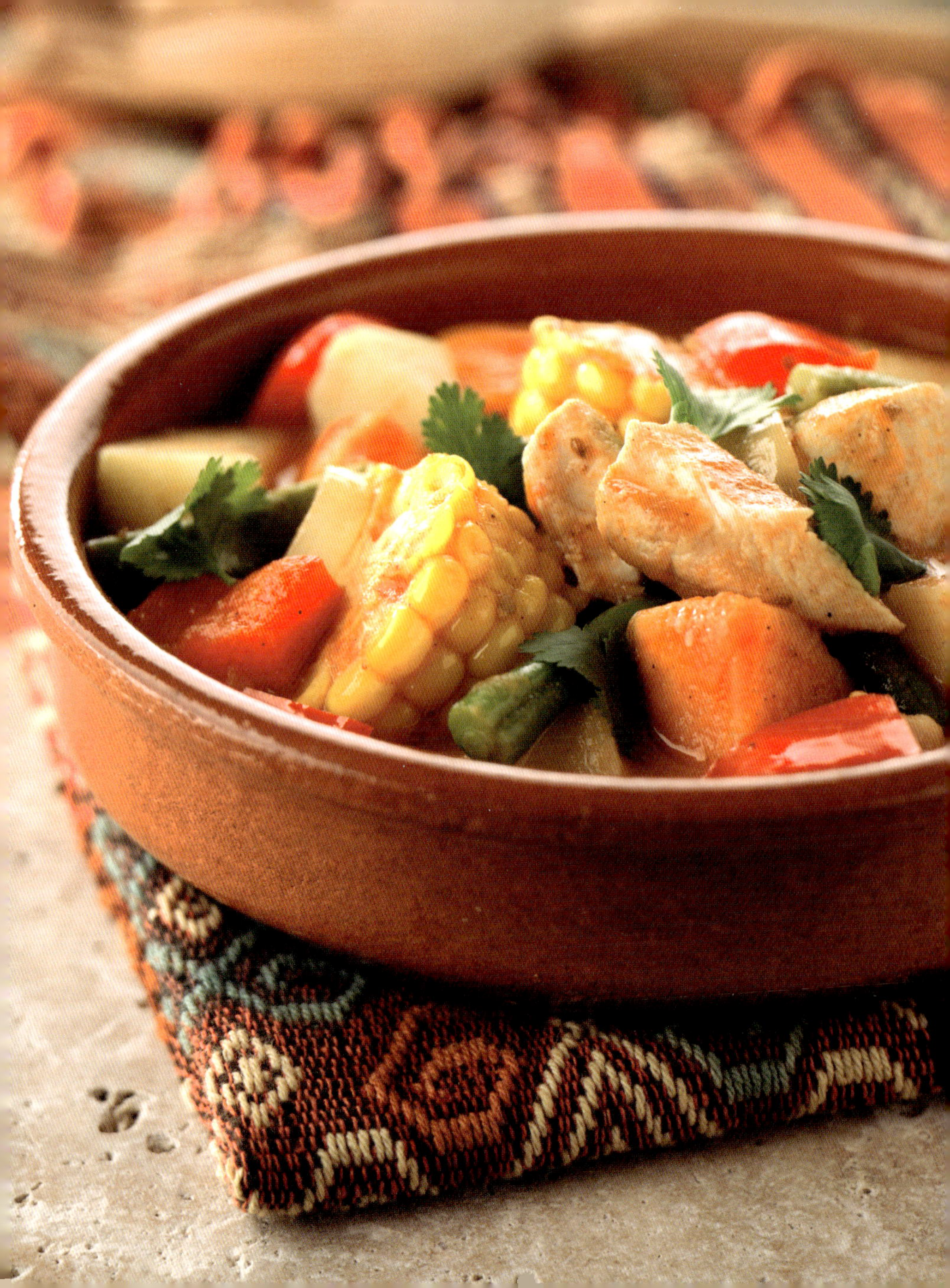

Chicken and vegetable stew

SERVES 4

¼ cup olive oil
1½ lbs/600g chicken breast fillets, cut into 1 ins/3cm pieces
1 onion, sliced
2 cloves garlic, crushed
2 jalapeño chilies, deseeded and finely diced
1 red pepper/capsicum, deseeded and diced
1 teaspoon ground cummin
1 teaspoon ground cilantro/coriander
2 teaspoons dried oregano

2 tomatoes, diced
2 cups chicken stock
2 potatoes, peeled and diced
12 oz/300g sweet potato, peeled and diced
5¼ oz/150g green beans, sliced
1 corn cob, husk removed and sliced
¼ cup fresh cilantro/coriander, chopped
salt and freshly ground black pepper
rice to serve

1. Heat 2 tablespoons of the oil in a large saucepan over medium to high heat. Cook chicken in batches until golden. Remove and set aside.
2. Heat remaining oil over medium heat. Cook onion, garlic, chili and pepper until soft. Stir in ground cumin and cilantro and cook until aromatic.
3. Add oregano, tomatoes, chicken stock, potatoes and sweet potato. Bring to the boil. Return chicken to the pan. Reduce heat to low, cover and simmer for 15 minutes. Add beans and corn and simmer for a further 6 minutes or until chicken and vegetables are tender.
4. Stir through the fresh cilantron and season with salt and pepper. Serve with rice.

Chicken, baby corn and green pea casserole

SERVES 4

2 lbs/1kg chicken drumsticks
12 1/3 oz/350g jar tomato and pesto pasta sauce
1/2 cup water
4 medium potatoes, peeled and quartered

2 tablespoons olive oil
1/2 cup parsley, finely chopped
9 oz/250g frozen peas
15 oz/425g canned baby corn
crusty bread, to serve

1. Preheat oven to 360°F/180°C. Remove skin from drumsticks. Pour the pasta sauce into a casserole or baking dish and stir in the water. Place drumsticks in one layer and arrange potato quarters in between. Drizzle over the olive oil and sprinkle with parsley. Cover dish with lid or foil.
2. Cook in the oven for 30 minutes. Remove from oven and turn the chicken and potatoes. Add the peas and baby corn. Return to oven and cook uncovered for 25 minutes more or until drumsticks and potatoes are tender.
3. Serve hot with crusty bread.

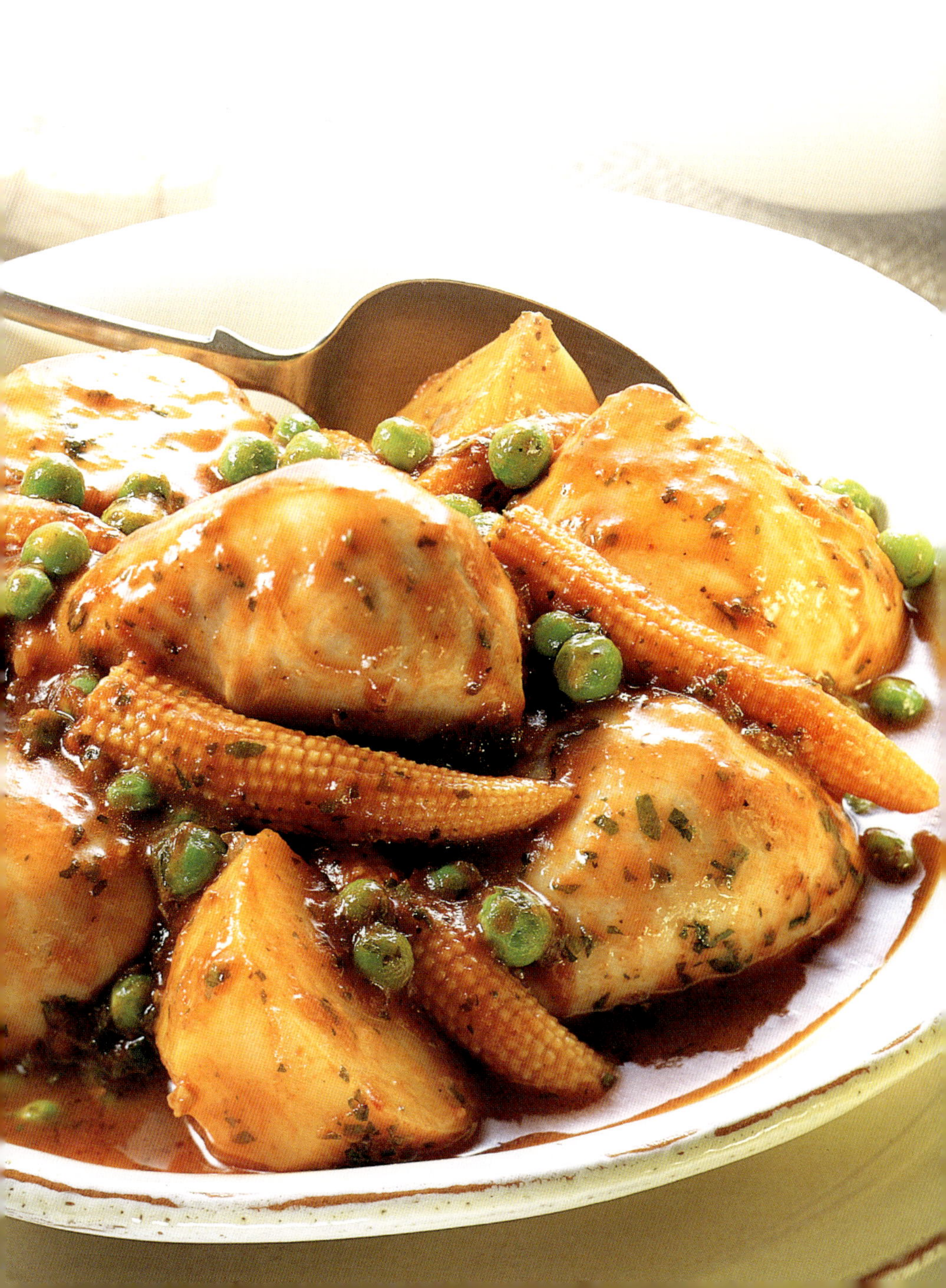

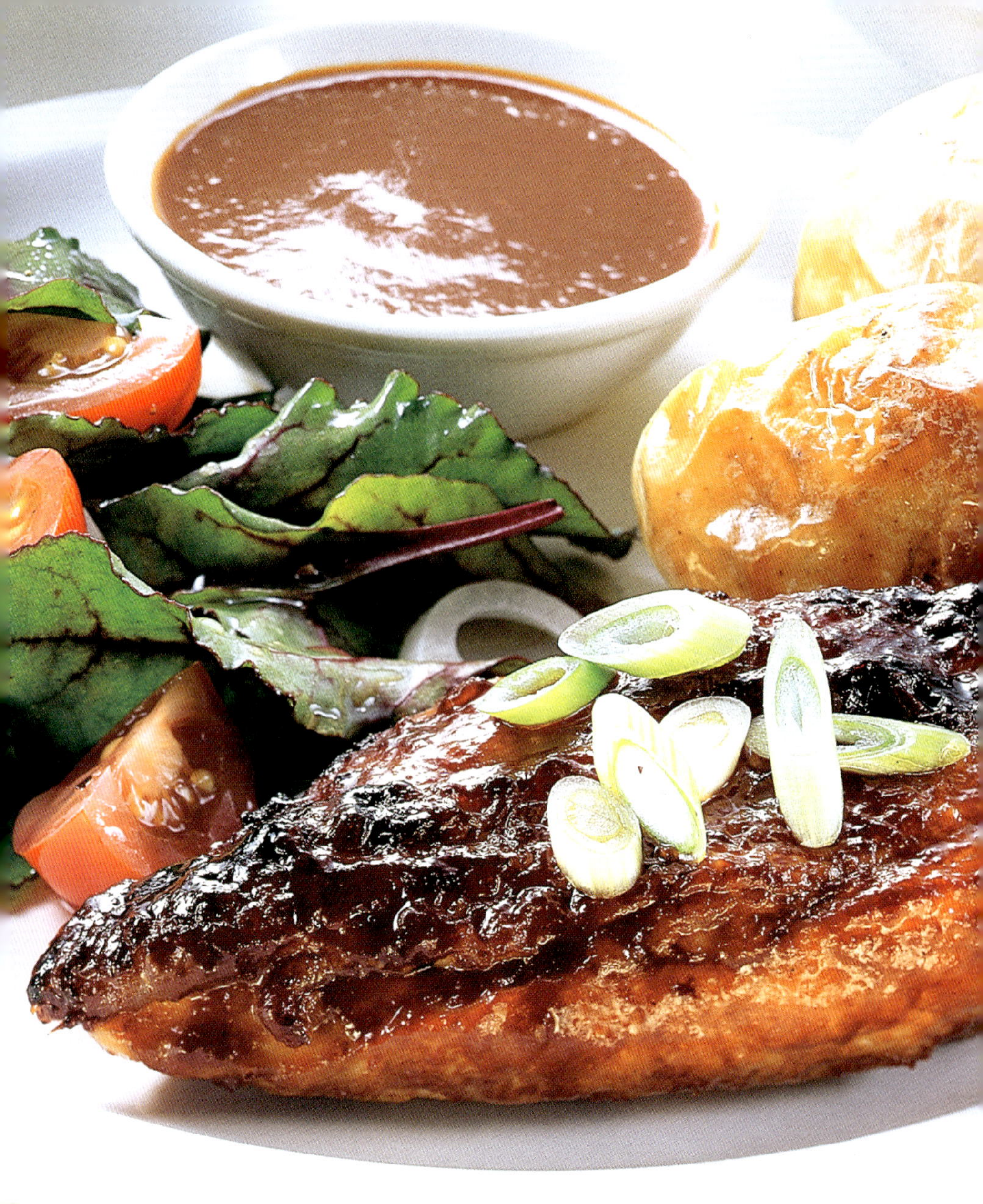

Southern barbecued chicken

SERVES 4

2 lbs/1kg chicken pieces
oil for cooking
Barbecue sauce
1½ cups tomato purée
1 cup cider vinegar
½ cup canola oil
⅓ cup Worcestershire sauce

½ cup brown sugar
¼ cup corn/golden syrup
2 tablespoons French mustard
3 cloves garlic, minced
¼ cup lemon juice
jacket potatoes and salad, to serve

1. Place all sauce ingredients in a saucepan, stir to combine. Simmer over low heat for 15–20 minutes, stirring regularly.
2. Heat barbecue to moderate and oil the grill plate. Lightly sear chicken pieces on all sides over direct heat, about 4 minutes each side. Remove the chicken to a plate.
3. Place 1 cup of the sauce in a bowl by the barbecue. Place chicken on the grill and brush well with the sauce.
4. Close the barbecue lid and cook for 10 minutes, then lift the lid, brush with sauce, turn chicken and brush again with sauce, close lid and cook 10 minutes. Repeat this process every 10 minutes for a total of approximately 40–50 minutes until chicken is rich brown and cooked through. If chicken is cooking too quickly, reduce heat. Heat extra sauce in a small saucepan on the barbecue.
5. Serve chicken with hot sauce and jacket potatoes. Accompany with a salad.

Store remaining barbecue sauce in the refrigerator for later use.

Teriyaki chicken with kinpira vegetables

SERVES 4

4 chicken breast fillets, skin on
1 cup teriyaki sauce
4 green asparagus spears, cut into quarters
4 white asparagus spears, cut into quarters
4 baby carrots, cut into quarters lengthwise
4 baby corn, cut into quarters lengthwise
1 tablespoon sugar
1 tablespoon light soy sauce
2 teaspoons sesame oil
2 teaspoons white sesame seeds

1. Place chicken under a hot grill and cook for two minutes each side. Heat teriyaki sauce in a large frying pan. Place chicken into pan and cook for a further two minutes on each side. Slice each chicken fillet into ½ ins/1cm strips. Arrange carefully onto warmed serving plate.
2. Combine vegetables with sugar, light soy sauce and sesame oil. Stir-fry over a high heat for 1–2 minutes.
3. Arrange vegetables beside the chicken, sprinkle with sesame seeds and serve.

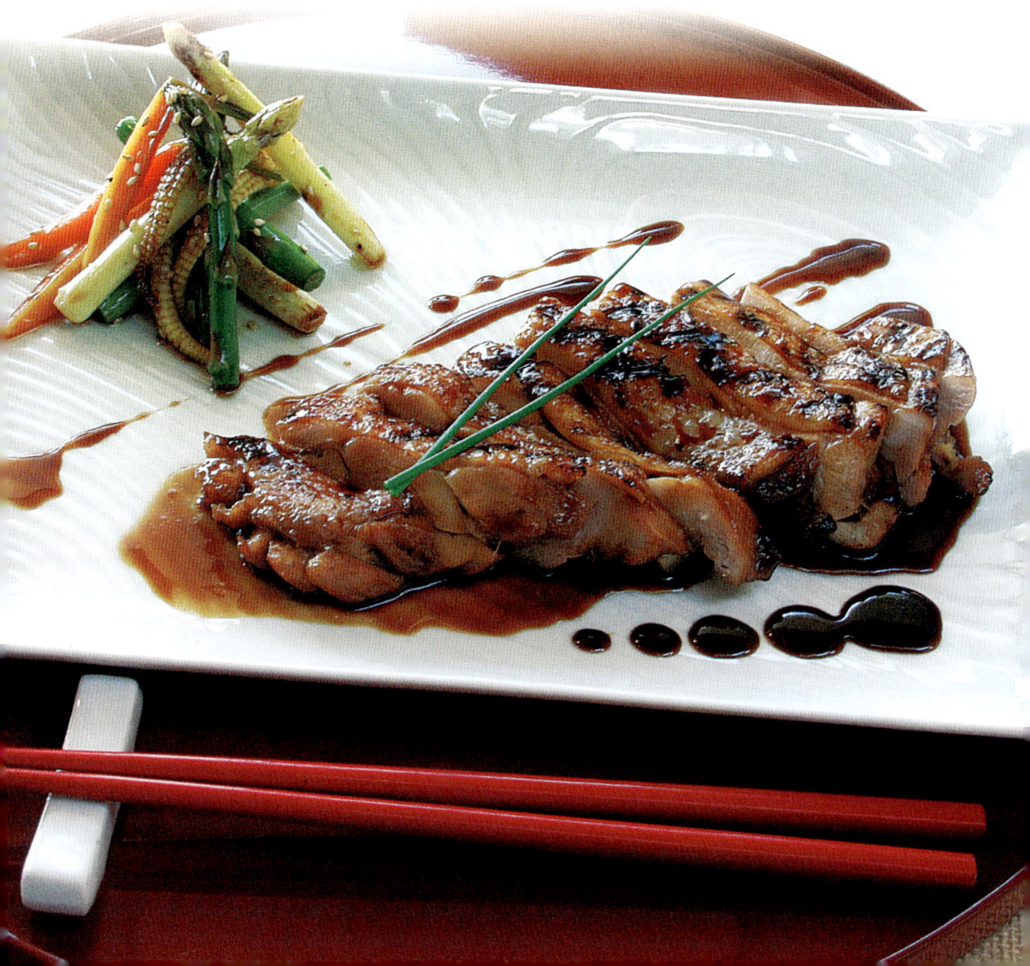

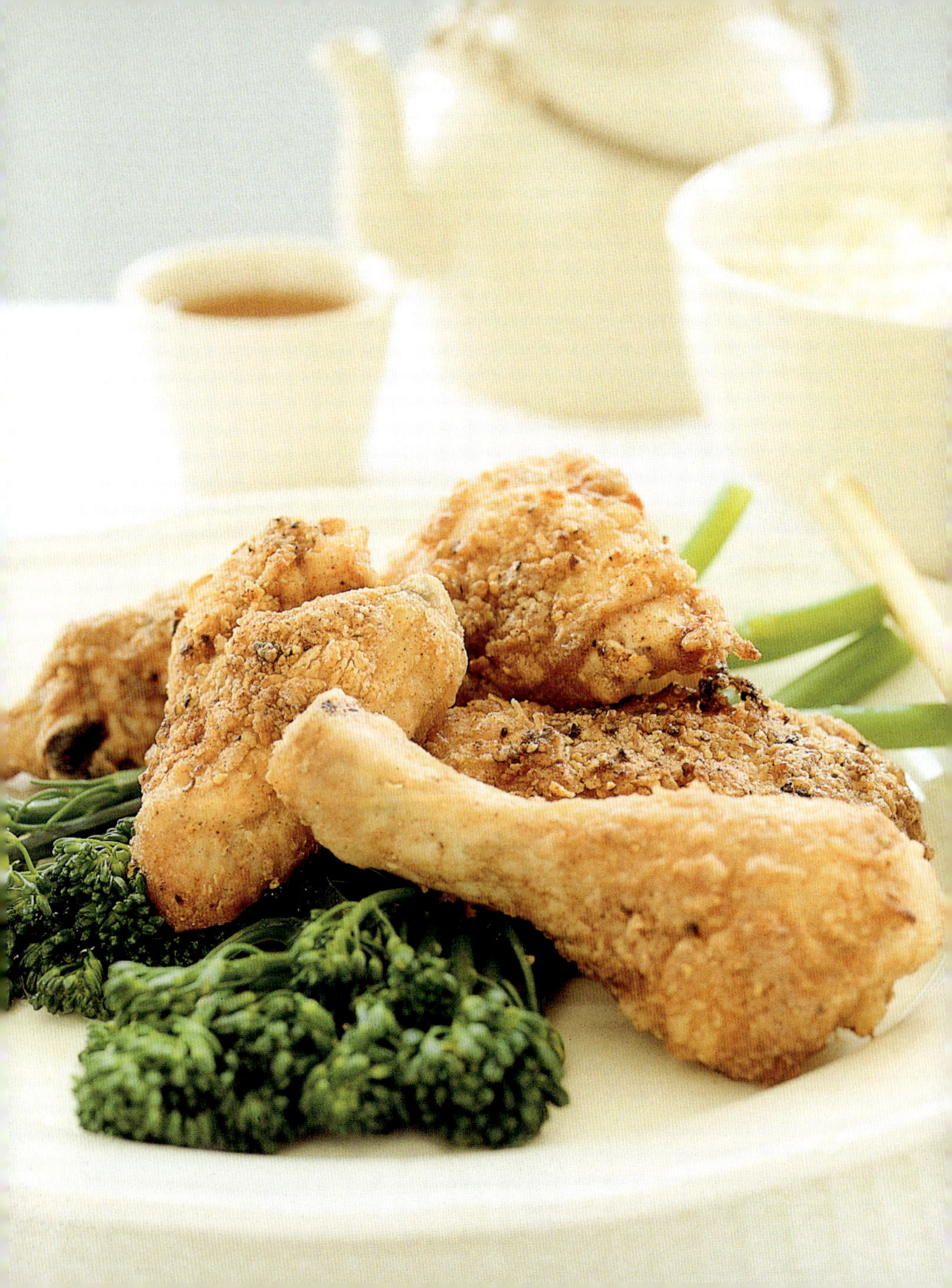

Chinese five spice chicken

SERVES 4

3 lbs/1½kg chicken pieces
⅔ cup cornflour
1 tablespoon Chinese five spice powder
2 teaspoons freshly ground black pepper

2 teaspoons garlic and herb salt
¼ cup lemon juice
olive oil spray
broccolini or Asian greens, to serve

1. Preheat the oven to 410°F/210°C. Cut larger chicken pieces in half so all the pieces are the same small size. Mix together the cornflour, five spice powder, pepper and garlic and herb salt.
2. Brush each chicken piece with lemon juice, spray with olive oil and coat lightly in flour mixture.
3. Place the chicken on a rack over a baking tray. Bake for 30–40 minutes or until golden and crisp. Spray again with olive oil halfway through cooking.
4. Serve with broccolini or Asian greens.

Honey balsamic barbecued drumsticks

SERVES 4

2 lbs/1kg chicken drumsticks
salt and freshly ground black pepper
½ cup honey

3 tablespoons balsamic vinegar
¾ ins/2cm piece ginger, grated
oil for cooking

1. Season drumsticks with salt and pepper. Place in a single layer in a non-metallic dish. Mix honey, vinegar and ginger together and pour over drumsticks. Stand 1 hour or longer in refrigerator.
2. Heat barbecue until hot. Place a wire cake rack over barbecue grill bars and lightly oil. Arrange drumsticks on rack and cook 20–25 minutes, turning frequently and brushing with honey mixture.
3. Remove cake rack from barbecue and place drumsticks directly on grill bars. Cook approximately 5–10 minutes more until brown and crisp, turning occasionally. Serve hot.

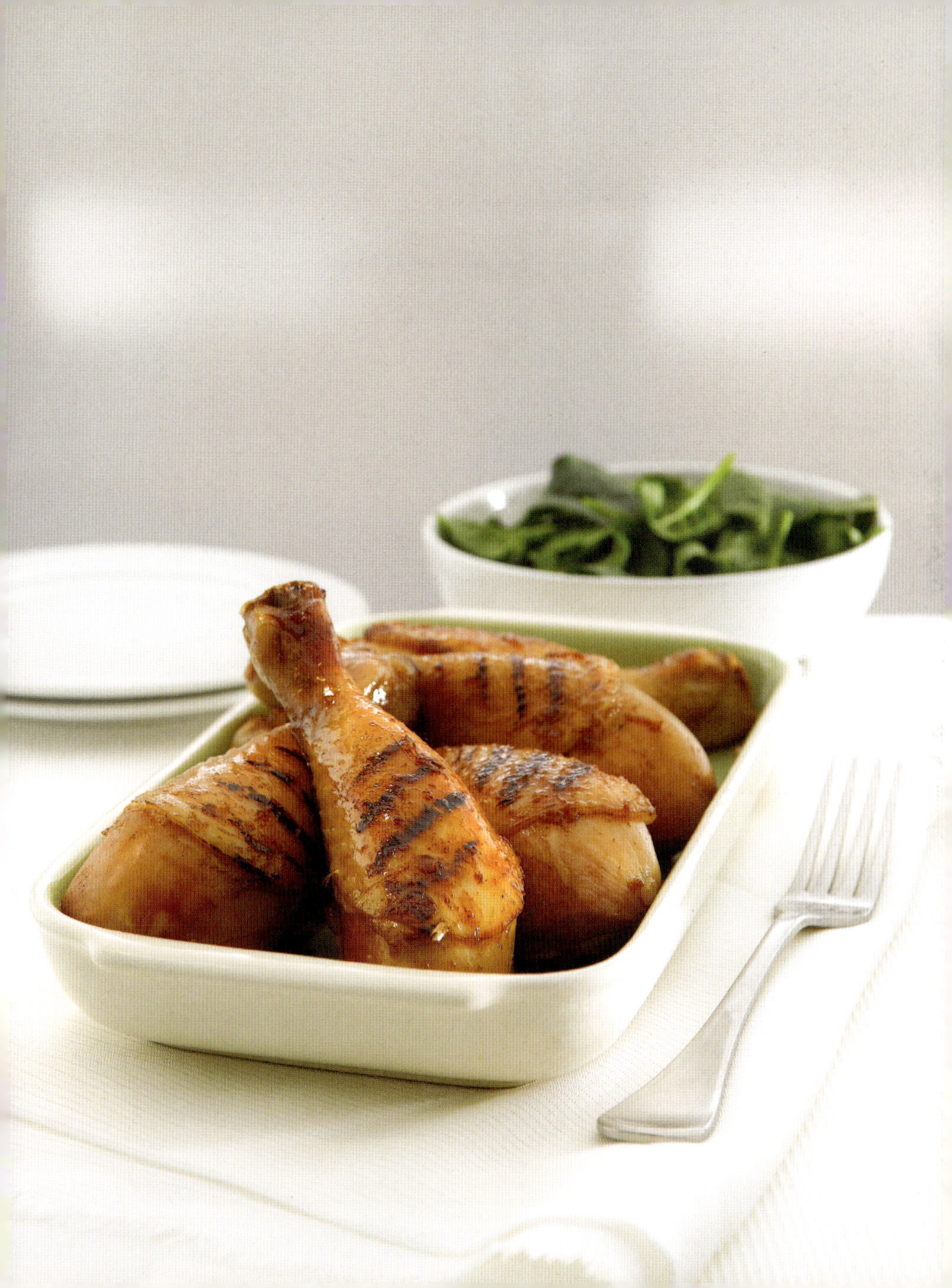

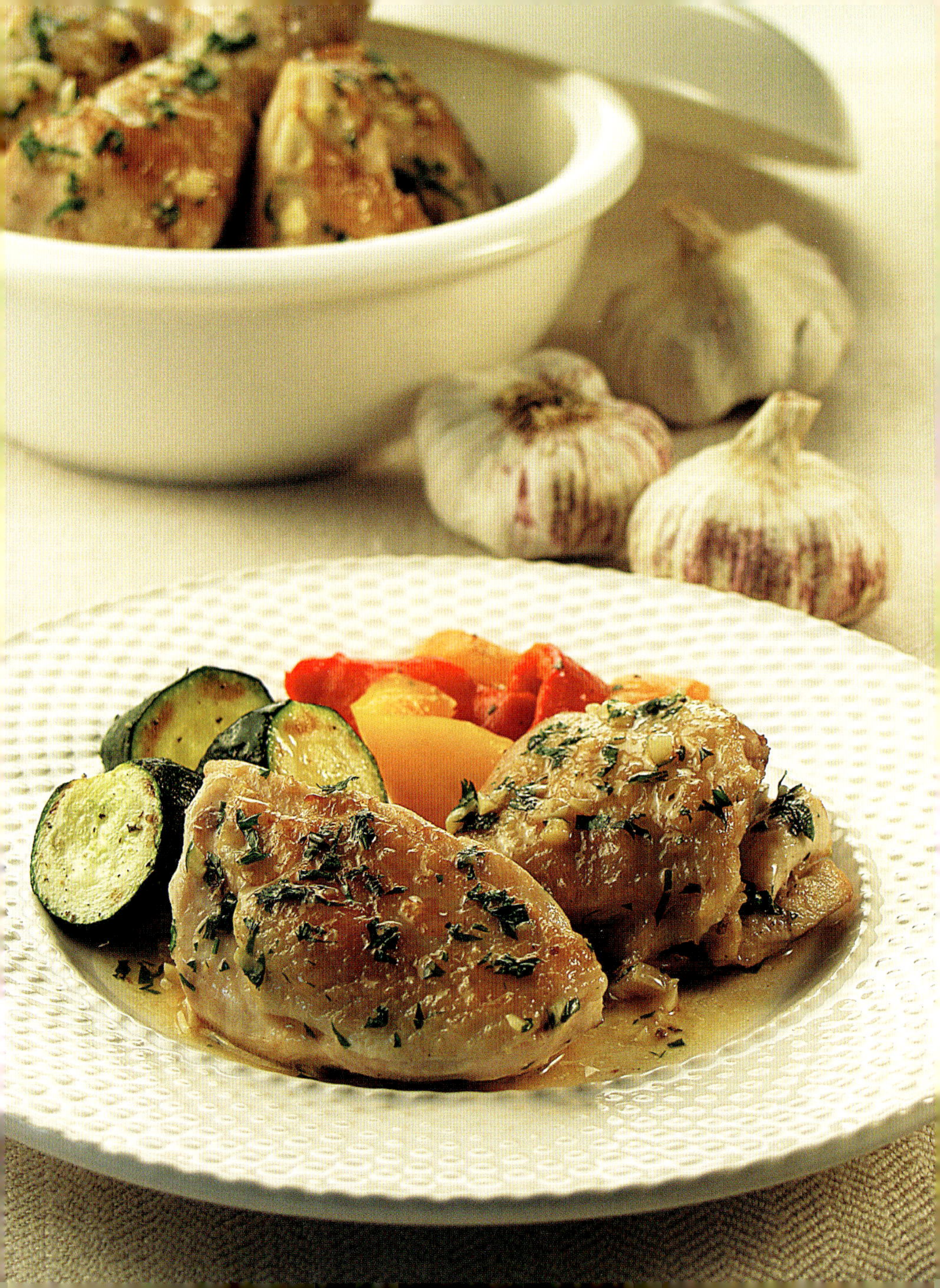

Chicken in garlic sauce

SERVES 4

3 lbs/1½kg chicken pieces
salt
5 tablespoons olive oil
6 garlic cloves, chopped, plus 1 clove, minced

¼ cup parsley, very finely chopped
2 tablespoons dry white wine

1. Cut the larger chicken pieces in half, so all pieces are a similar size. Sprinkle with salt. Heat the oil in a shallow flameproof casserole dish and brown the chicken over a medium-high heat on all sides. Add the chopped garlic, reduce heat to medium, and cook, stirring occasionally, for 30 minutes. Stir in the minced garlic, parsley, and wine. Cover and cook for 15 minutes more, or until chicken is done and the juices run clear when a thigh is pierced with a skewer.

Vineyard chicken

SERVES 4

4 chicken breast halves
2 tablespoons all-purpose/plain flour
8 basil leaves, shredded
¼ teaspoon dried tarragon
¼ teaspoon ground paprika
salt and freshly ground pepper
1 tablespoon olive oil

1 tablespoon butter
2 small cloves garlic, chopped
½ cup dry white wine
1 cup red grapes, halved and seeded
½ cup chicken stock
1 teaspoon fresh lemon juice
¼ cup parsley, chopped

1. Trim any excess fat from the chicken. In a wide bowl combine the flour, basil, tarragon, paprika and salt and pepper. Add chicken and toss gently to coat. Heat oil and butter in a large heavy frying pan over a moderately high heat. Add chicken and sauté on each side until golden brown. Add garlic to the pan, cook a minute, then pour in wine. Cover and cook gently until chicken is just tender, about 5 minutes.
2. Add grapes, stock and lemon juice and continue cooking until sauce is hot. Transfer chicken and grapes to a heated serving platter and keep warm. Continue cooking sauce until reduced by half. When serving, spoon sauce over chicken and garnish with chopped parsley.

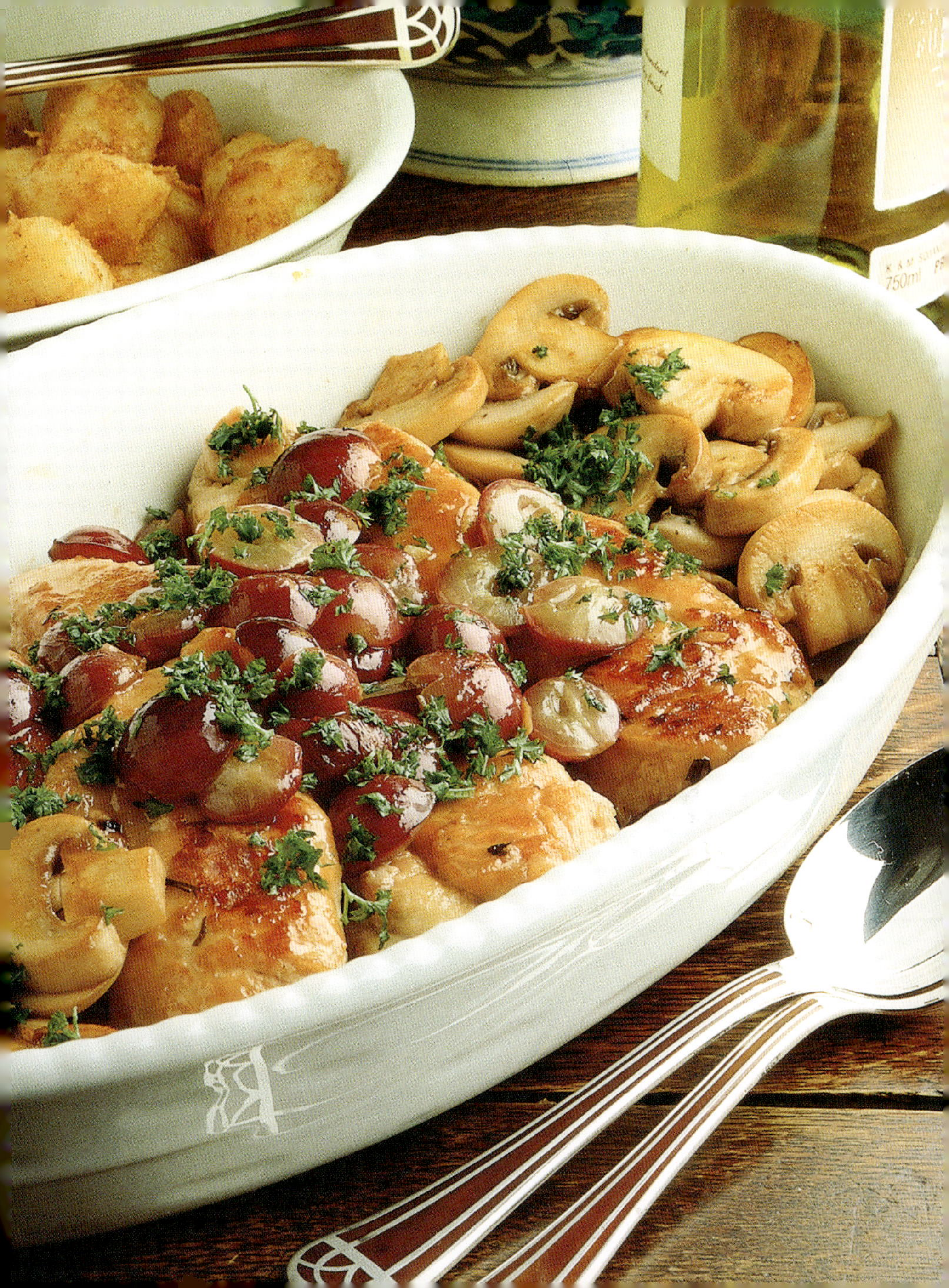
750ml

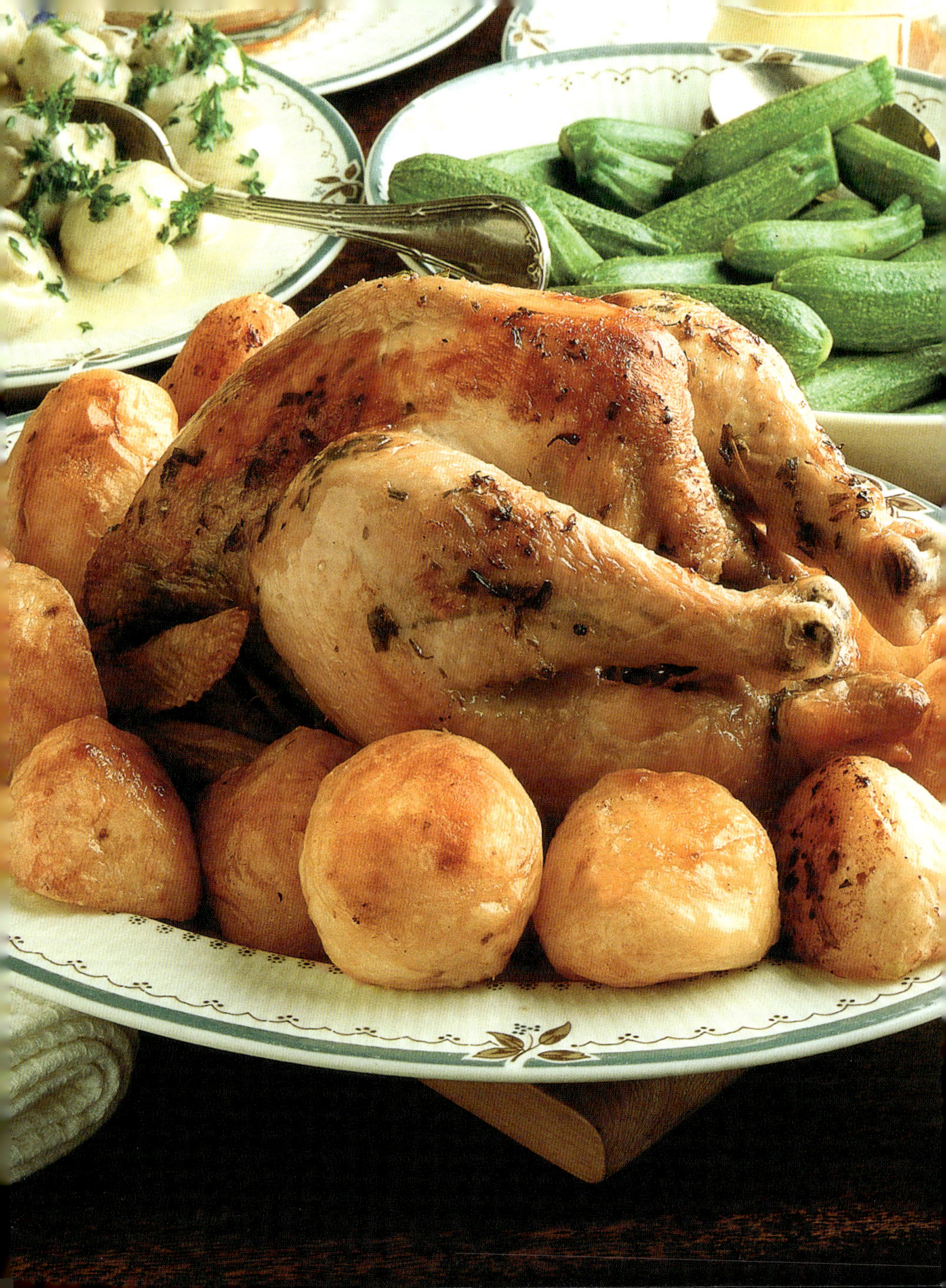

Lemon and tarragon roast chicken

SERVES 4

1 large free-range chicken
2 oz/60g butter
zest of 2 lemons
3 tablespoons lemon juice
¼ cup fresh tarragon, chopped

salt and freshly ground pepper
2 tablespoons oil
6 potatoes, halved and boiled for 5 minutes
baby courgettes/zucchini and buttered mushrooms, to serve

1. Preheat oven to 390°F/200°C. Carefully loosen skin of chicken from flesh, without piercing skin. This can be done by starting at the neck and slipping fingers between skin and flesh. Work towards tail, including tops of drumsticks. Cream butter with lemon zest. Gradually add 1 tablespoon of the lemon juice and the tarragon, then season with salt and pepper.
2. Spread two-thirds of the butter mixture under skin and pat chicken to smooth butter into an even layer. Truss chicken and rub with remaining butter mixture.
3. Add the oil to a large baking dish, add the potatoes and roll to coat evenly in the oil. Place chicken breast-side down on an oiled rack and place in the baking dish. Roast for 20 minutes. Turn potatoes and chicken and sprinkle with remaining lemon juice. Continue to cook, basting every 20 minutes, for 1¼ hours.
4. Let chicken rest for 15 minutes and cut into joints if desired. Transfer to a heated platter with potatoes and serve with baby courgettes and buttered mushrooms.

Apricot-glazed chicken with savoury stuffing

SERVES 4

2 lbs/1kg fresh chicken
1 tablespoon ground white pepper
1 cup apricot dipping sauce
  (see Spring rolls)
1 tablespoon soy sauce
½ lemon
1 tablespoon all-purpose/plain flour

Stuffing
3 rashers bacon, chopped
1 onion, finely chopped
1 cup long-grain rice, rinsed
2 cups boiling water
2 tablespoons apricot dipping sauce
2 teaspoons soy sauce
2 teaspoons mixed dried herbs
¼ cup parsley, chopped

1. Preheat oven to 360°F/180°C. Sprinkle the chicken with the white pepper, inside and out. Mix together the apricot dipping sauce and soy sauce, then brush over the chicken, including inside the cavity. Place the lemon in the cavity. Place chicken on an adjustable rack, breast-side down. Add a cup of water to the dish and bake for 40 minutes. Brush with sauce and turn breast-side up, brush again with sauce and cook for 40–50 minutes more until cooked when juices run clear when pierced with a skewer.
2. When chicken is placed in the oven, prepare the stuffing. Combine all ingredients in a lidded casserole dish and place on a shelf in the oven under the chicken. Cook for 40 minutes then remove from oven and stand covered for 10 minutes.
3. When chicken is cooked, remove from dish and cover with foil to rest. Skim fat from roasting pan and add about 1 cup of water to dissolve any cooked-on pan juices. Pour into a small saucepan. Add flour blended with a little water and stir until it thickens and boils. Serve at the side of the whole chicken.

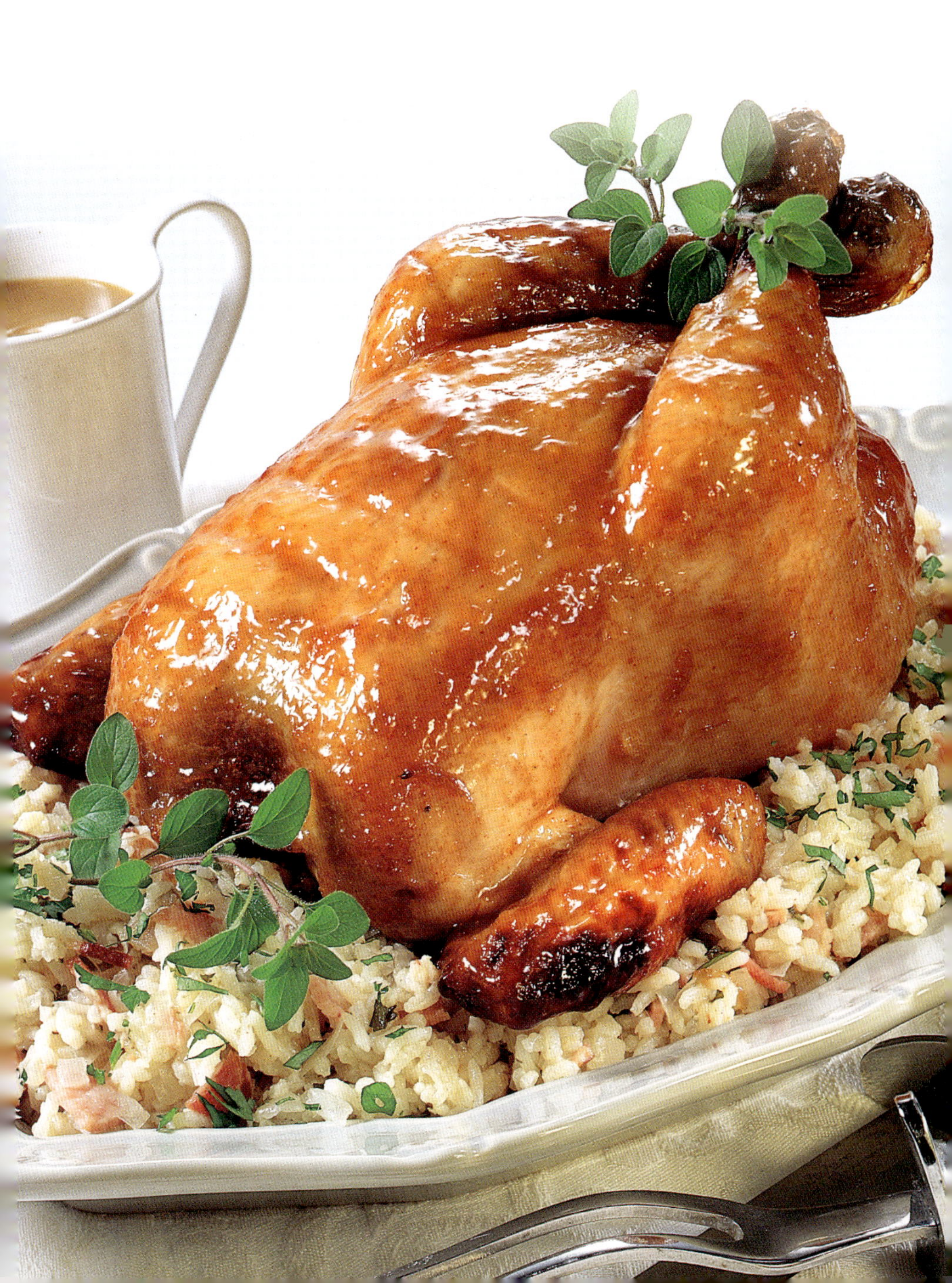

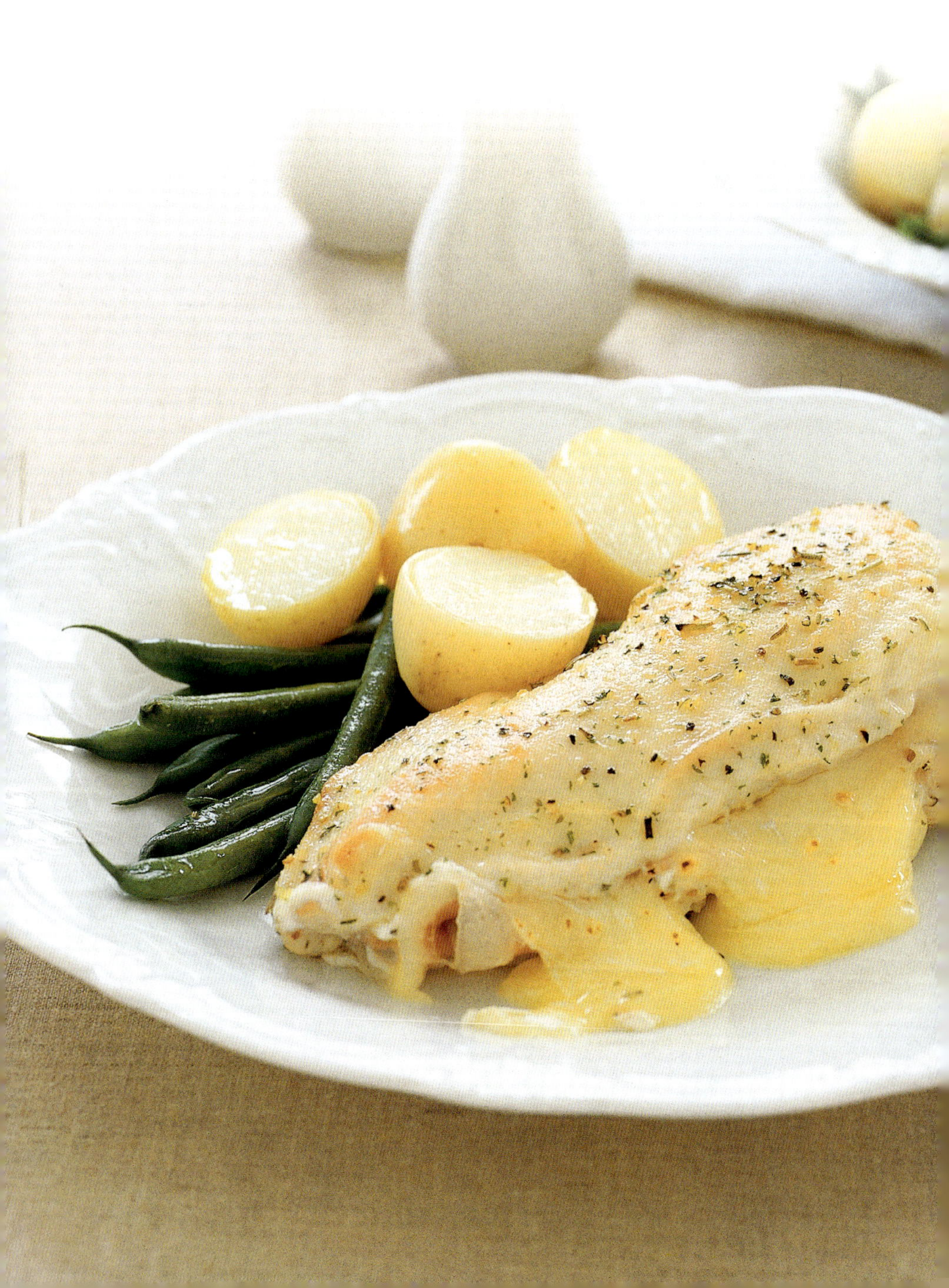

Tuscan chicken with mozzarella and prosciutto

SERVES 4

4 single chicken breast fillets, without tenderloins
8 slices mozzarella or other soft cheese
8 slices prosciutto or bacon
freshly ground black pepper
¼ cup plain flour

1 tablespoon Tuscan seasoning
2 tablespoons olive oil
7 oz/200g green beans, trimmed
½lb/500g baby potatoes
¾ oz/20g butter, melted

1. Trim the chicken breasts and slice nearly in half horizontally to make a slit.
2. Place 2 slices of mozzarella and prosciutto in each chicken breast. Season with freshly ground black pepper and secure with toothpicks. Combine the flour and Tuscan seasoning. Lightly coat each chicken breast.
3. Heat the oil in a large frying pan. Cook the chicken over medium-low heat for 4–5 minutes on each side or until golden and cooked. Meanwhile, cook the beans and potatoes until tender.
4. Remove the chicken from the pan and serve with the beans, potatoes and butter.

Tandoori chicken

SERVES 4-6

2 x 1¾ lb/800g fresh chickens
3 tablespoons tandoori paste
7 oz/200g natural yoghurt
2 tablespoons lemon juice
1 oz/30g butter, melted

1 small lettuce
1 red onion, cut into rings
2 small tomatoes, quartered
1 lemon, quartered

1. Make deep gashes in the chicken thighs and on each side of breast. Pin back the wings.
2. Mix tandoori paste, yoghurt, lemon juice and melted butter together. Place chickens in a non-metallic dish and spread mixture all over, rubbing well into the gashes. Cover and refrigerate for 12 hours or more. Place chickens on a roasting rack in a baking dish and spoon any remaining marinade over chickens.
3. Preheat oven to 375°F/190°C, add chicken and cook for 1 hour. Baste with pan juices during cooking. When cooked, cover with foil and rest for 10 minutes before serving.
4. Arrange crisp lettuce leaves on a large platter and cover with onion rings. Cut chicken into portions and place on the platter. Garnish with tomato wedges and lemon pieces.

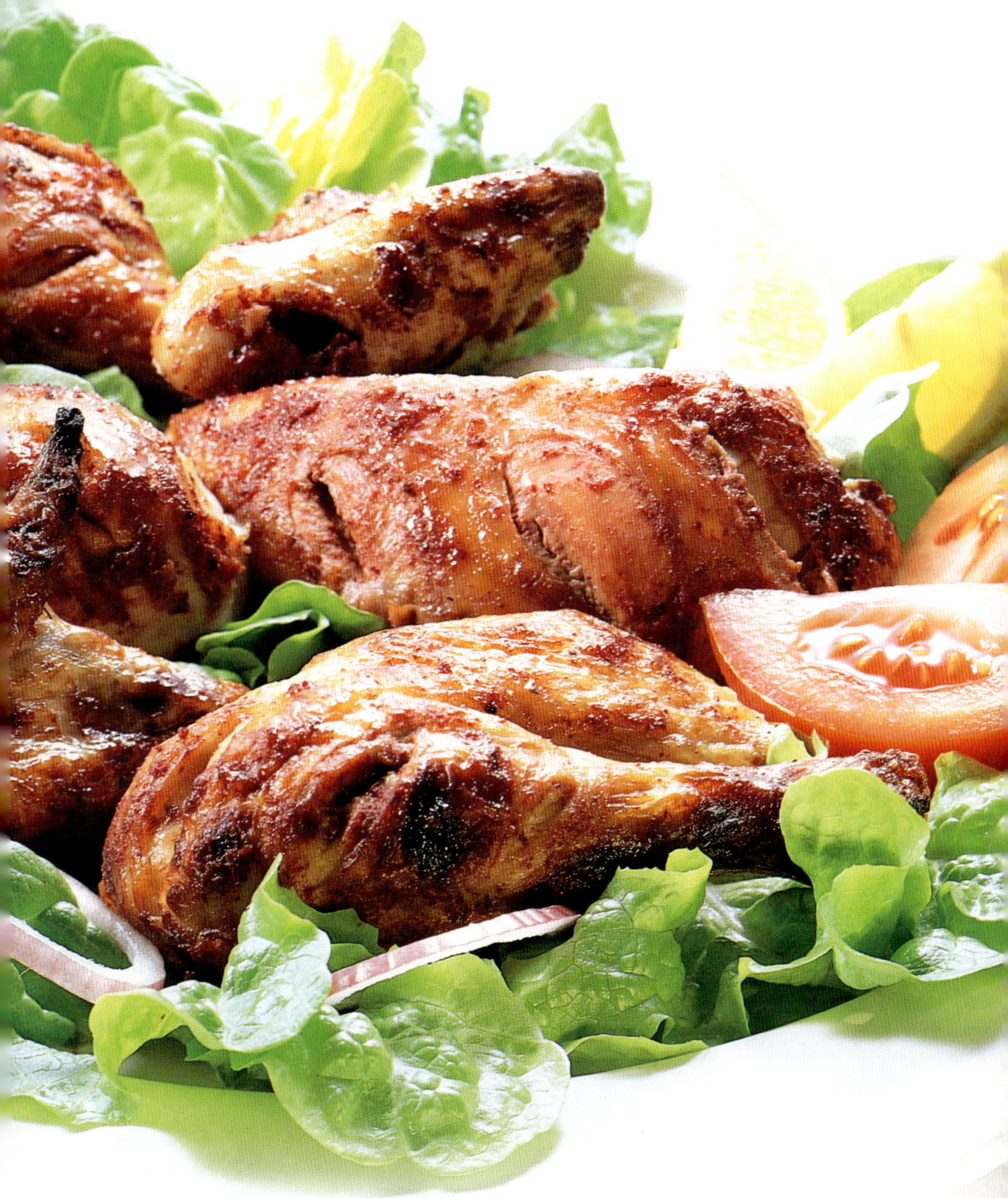

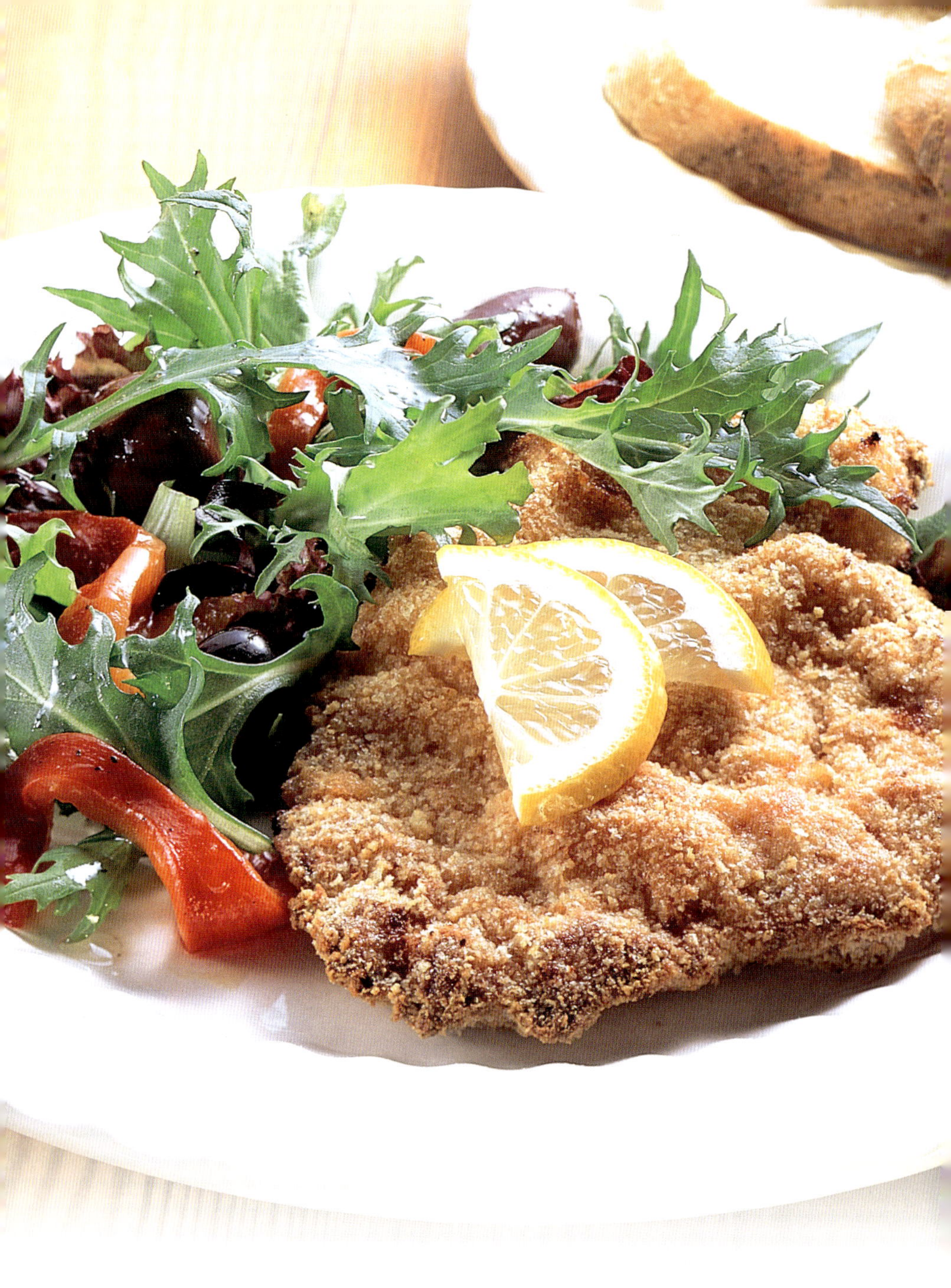

Oven-baked chicken schnitzels

SERVES 4

4 skinless chicken breast fillets
salt and freshly ground black pepper
juice of 1 lemon
2 tablespoons sweet chili sauce
¾ cup plain flour

2 eggs
1½ cups dried breadcrumbs
olive oil spray
salad, to serve

1. Place each chicken fillet between 2 pieces of cling film and flatten to even thickness with the side of a meat mallet or rolling pin. Place on a platter. Mix the salt, pepper, lemon juice and chili sauce together, pour over the chicken. Cover and refrigerate for 20 minutes.
2. Preheat oven to 360°F/180°C. Spread flour onto a sheet of baking paper. Beat eggs with one tablespoon water and place in a shallow tray or dish. Spread breadcrumbs onto a separate sheet of baking paper. Coat each side of chicken fillets in flour (shaking off any excess) then egg, and press into the breadcrumbs to coat both sides. Place on a flat surface in single layer. Lightly spray with oil.
3. Place oiled-side down on a rack over an oven tray (a cake rack is suitable). Lightly spray top side with oil. Bake chicken for 8 minutes, turn with tongs and cook for 8 minutes more.
4. Serve with a salad.

Crisp curried wings with steamed rice

SERVES 4

2lbs/1kg chicken wings
2 tablespoons mild curry paste
1½ cups basmati rice, rinsed
½ teaspoon salt

3 cups boiling water
2 tomatoes, blanched and skinned
1 small cucumber
1 cup fruit chutney

1. Rub the the chicken wings all over with the curry paste. Pin back the wing tips to form a triangle. Place in single layer on a tray and stand for 30 minutes in refrigerator, uncovered.
2. Meanwhile, preheat oven to 360°F/180°C. Place the rice in an 8-cup casserole dish, add salt and boiling water. Cover with lid or foil and place on lower shelf of oven for 40 minutes. Remove from oven and stand covered 5 minutes.
3. Transfer chicken wings to a wire rack placed over a baking tray. Place on top shelf of oven above the rice. Cook for 20 minutes, turning once. When rice has been removed, increase oven temperature to 390°F/200°C for 5 minutes to crisp the wings.
4. Halve the tomatoes and remove the seeds then cut into small dice. Peel cucumber, slice in half lengthwise and remove the seeds. Dice the cucumber and mix with the tomato. Place in a suitable dish, place chutney in a similar dish. Serve with the crisp curried wings and the rice.

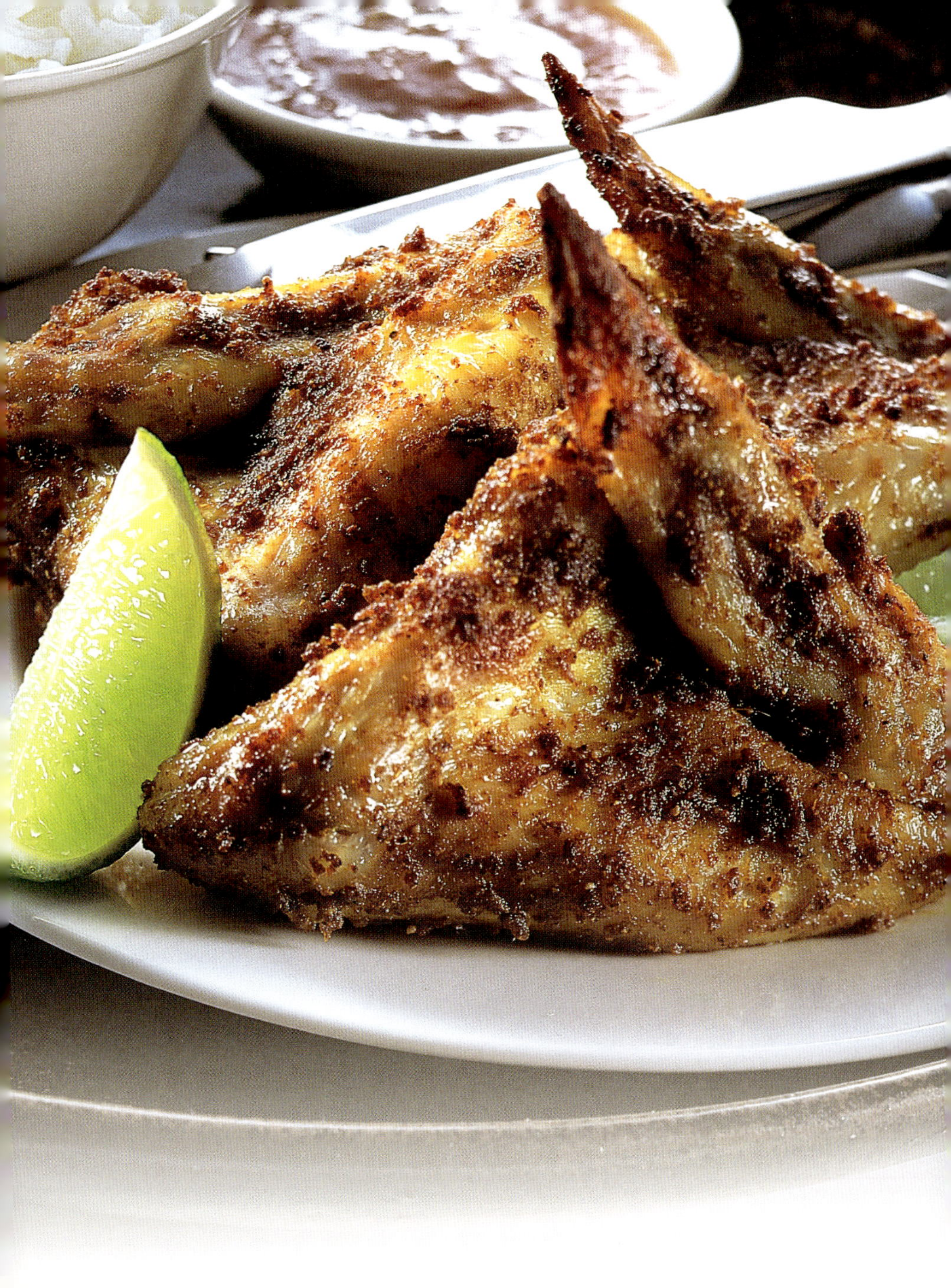

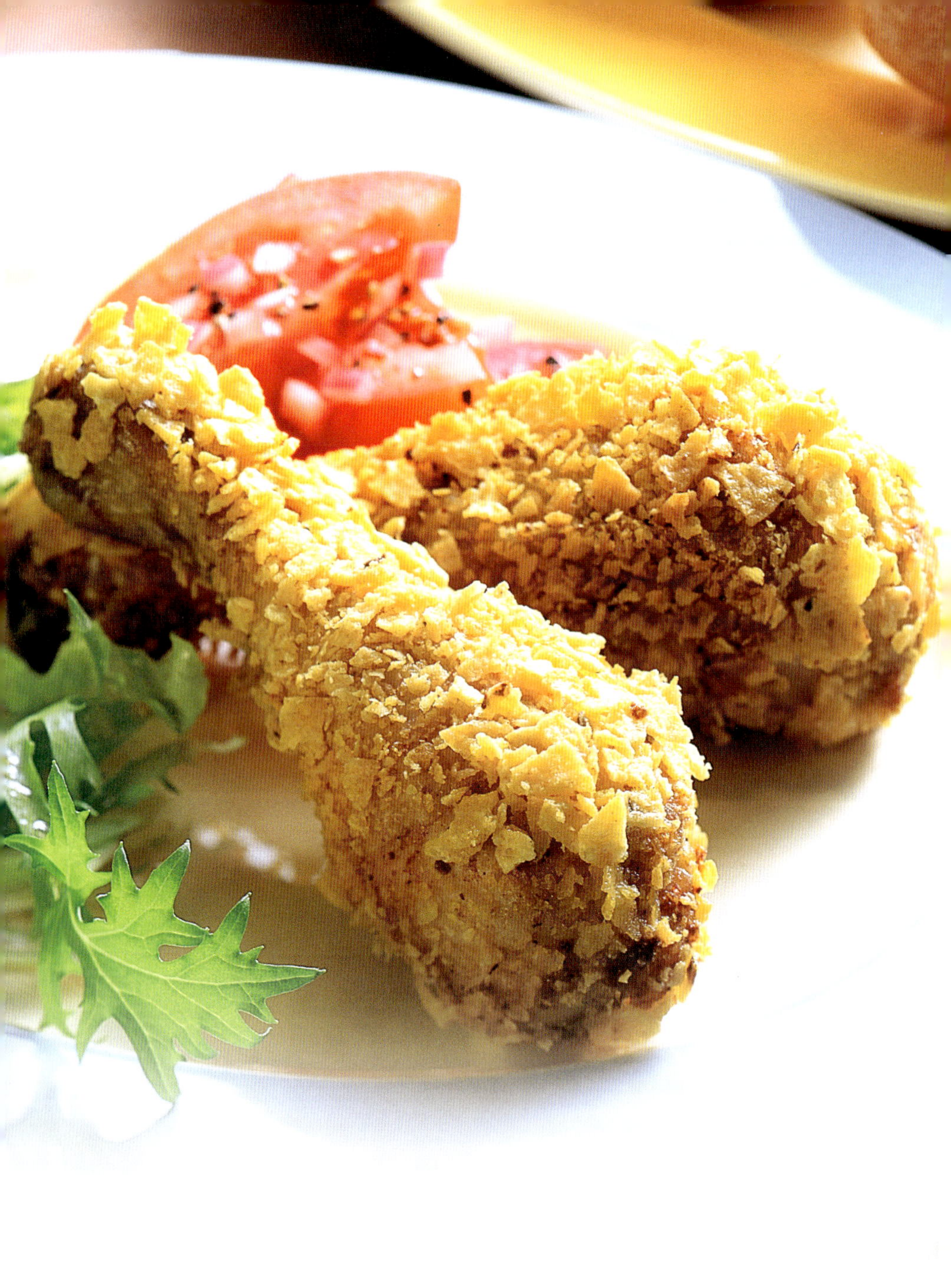

Crunchy drumsticks

SERVES 4

2 lbs/1kg chicken drumsticks
2 tablespoons curry paste
2 cups vinegar-flavoured corn or potato chips

1. Using your fingers, rub the drumsticks all over with the curry paste.
2. Crush the corn or potato chips and press onto drumsticks. Place on a rack over a shallow baking tray.
   Preheat oven to 360°F/180°C, add chicken and bake for 35–40 minutes.
3. Serve hot with boiled rice and a portion of chutney on the side. They may also be served cold with salad.
4. A shallow dish is recommended as it aids the crisping process.

Tangy tenderloins

SERVES 4

1 lb/500g chicken tenderloins
salt and pepper
olive oil spray
7 oz/200g mange tout/sugar snap peas

15 oz/425g canned baby corn
½ cup apricot nectar
2 tablespoons cider vinegar
2 tablespoons sweet chili sauce

1. Flatten the tenderloins slightly and sprinkle with salt and pepper. Heat a heavy-based frying pan and spray lightly with oil spray. Add tenderloins and cook 2 minutes on each side. Remove from pan.
2. Add the sugar snap peas and stir around pan until they turn bright green. Add the drained corn.
3. Return the chicken to the pan and toss with the vegetables. Combine the apricot nectar, vinegar and sweet chili sauce. Pour over chicken and vegetables and heat through. Pile onto serving plates. Serve immediately.

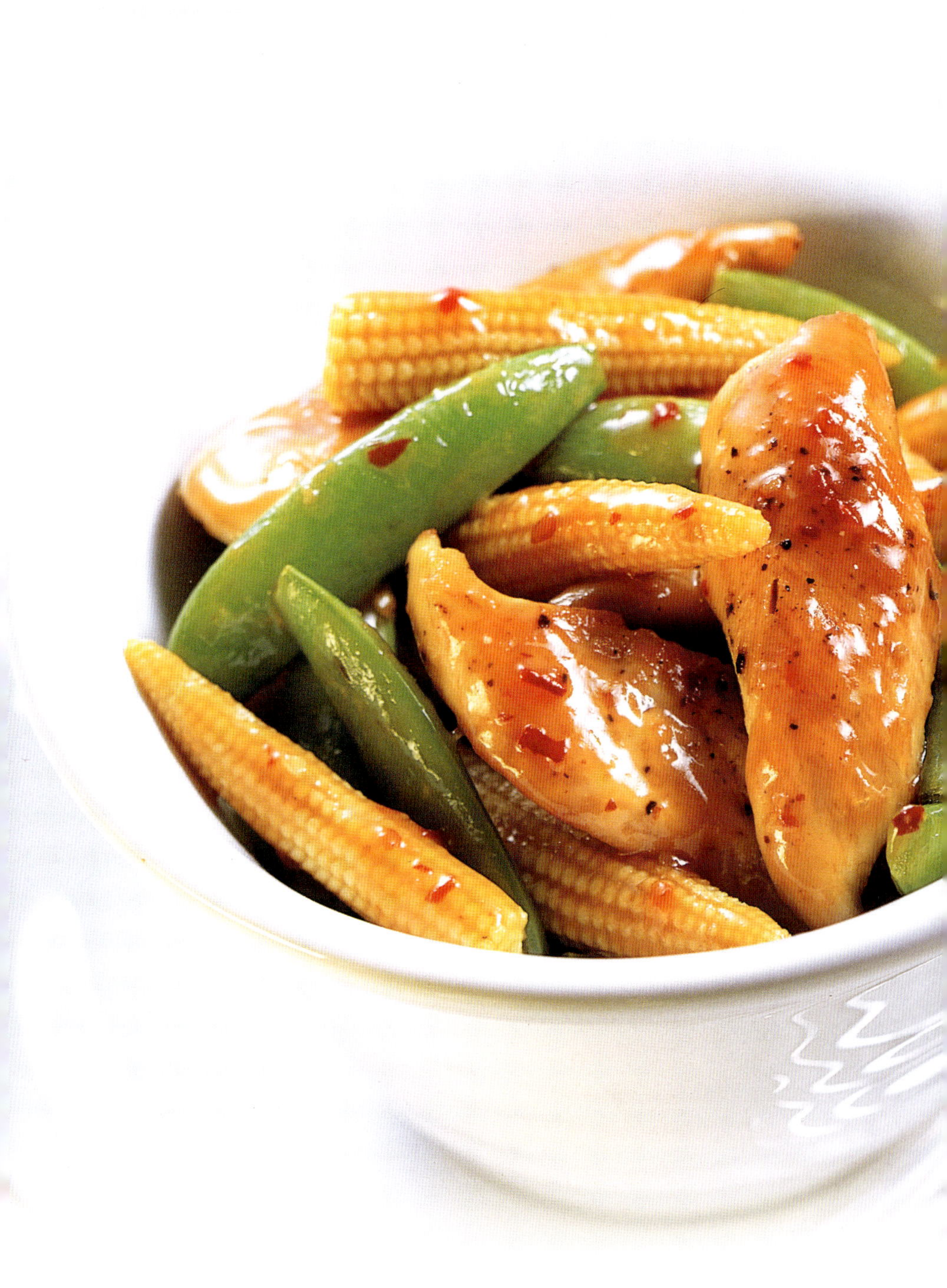

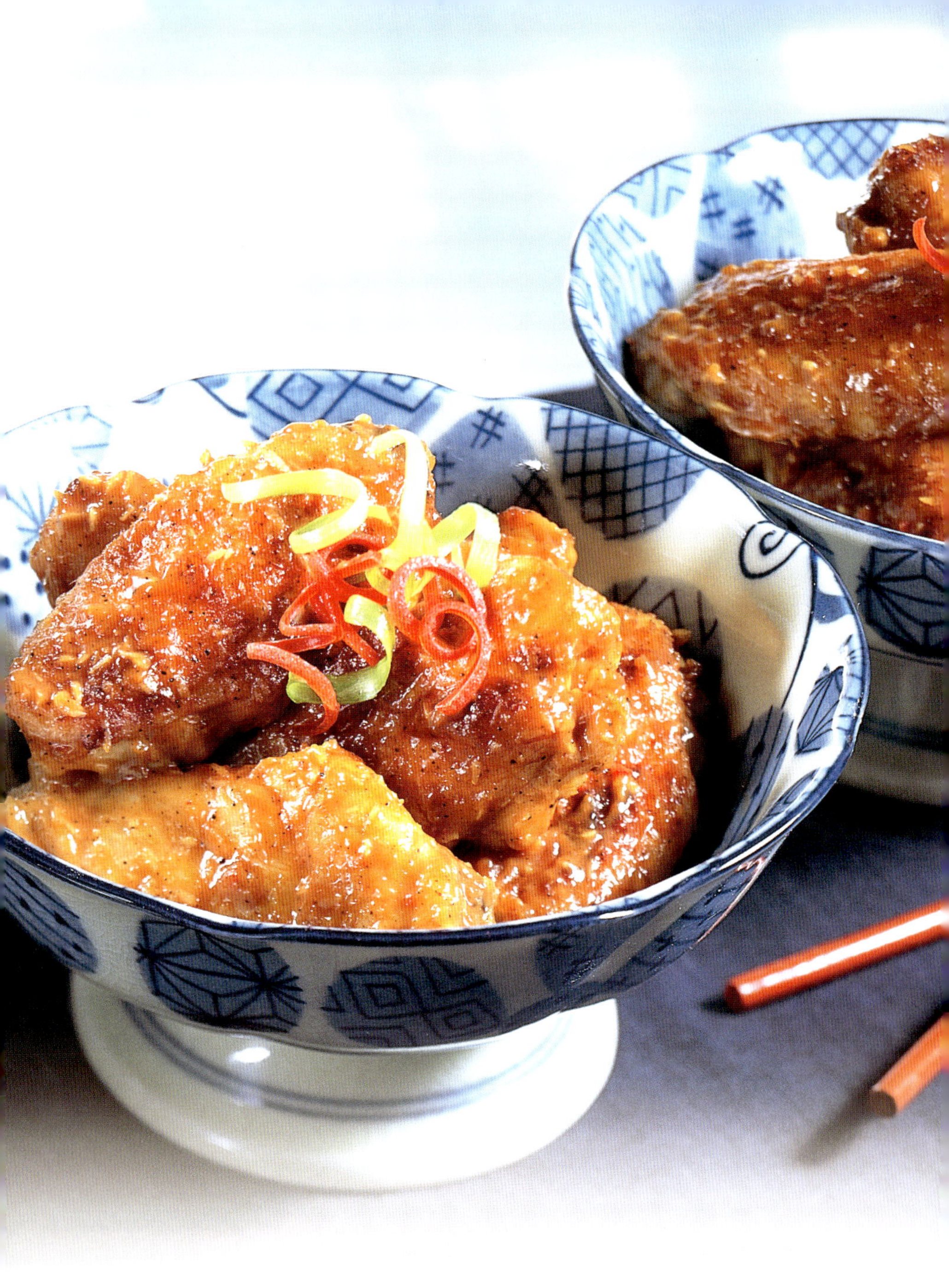

Satay wings

MAKES 32

2 lbs/1kg chicken wings
¾ cup satay sauce
zest of 2 lemons

1. Cut off the wing tips and discard. Cut through next joint to make two pieces. Place all the wings in a bowl and stir through the satay sauce. Cover and marinate for 2 hours or more – they may be left overnight.
2. Preheat the oven to 360°F/180°C. Arrange wing pieces on a rack over a shallow dish or tray lined with foil. Place in oven for 15 minutes. Brush some of the remaining marinade on wing pieces, then turn over and brush again. Cook 20 minutes more. Brush with marinade, increase heat to 390°F/200°C and cook approximately 5 minutes more.
3. Remove from oven. Brush with 1 tablespoon fresh satay sauce (do not use any remaining marinade) to intensify the flavour. Serve topped with lemon zest, either on a platter or in small Asian bowls as individual serves.

Thigh steaks with fruity mint salsa

SERVES 4

1 lb/500g chicken thigh fillets
salt and pepper
½ teaspoon dried oregano
canola oil spray
1 pear, peeled and diced

1 banana, peeled and diced
2 tablespoons lemon juice
½ cup mint, finely chopped
2 teaspoons sweet chili sauce
mashed potatoes or rice, to serve

1. Pound thigh fillets on both sides with a meat mallet to flatten. Sprinkle with salt, pepper and oregano.
2. Heat a non-stick frying pan and lightly spray with oil, add the thigh steaks and cook for 3 minutes on each side. Remove to a heated plate and keep hot. Add pear, banana, lemon juice, mint and chilli sauce to the pan. Scrape up pan juices and stir to heat fruit.
3. Pile hot fruit salsa on top of thigh steaks. Serve immediately with mashed potatoes or rice.

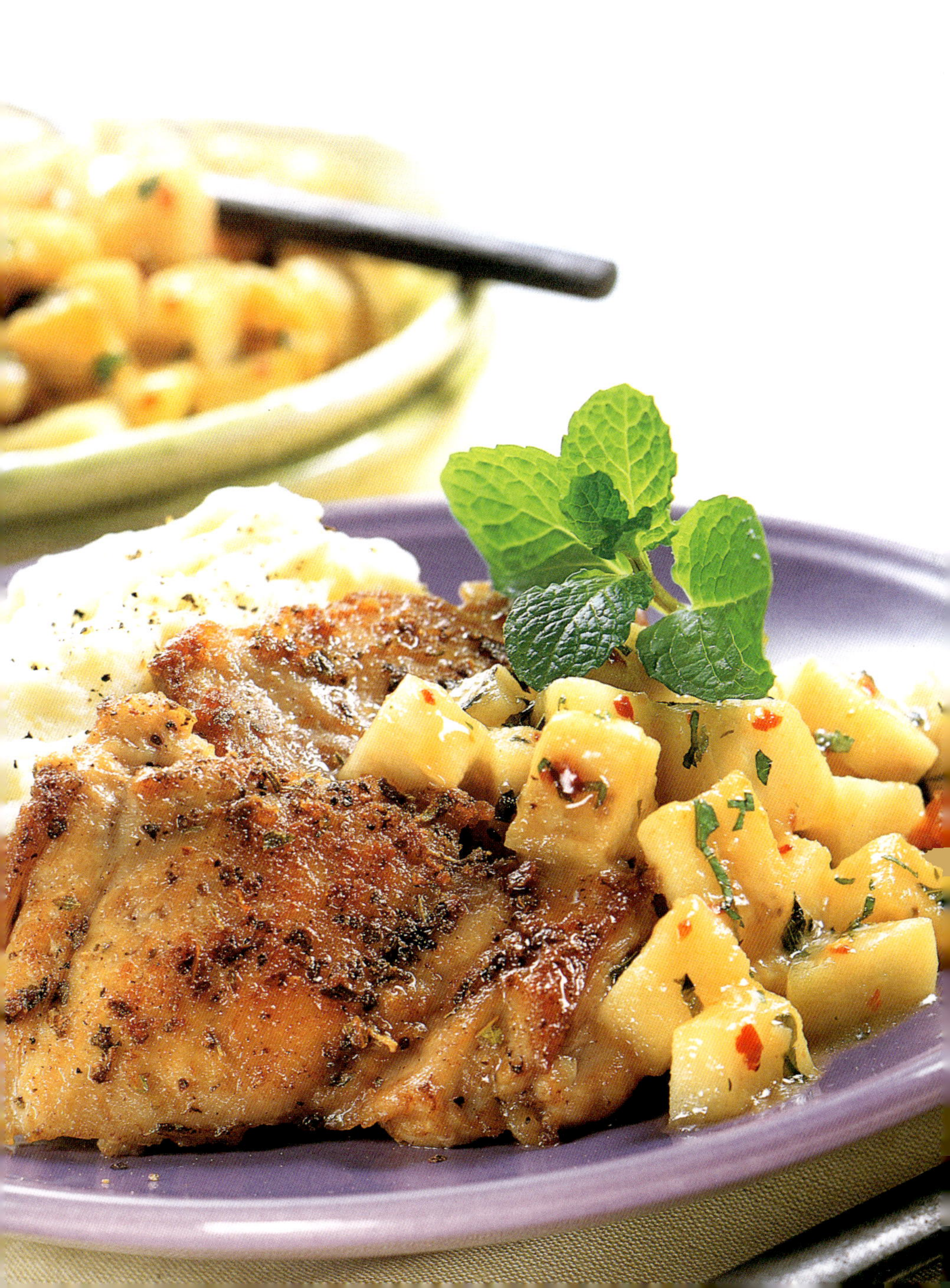

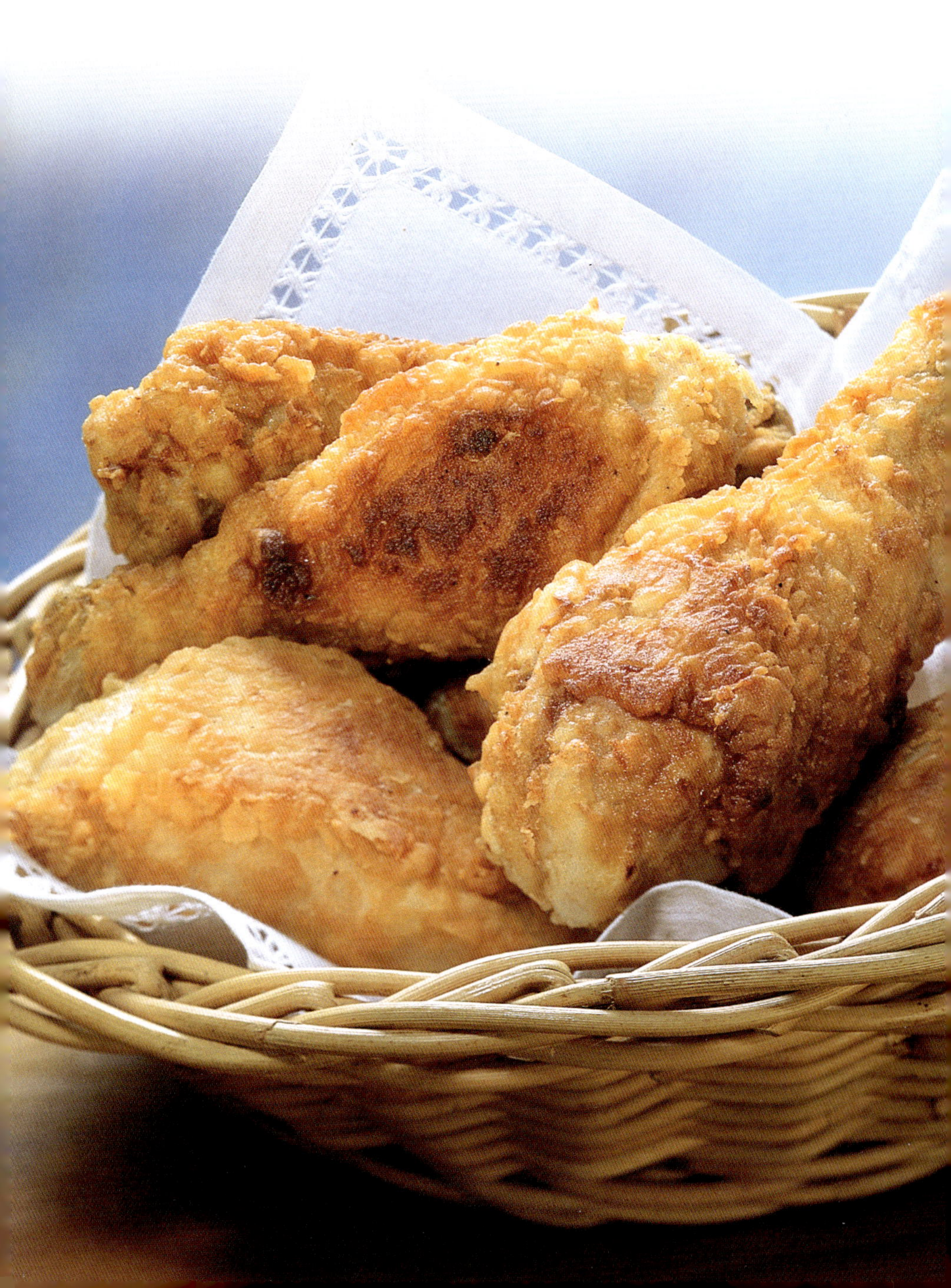

Southern-fried chicken drumsticks

SERVES 4

2 lbs/1kg chicken drumsticks
1 teaspoon salt and pepper
1½ cups all-purpose/plain flour
2 eggs
⅓ cup milk
½ cup vegetable oil
vegetables, to serve

1. Smooth the skin over the drumstick if needed and season with salt and pepper. Sprinkle flour on a flat, paper-lined plate. Beat eggs and milk well together in a deep plate.
2. Dip the drumsticks in the flour then into the egg, turning to coat both sides. Place again into the flour and roll until well covered. Place in single layer on a clean, flat tray.
3. Heat oil in a large frying pan. Add drumsticks and fry a few minutes on each side until just beginning to brown. Reduce heat, place a lid on the pan and cook slowly for 20 minutes, turning chicken after 10 minutes.
4. Remove lid and increase heat, continue cooking until golden brown and crisp, turning frequently. Remove from pan, drain on absorbent paper. Serve hot with vegetable accompaniments.

Chicken steaks with herb sauce

SERVES 4

1 lb/500g chicken thigh fillets
1 oz/30g butter
1 clove garlic, finely chopped
1 medium onion, finely chopped

salt and black pepper
$1/4$ cup lemon juice
$1/4$ cup parsley, chopped
vegetables, to serve

1. Pound thigh fillets on both sides with a meat mallet to flatten.
2. Heat enough butter to coat base of a large heavy-based frying pan. Add thigh fillets and cook 3 minutes on each side over medium heat. Remove to a heated plate.
3. Add garlic and onion and fry over gentle heat until soft. Add salt, pepper, lemon juice and parsley. Stir quickly to lift pan juices and pour over chicken steaks. Serve immediately with vegetable accompaniments.

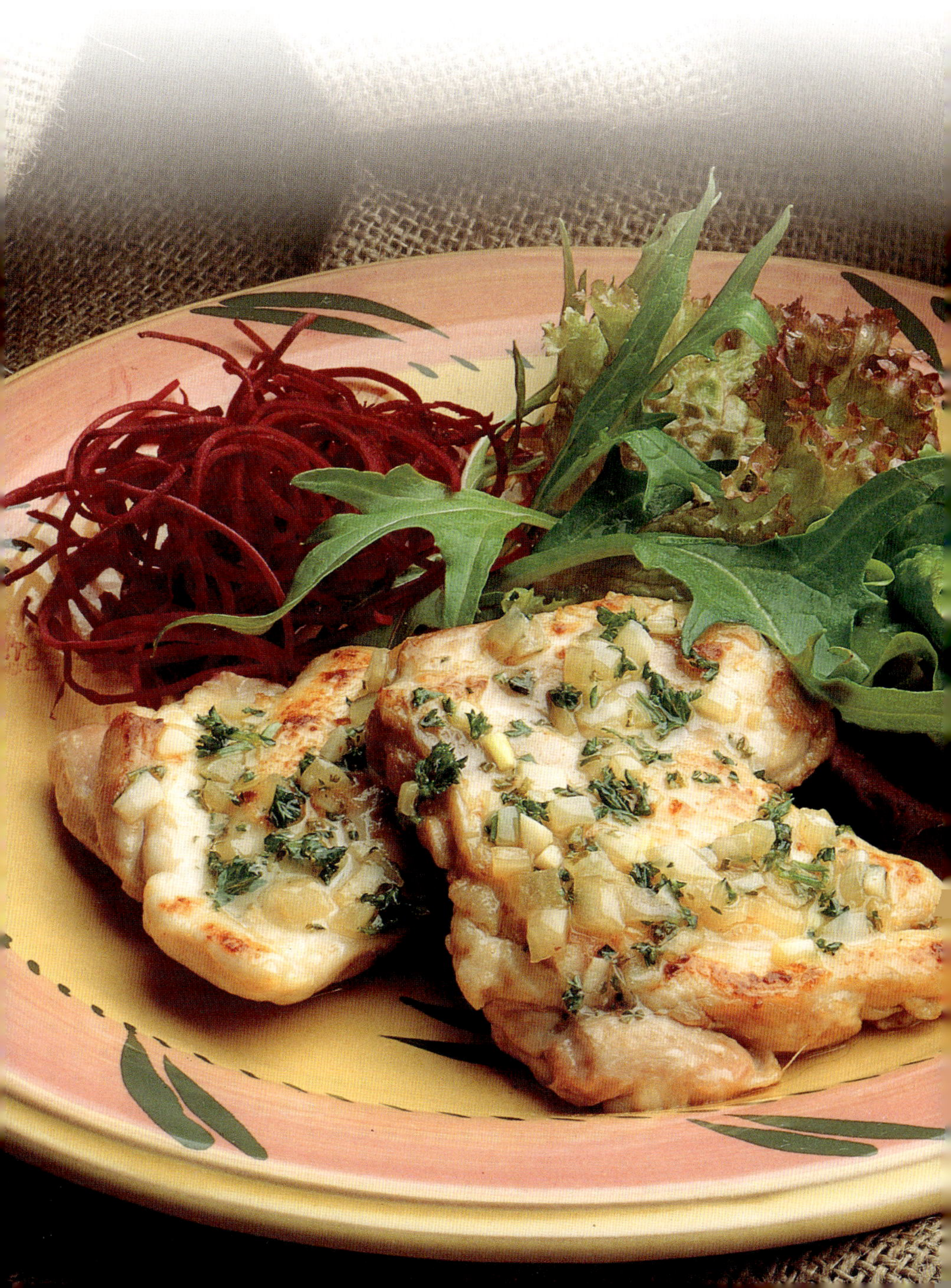

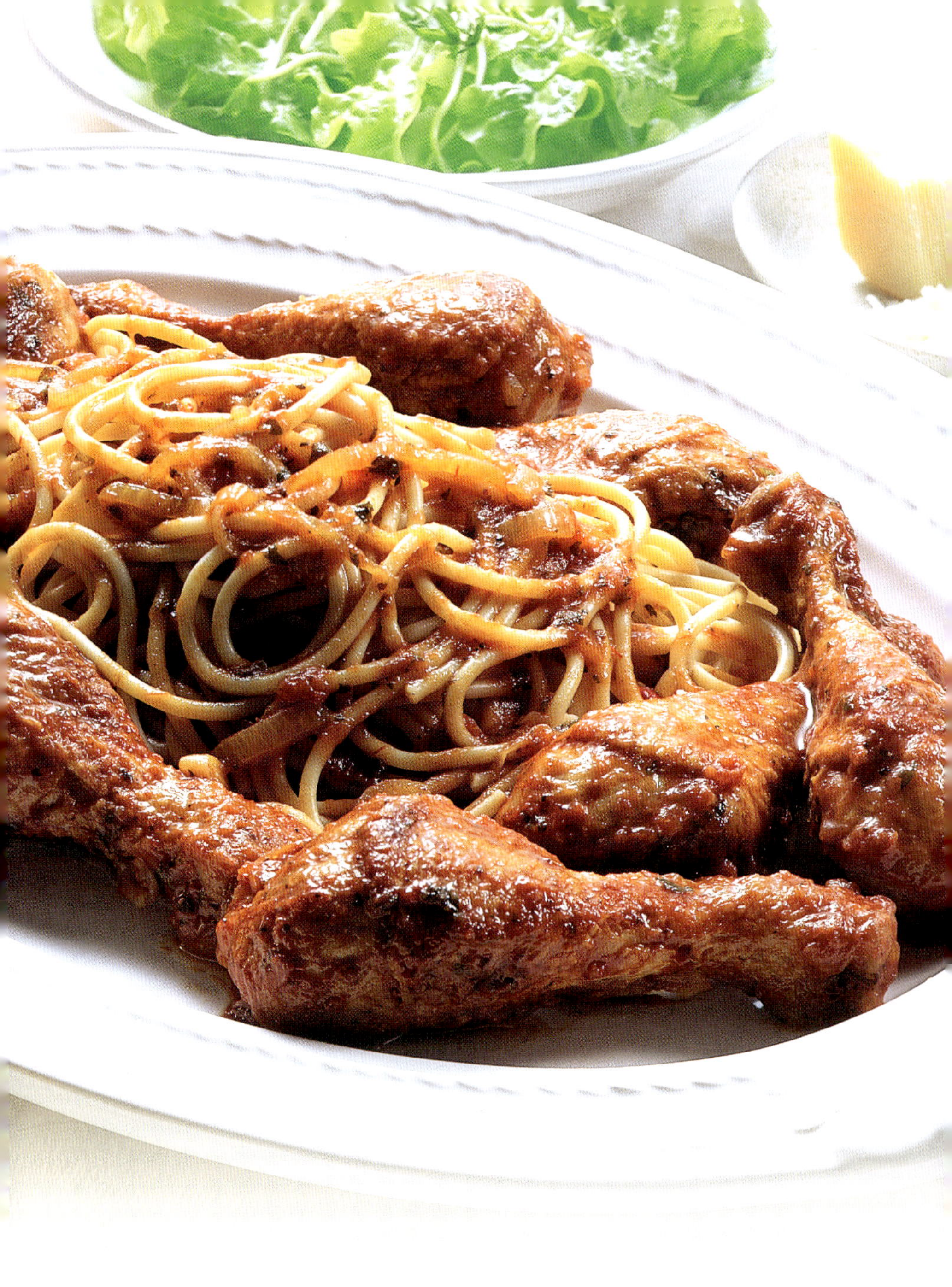

Drumsticks in tomato sauce

SERVES 4

2 lbs/1kg chicken drumsticks
salt and freshly ground black pepper
1 tablespoon canola oil
12 1/3 oz/350g jar tomato pasta sauce
1/2 cup water
1 cinnamon stick

1 large onion, sliced into rings
1/4 cup parsley, finely chopped
9 oz/250g spaghetti
1 3/4 oz/50g parmesan cheese, grated
side salad, to serve

1. Season the drumsticks with salt and pepper. Heat oil in a wide-based saucepan and lightly brown the drumsticks 3 at a time. Remove from pan as they brown and wipe fat from the pan when finished.
2. Pour in the pasta sauce, add the water and the cinnamon stick. Heat the sauce then return drumsticks to the pan. Add the onion rings and the parsley. Cover and bring to the boil, turn down to a simmer and cook for 35 minutes until chicken is tender.
3. Boil and drain the spaghetti and stir through a teaspoon of oil to keep strands separate. Place in a large serving dish, arrange drumsticks around spaghetti and smother with the sauce. Sprinkle with extra parsley.
Serve immediately with parmesan cheese. Accompany with a tossed side salad.

Poached chicken with tomato and mushroom sauce

SERVES 4

4 chicken breast fillets
1 medium onion, finely chopped
1 clove garlic, finely chopped
4 large ripe tomatoes, blanched, peeled and chopped
3½ oz/100g mushrooms, sliced
¼ cup fresh basil, chopped

¾ cup water
1 teaspoon dried oregano
freshly ground black pepper
2 cups spiral shaped pasta
½ teaspoon olive oil
1½ oz/40g parmesan cheese, grated

1. Remove the skin from the chicken breasts. Place onion, garlic, tomatoes and mushrooms in a wide-based saucepan over moderate heat. Stir until they begin to soften. Add basil, water, oregano and pepper, heat a little and add the chicken breasts. Cover and simmer slowly for 20 minutes until chicken is tender. Do not allow to boil.
2. In another saucepan cook pasta spirals according to the directions on the packet. Drain and stir through the olive oil.
3. When chicken is cooked, remove to a plate. If sauce is too thin, increase heat and boil until it reduces and thickens. Pour over chicken and serve with pasta spirals. Sprinkle with parmesan cheese.

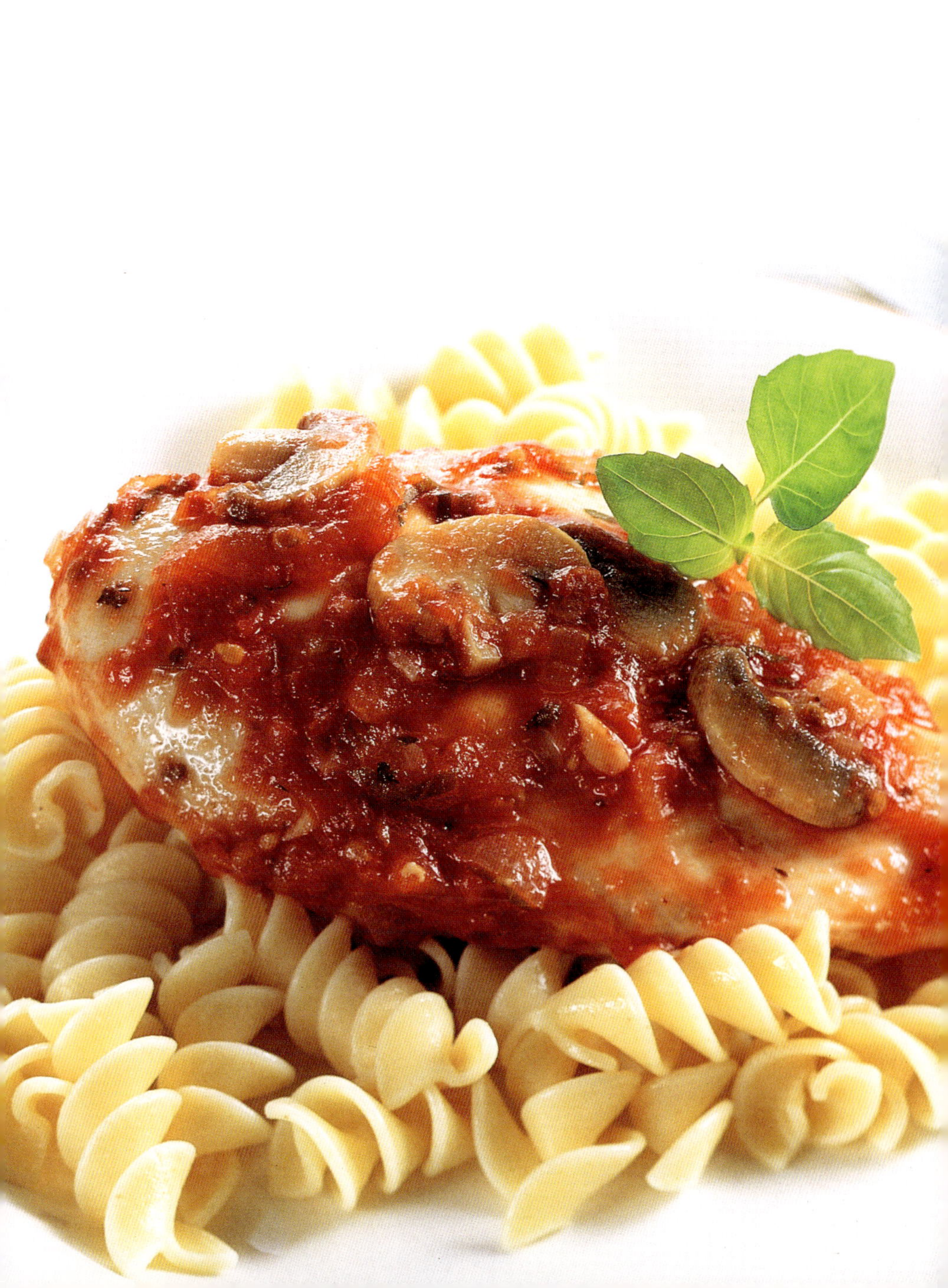

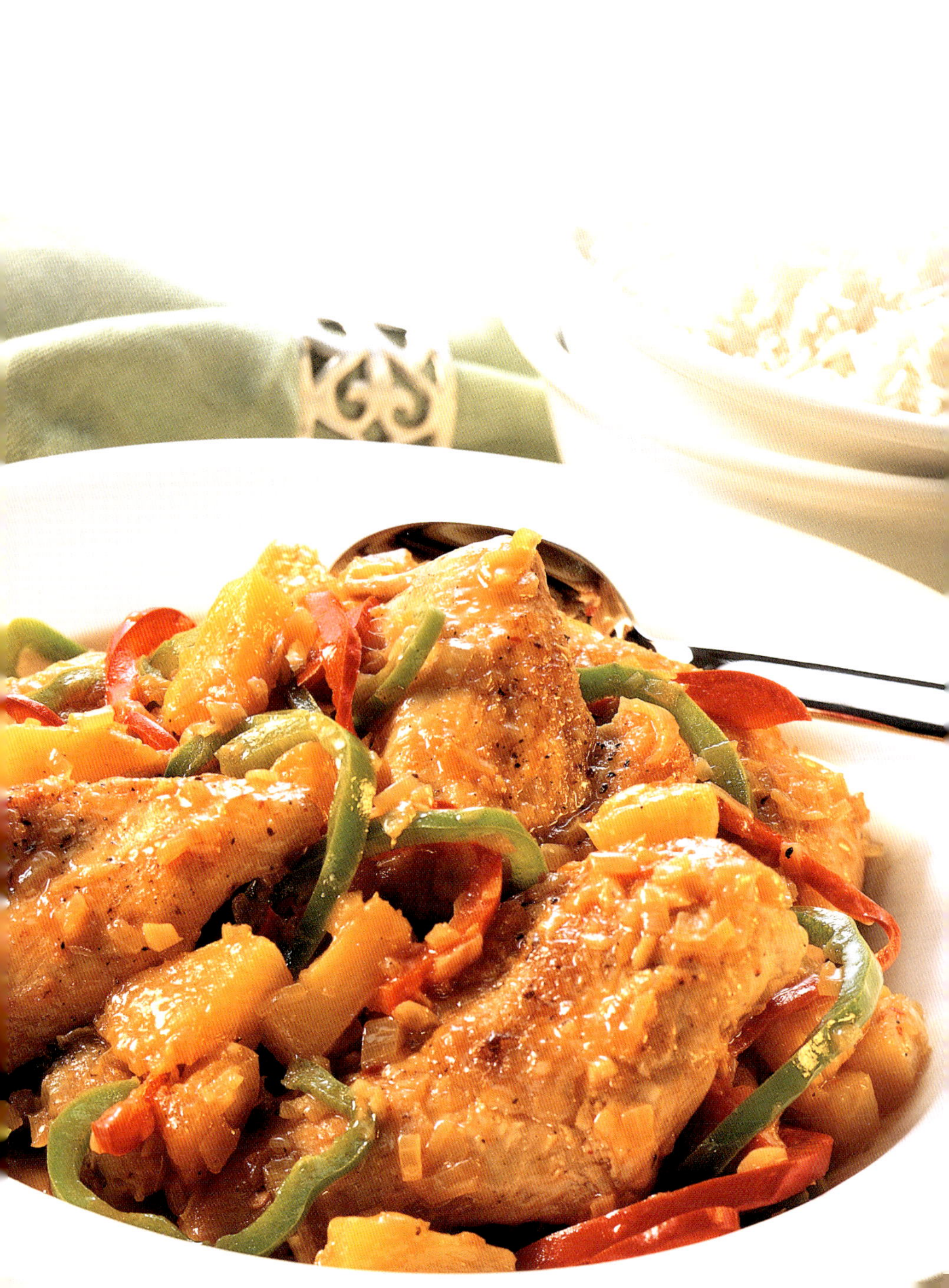

Hawaiian poached chicken

SERVES 4

2 lbs/1kg chicken pieces
salt and pepper
1 teaspoon paprika
2 tablespoons oil
1 large onion, chopped
1 clove garlic, crushed
¼ cup water
1 tablespoon Worcestershire sauce
2 teaspoons sweet chili sauce
¼ cup apple cider vinegar

1½ tablespoons brown sugar
½ medium pineapple, peeled and diced
1 green bell pepper/capsicum, cut into thin strips
1 red pepper/capsicum, cut into thin strips
1 tablespoon rum
1½ tablespoons cornflour
boiled rice, to serve

1. Season the chicken with salt, pepper and paprika. Heat the oil in a large saucepan. Add chicken pieces a few at a time and brown on all sides. Remove to a plate lined with absorbent paper.
2. Add the onion and garlic to the saucepan and cook, stirring for 2 minutes. Return chicken to the saucepan. Combine the water, the two sauces, vinegar and brown sugar and pour over the chicken. Add the pineapple and capsicum. Simmer for 25–30 minutes until chicken is tender.
3. Warm and flame the rum and pour onto the chicken. Blend the cornflour with a little water, add to the chicken and stir through. Allow to simmer until the mixture thickens. Increase the heat until boiling then turn off immediately. Serve with boiled rice.

Indonesian chicken rolls

SERVES 4

2lbs/1kg chicken thigh fillets
10 oz/285g can rendang curry sauce
2 bananas
2 tablespoons vegetable oil
½ cup water
½ cup coconut milk
1 small pineapple, peeled and thinly sliced

freshly ground black pepper
¾ oz/20g butter
2 tablespoons shredded coconut, toasted
steamed white rice, to serve

1. Open out the thigh fillets on a large chopping board. Flatten with a meat mallet to an even thickness. Spread each with a teaspoon of rendang curry sauce.
2. Peel bananas and slit in half lengthwise then cut in half to make 4 pieces. Place a piece of banana in centre of each fillet and form into a roll. Fasten with a toothpick. Heat oil in a wide-based saucepan and brown the rolls on all sides, a few at a time, removing rolls to a plate as they brown. Drain all the oil from the saucepan.
3. To the same saucepan, add remaining curry sauce and the water. Bring to the boil, turn down heat to a simmer and add the chicken rolls. Cover and simmer 35 minutes, turning rolls once during cooking.
4. Remove rolls to a heated platter and keep hot. If sauce is thin, increase heat and reduce sauce to a thicker consistency. Reduce heat and stir in the coconut milk and simmer 2 minutes. Return rolls to the saucepan to reheat.
5. Sauté the pineapple rings in the butter until lightly coloured and grind over some black pepper. Arrange 1 or 2 slices of pineapple and a chicken roll on each plate, spoon sauce over the roll and sprinkle with a little toasted coconut. Accompany with steamed rice.

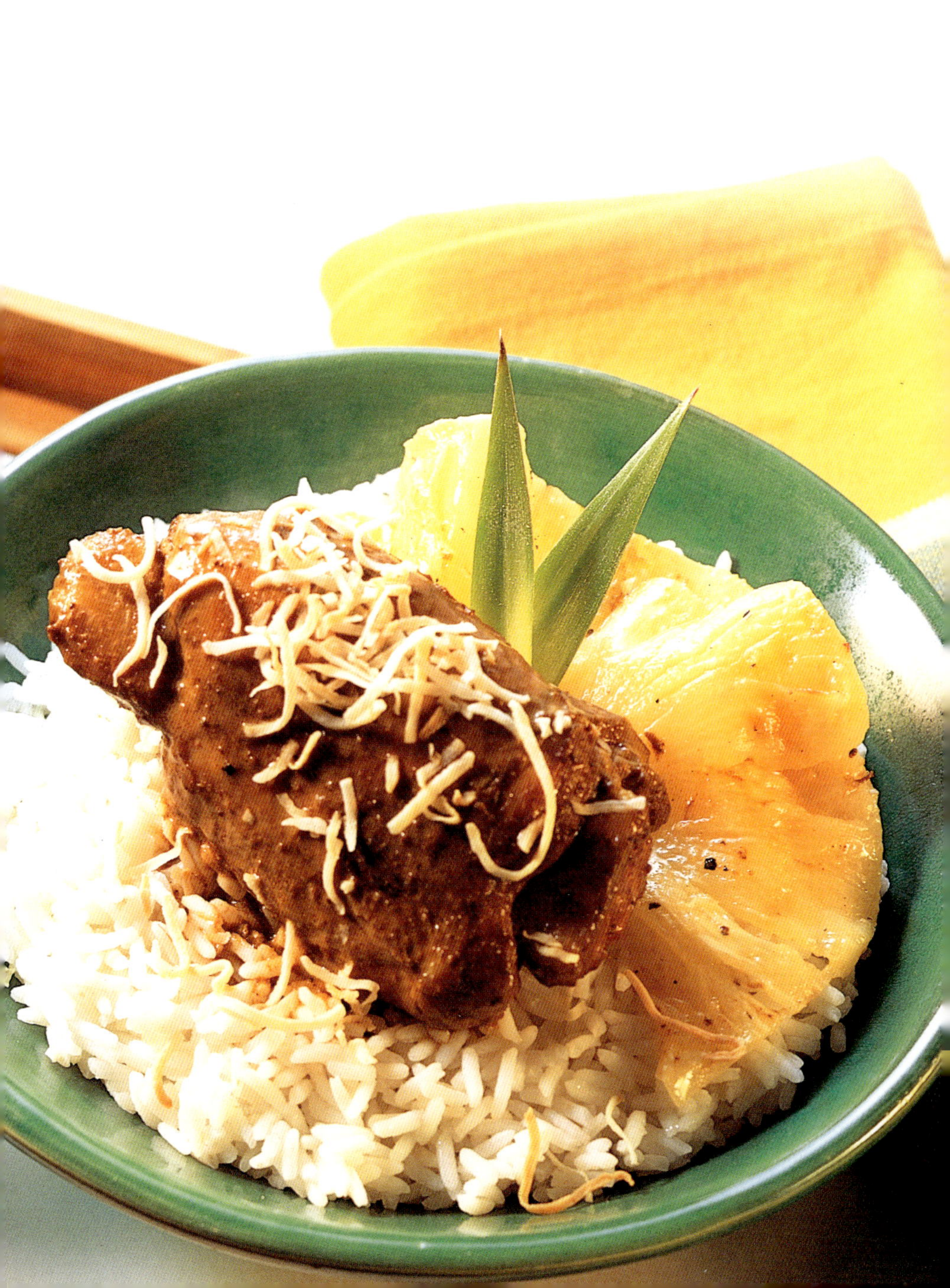

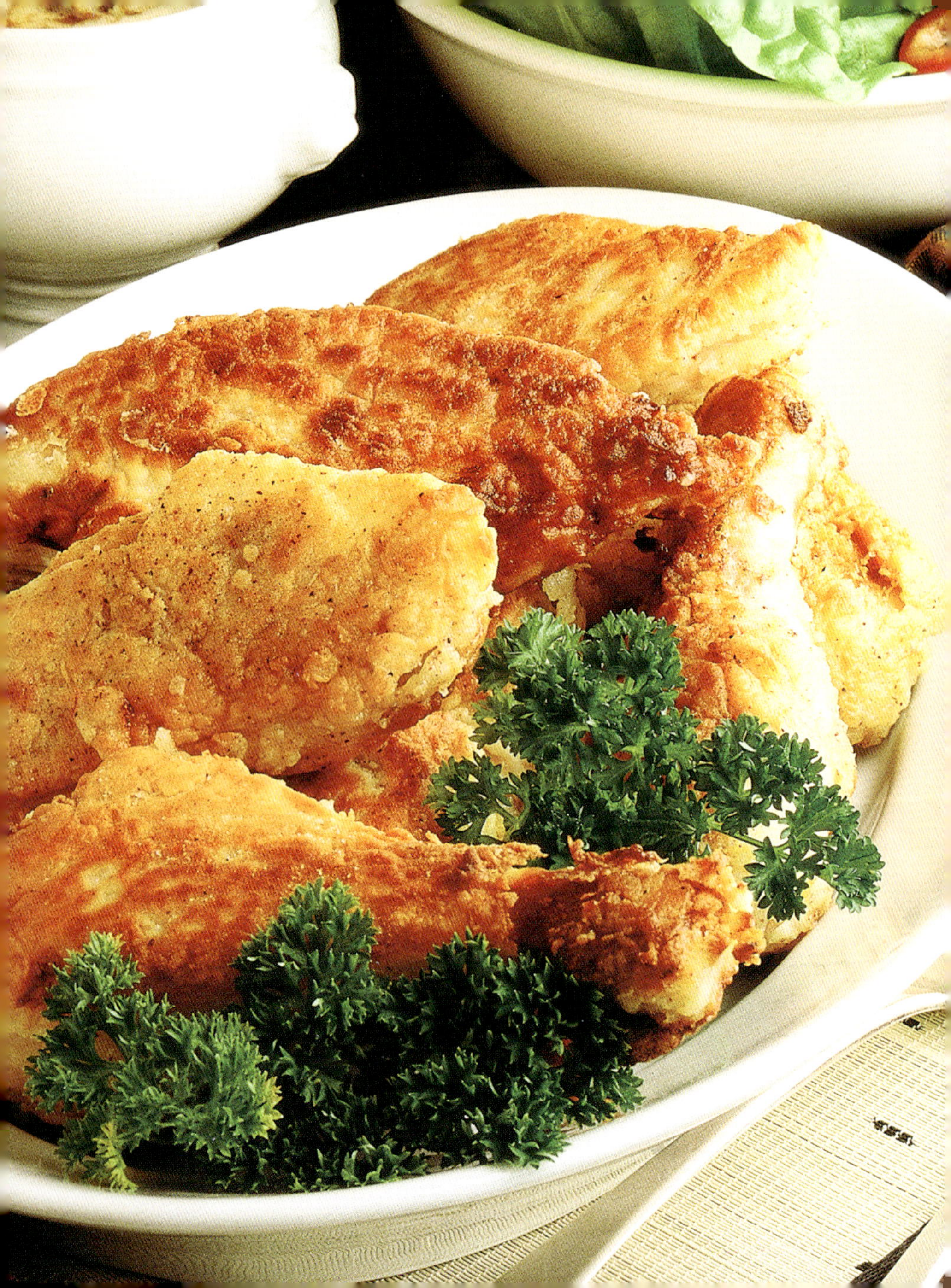

Mustard chicken

SERVES 4

4 chicken Marylands
Glaze
1 tablespoon Dijon mustard
1 tablespoon English mustard
¼ cup superfine/caster sugar

5 tablespoons lemon juice
2 tablespoons oil
2 teaspoons Worcestershire sauce
salt and pepper
mashed potato and green vegetables, to serve

1. Arrange the chicken, skin-side down, on a grilling pan. Place the ingredients for the glaze in a bowl and mix well. Spoon ¼ of the glaze over the chicken and cook under a moderate grill for 15 minutes.
2. Spoon over more glaze halfway through cooking. Turn the chicken pieces, then glaze the skin side and cook for 15–20 minutes until tender. Spoon over the remaining glaze during cooking. Serve with mashed potato and green vegetables.

Drumsticks in dill sauce

SERVES 4

8 chicken drumsticks
salt and white pepper
1 oz/30g butter
1 bunch spring onions/shallots, chopped
½ cup dill, finely chopped
¼ cup lemon juice

1 bunch Dutch/baby carrots, peeled
2 cups water
1 chicken bouillon cube
2 tablespoons cornflour
2 tablespoons water

1. Season drumsticks liberally with salt and pepper. Heat butter in a wide-based saucepan. Add drumsticks a few at a time and brown lightly on all sides. Remove to a plate while browning the remainder.
2. Add spring onions and sauté for one minute. Stir in dill and lemon juice, then return drumsticks to saucepan.
3. Arrange the carrots over the drumsticks. Add water and bouillon cube. Bring to a simmer, reduce heat, cover and simmer for 40 minutes until tender.
4. Remove drumsticks and carrots with a slotted spoon and arrange on a heated platter. Blend the cornflour with the water, stir into the juices remaining in the pan. Stir over heat until sauce boils and thickens. Pour over drumsticks and carrots. Serve immediately.

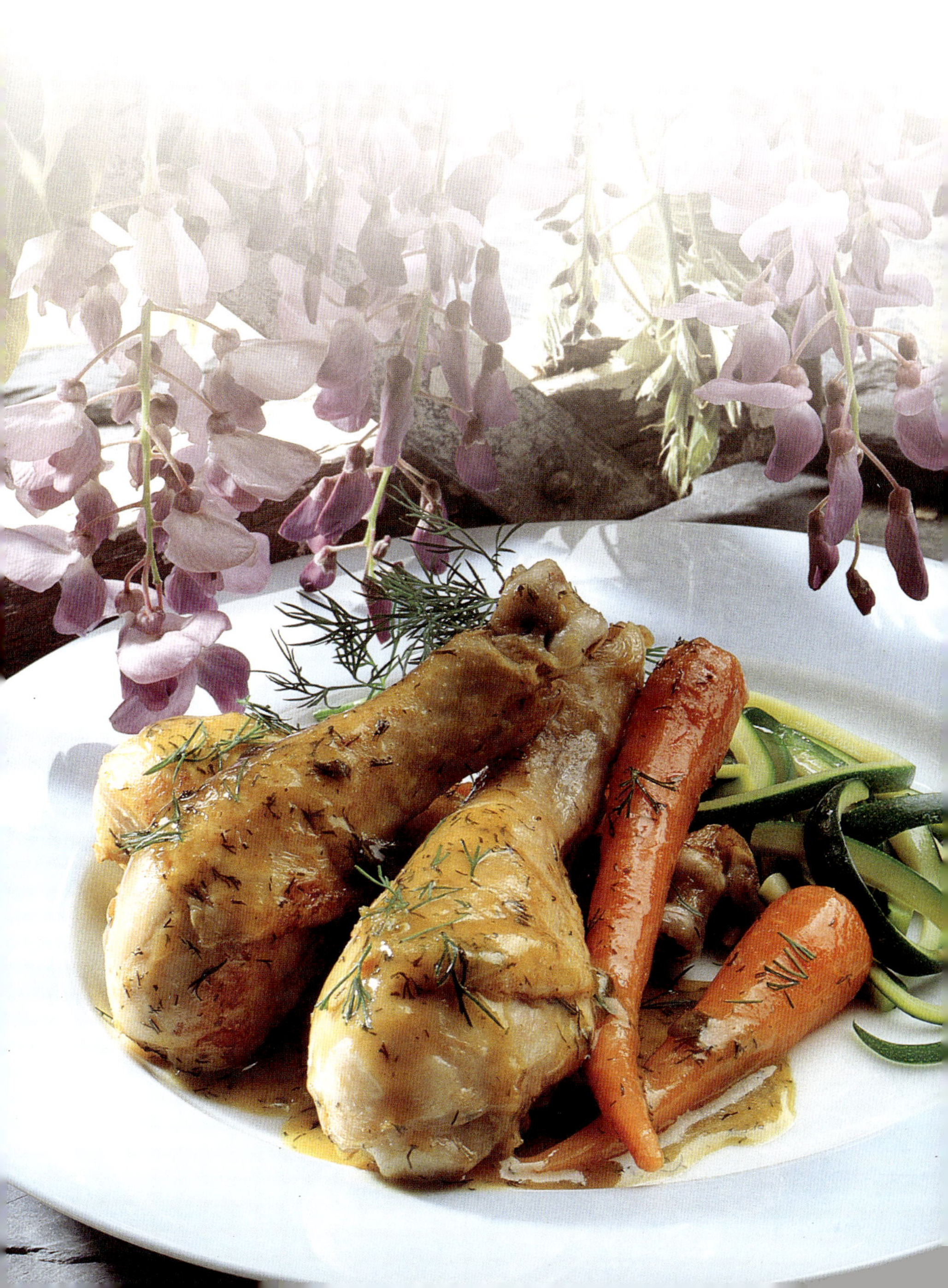

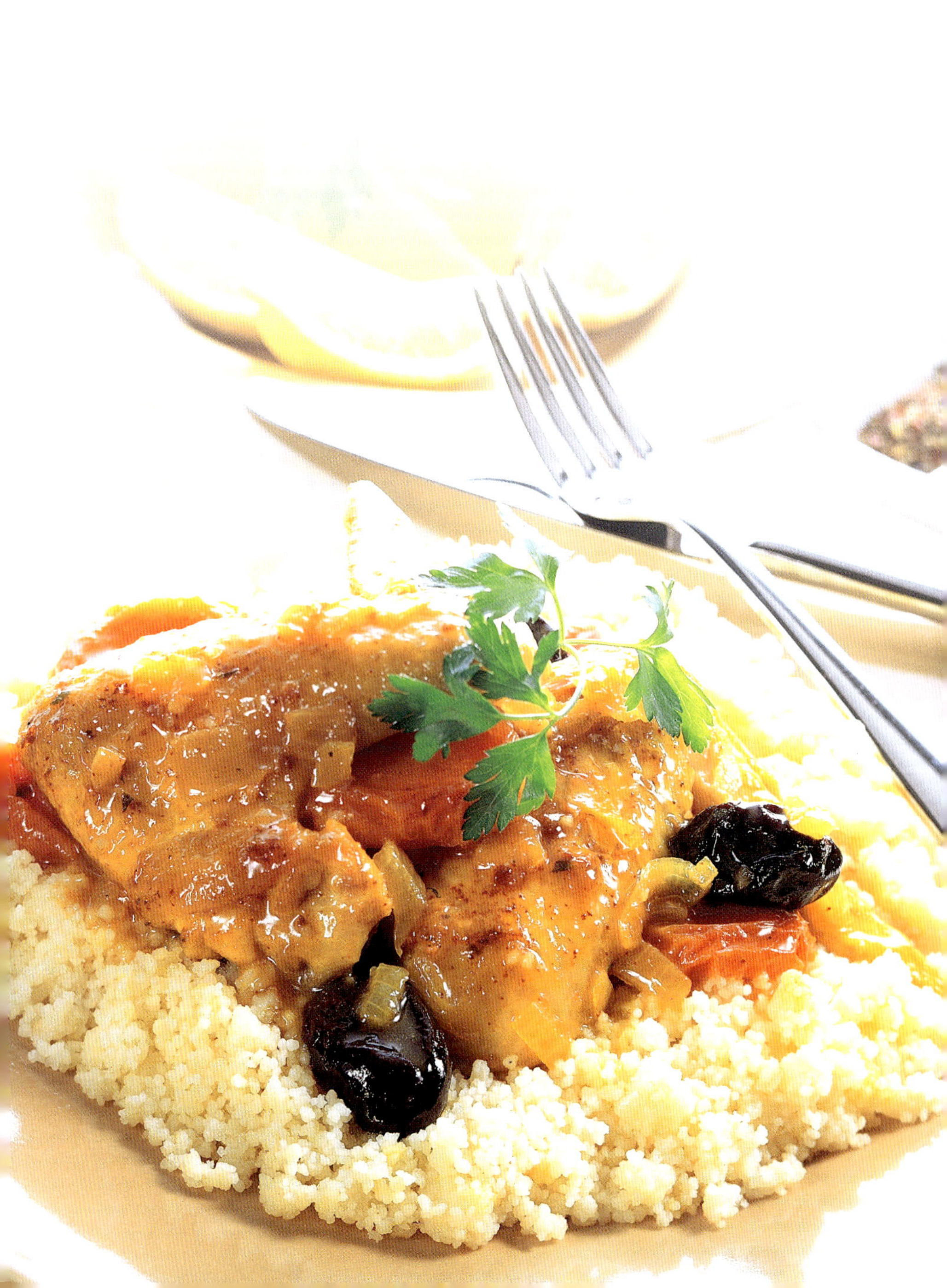

Chicken wings Moroccan style

SERVES 4

2 lbs/1kg chicken wings
salt and pepper
2 tablespoons canola oil
1 large onion, finely chopped
1 clove garlic, crushed
¾ ins/2cm piece fresh ginger, chopped
½ teaspoon ground turmeric
½ teaspoon cummin

½ cinnamon stick
¼ cup cider vinegar
2 cups apricot nectar
3½ oz/100g pitted prunes
3½ oz/100g dried apricots
1 tablespoon honey
¼ cup lemon juice
steamed couscous or rice, to serve

1. Season chicken wings with salt and pepper. Heat oil in a wide-based saucepan, add chicken wings a few at a time and brown lightly on both sides. Remove to a plate as they brown.
2. Add onion and fry for 2 minutes. Stir in garlic, ginger and spices and cook for 1 minute, stirring. Return chicken to the pan, stir and turn the wings to coat with spices. Add vinegar and apricot nectar, season to taste. Cover and simmer for 25 minutes.
3. Add prunes, apricots, honey and lemon juice. Cover and simmer 10 minutes, remove lid and simmer uncovered for 5 minutes. If a thicker sauce is desired, remove wings and fruit to a serving platter, increase heat and boil until sauce reduces and thickens, stirring occasionally. Pour sauce over wings. Serve immediately with steamed couscous or rice.

Quick chicken cacciatore

SERVES 4

1½ lb/750g chicken tenderloins
2 tablespoons canola oil
1 medium onion, finely chopped
12 ⅓ oz/350g jar tomato pasta sauce
½ cup water
1 teaspoon chicken bouillon powder

1½ tablespoons balsamic vinegar
¼ cup parsley, chopped
3 anchovy fillets, chopped
2 oz/60g pitted black olives
fettuccine or rice, to serve

1. Remove any excess fat from the tenderloins and cut into ¾ ins/2cm cubes. Heat oil in a large, wide-based saucepan, add onion and cook, stirring until light golden. Pour in the pasta sauce, water, bouillon powder and vinegar. Stir well and bring to the boil.
2. Add the chicken tenderloins, stir then turn down heat until simmering gently. Cover and simmer for 20 minutes. Add parsley, anchovy fillets and olives. Simmer uncovered for 5 minutes.
3. Place in a serving dish and sprinkle with extra chopped parsley. Serve with fettuccine or rice.

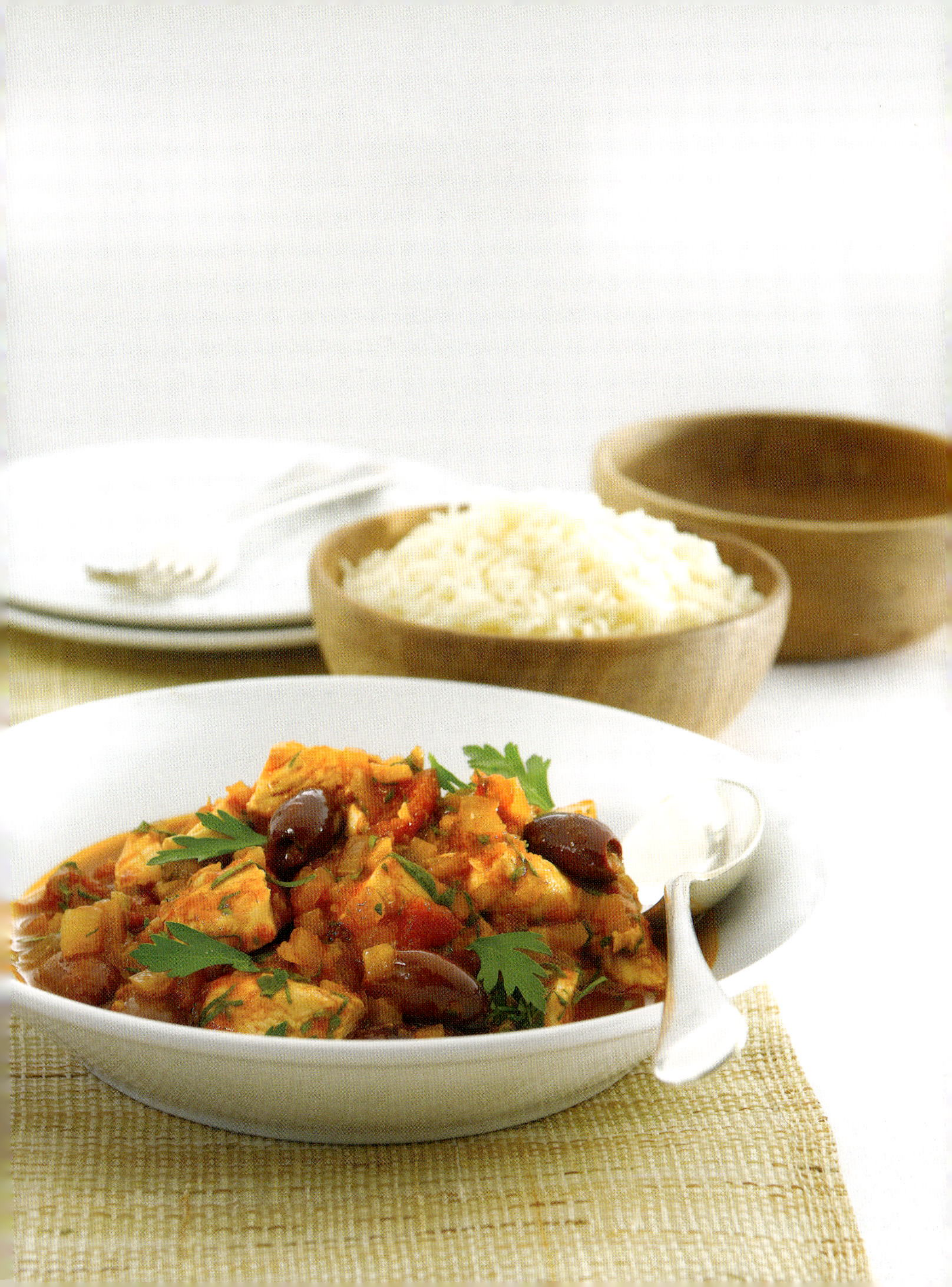

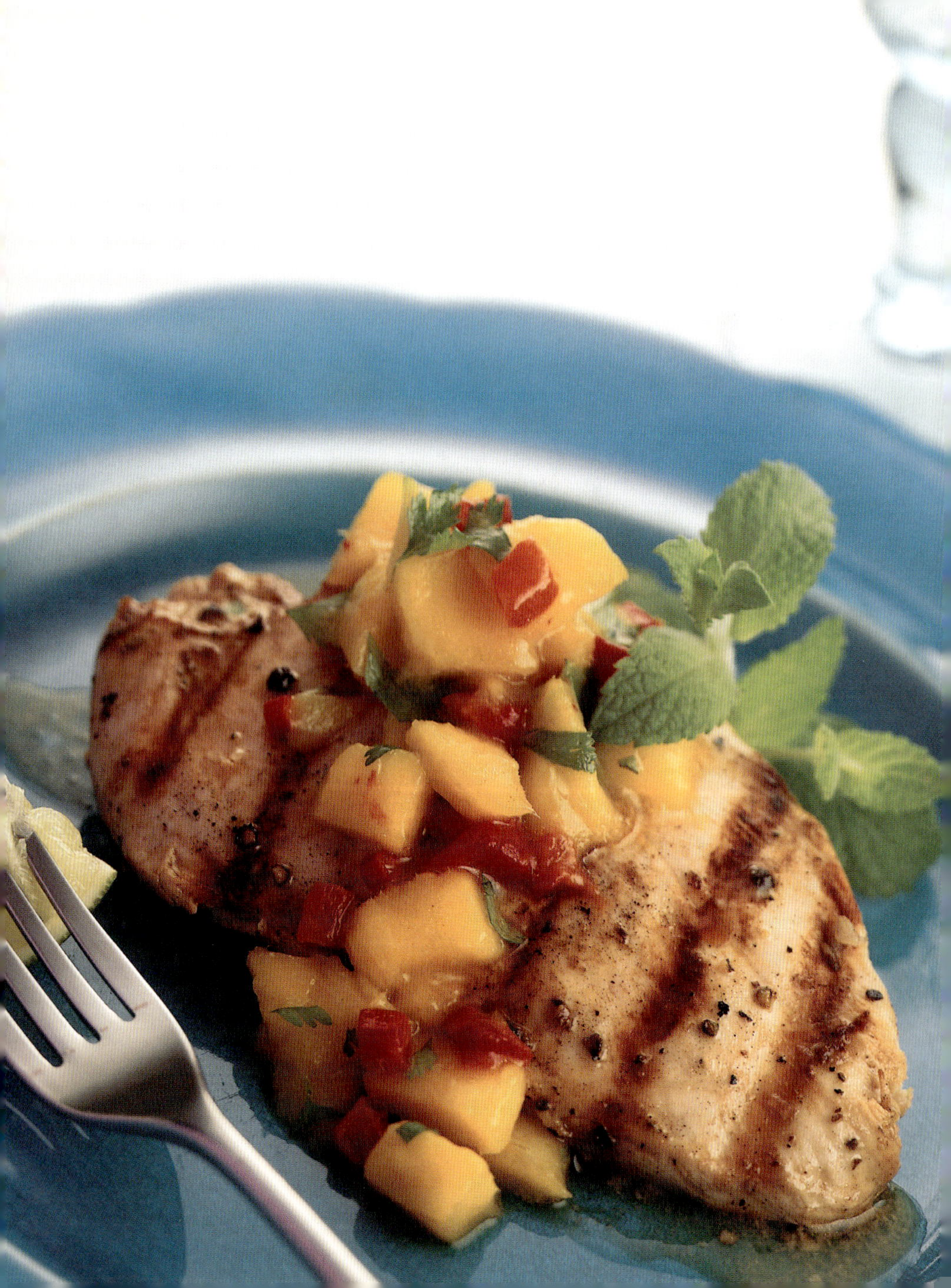

Char-grilled chicken with mango salsa

SERVES 4

4 skinless chicken breast fillets
1 tablespoon olive oil
2 tablespoons fish sauce
juice of 1 lime
salt and black pepper
Salsa
1 red pepper/capsicum, quartered
1 mango
1 small red chili, deseeded and finely chopped
1 tablespoon olive oil
juice of 1 lime
¼ cup cilantro/coriander, chopped
¼ cup mint, chopped

1. Place the chicken breasts between cling film and pound with a rolling pin to flatten slightly. Unwrap and place in a non-metallic dish. Combine the oil, fish sauce, lime juice and seasoning and pour over the chicken. Cover and leave to marinate in the refrigerator for 1 hour.
2. Meanwhile, make the salsa. Preheat the grill to high. Grill the red pepper for 10 minutes, cool, then peel off the skin and dice. Peel the mango, cut the flesh away from the stone and chop. Combine the chopped mango, red pepper, chili, oil, lime juice and herbs in a bowl. Cover and refrigerate.
3. Heat a ridged cast-iron pan over a medium-high heat. Wipe with the marinade, using a folded piece of absorbent paper. Add the chicken and fry for 3–5 minutes on each side, until cooked through (you may have to do this in batches). Serve with the salsa and garnish with mint and lime.

Honey and sesame chicken

SERVES 4

1 lb/500g chicken tenderloins
¼ teaspoon sesame oil
¼ teaspoon Chinese five spice powder
½ cup peanut oil
2 tablespoons cornflour
3 tablespoons honey
1 tablespoon lemon juice

2 tablespoons sesame seeds
Batter
¼ cup cornflour
¾ cup bakers/self-raising flour
1¼ cups water
1 egg white

1. Cut tenderloins in half. Mix with sesame oil and five spice powder and stand 15 minutes. To prepare the batter, sift the 2 flours into a bowl. Add water and mix until free of lumps. Stiffly beat the egg white and fold into the batter.
2. Place oil in wok to heat. Dip a piece of chicken into the cornflour, shake off excess, dip into the batter and place immediately into the hot oil. Repeat with 5 or 6 more pieces. Cook until golden brown, then remove to a tray lined with absorbent paper. Repeat with remainder. Drain all the oil from the wok.
3. Add honey and lemon juice to the wok and heat through on medium heat. Add chicken a few pieces at a time and coat with honey, remove to a serving platter and sprinkle with sesame seeds. Serve hot.

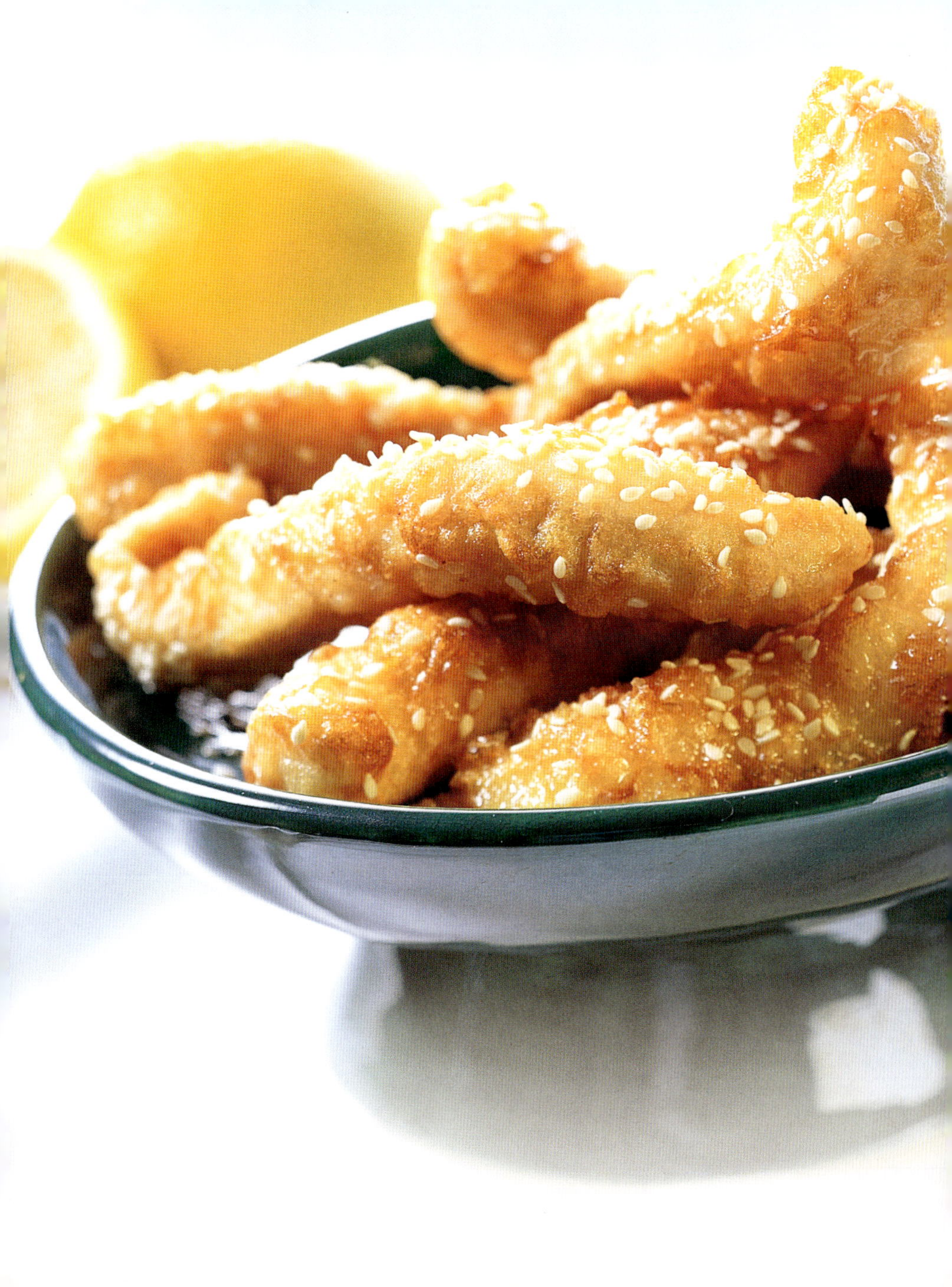

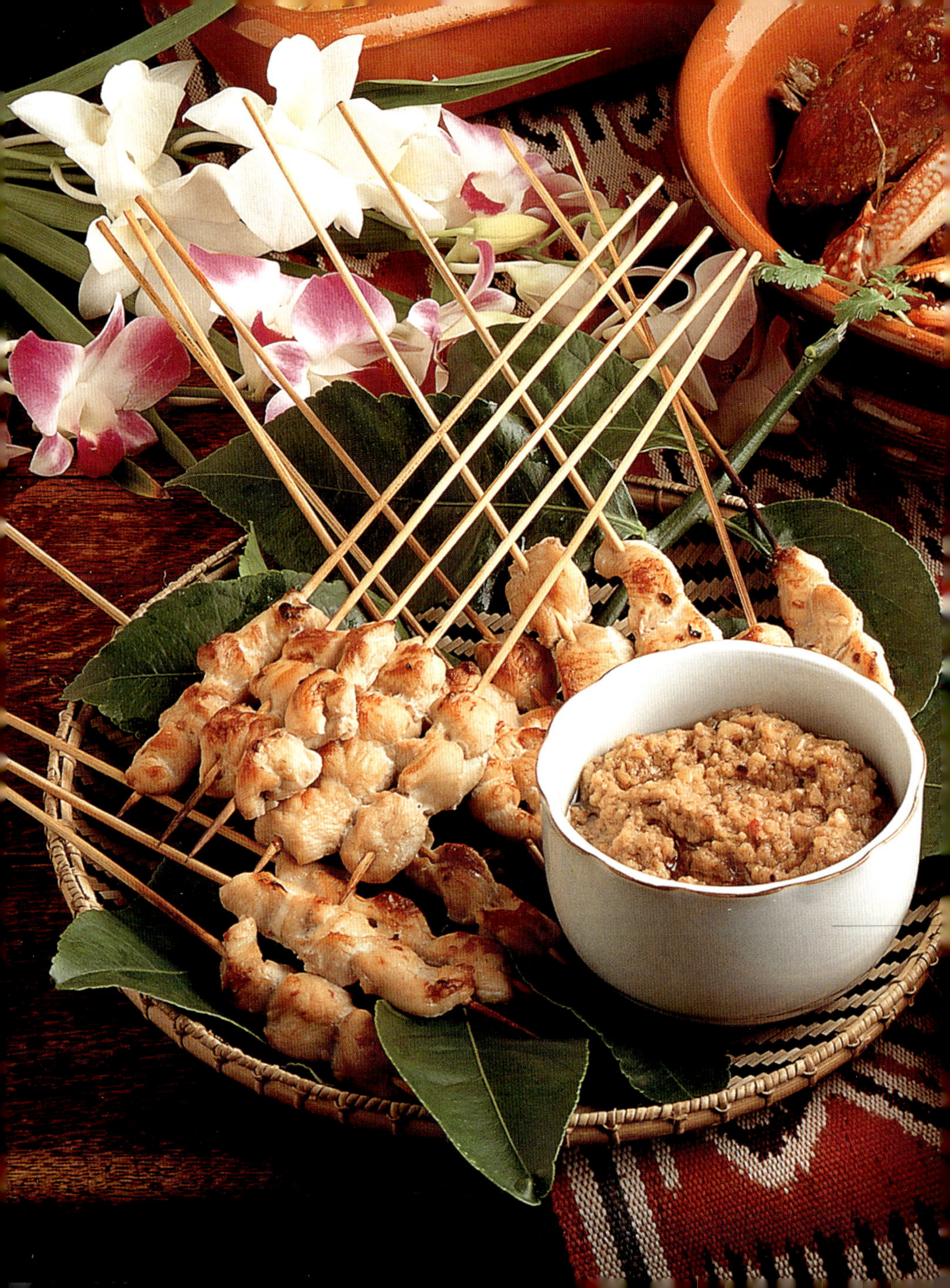

Chicken satay

SERVES 4

2lbs/1kg skinless chicken fillets
1 cup satay sauce
Marinade
1 tablespoon dark soy sauce
½ onion, finely sliced

1 garlic clove, crushed
pinch of chili powder
1 tablespoon lemon juice

1. Dice the chicken into ¾ ins/2cm cubes. Mix the marinade ingredients together in a bowl. Add the chicken and stir to coat thoroughly.
2. Cover and leave to marinate in the refrigerator for at least 1 hour.
3. Soak 16 bamboo skewers in water while the chicken is marinating. Divide the chicken pieces equally between the skewers and grill for 5–8 minutes, turning frequently. Serve hot with satay sauce for dipping.

Moroccan roast chicken with herbed couscous

SERVES 4–6

2 x 2lb/1kg chickens
¼ cup olive oil
zest of 1 lemon
¼ cup lemon juice
1 tablespoon Moroccan seasoning
2 teaspoons parsley flakes

Herbed couscous
1½ cups chicken stock
¾oz/20g butter
4 green onions/scallions, sliced
1½ cups couscous
¼ cup slivered almonds, toasted
¼ cup mixed fresh herbs, chopped

1. Preheat the oven to 390°F/200°C. Cut the chickens in half. Combine the olive oil, lemon zest, lemon juice, Moroccan seasoning and parsley in a small bowl.
2. Brush the chickens with the mixture. Place the chickens on a roasting rack over a baking tray. Bake in the oven for 1 hour or until cooked. Brush with the remaining mixture from time to time.
3. To make the couscous, place the stock, butter and green onions in a saucepan. Bring to the boil and simmer for 1 minute. Place the couscous in a heatproof bowl. Pour the stock over, stir with a fork and cover with cling film for 2 minutes or until the liquid is absorbed. Add the almonds and mixed herbs and stir through with a fork.
4. Serve the chicken with couscous.

To toast almonds, place on a baking tray lined with baking paper and bake at 360°F/180°C for 4–5 minutes or until golden.

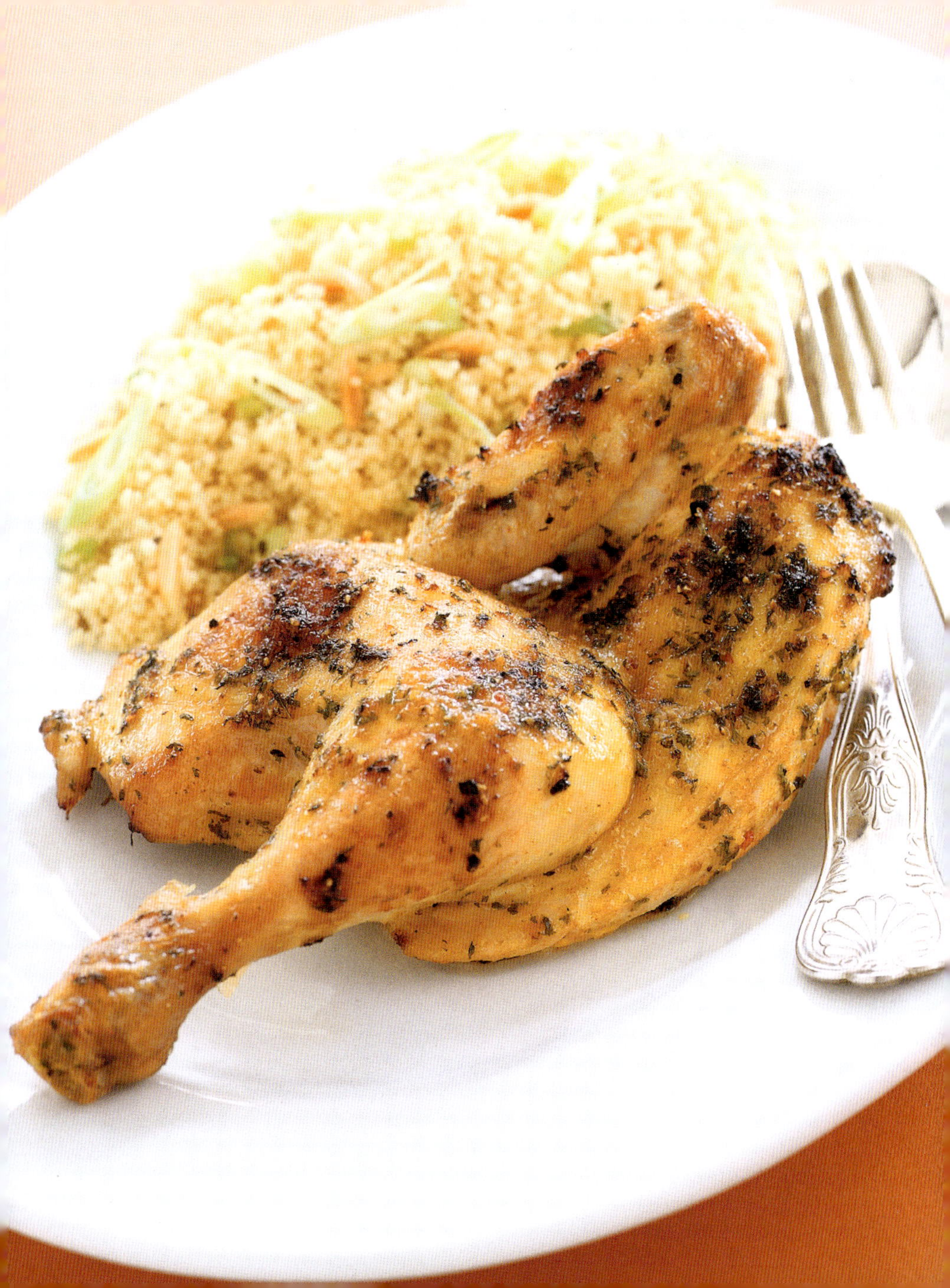

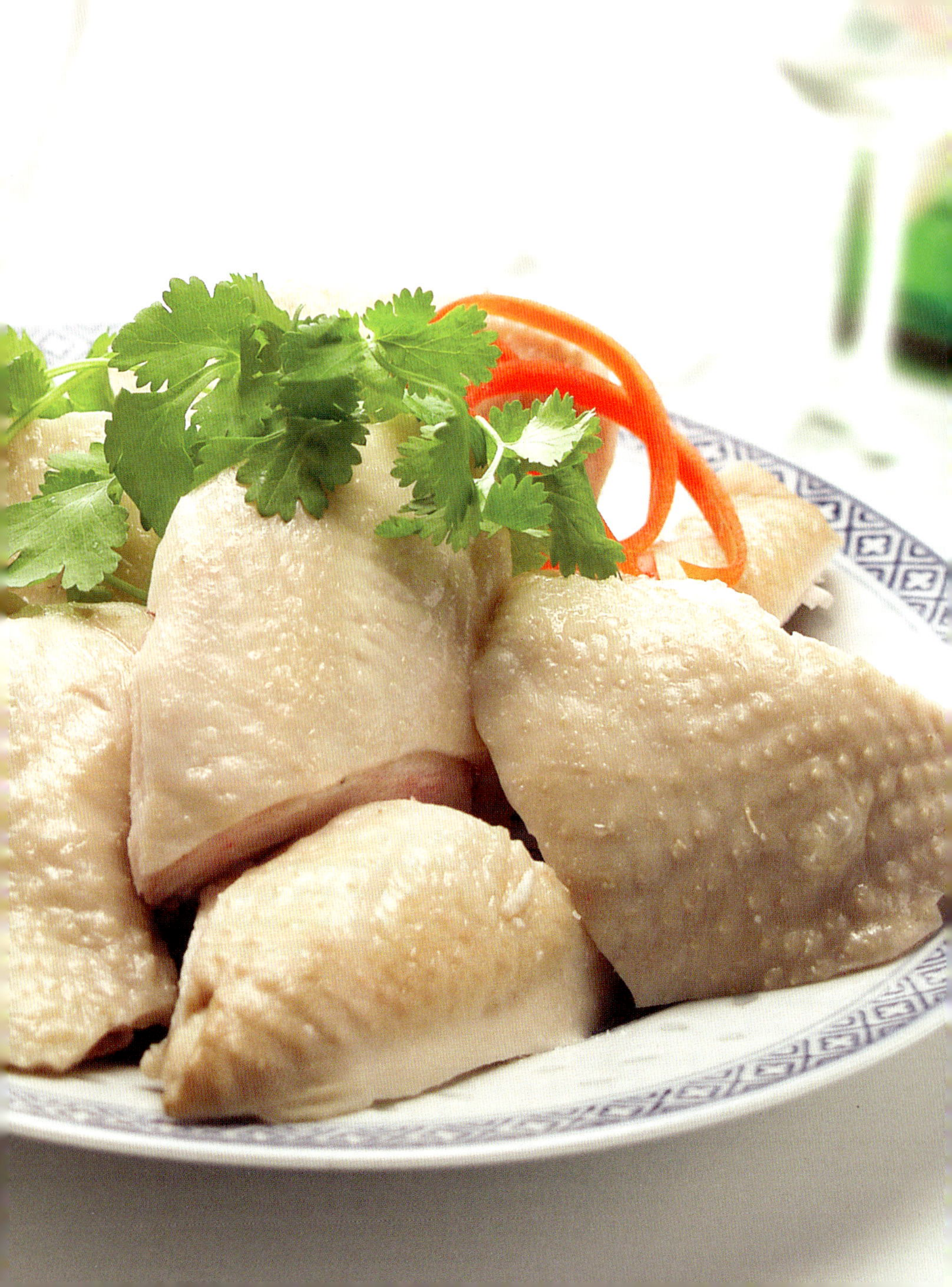

Drunken chicken

SERVES 4

2lb/1kg chicken
2 medium onions
2 teaspoons salt
2 ins/6cm piece fresh ginger, peeled and sliced

1¼ cups dry sherry
2 teaspoons sugar
cilantro/coriander leaves, to garnish

1. Cut the chicken into large serving-size pieces. Quarter onions and place in a pot with salt and ginger. Add chicken and enough hot water to cover and bring to the boil for 5 minutes. Cover and simmer for 15 minutes.
2. Transfer chicken to a large non-metallic bowl. Add sherry and sugar to cooking liquid, pour over chicken, stir thoroughly to ensure chicken is completely immersed and cover tightly with cling wrap. Refrigerate for 48 hours, stirring and cold basting with marinade occasionally.
3. Drain chicken, discarding onions. Serve cold, garnished with cilantro.

Balinese chicken

SERVES 4

1 small chicken, about 2lb/1kg
1 stalk lemongrass, bruised
   and tied in a knot
1 salam leaf
Marinade
½ teaspoon shrimp paste
1 teaspoon tamarind pulp, seeds
   removed
1 tablespoon light soy sauce
½ teaspoon salt
¼ teaspoon freshly ground black
   pepper

1 tablespoon peanut oil
Spice Paste
4 shallots/eschalots, roughly sliced
5 cloves garlic, sliced
1 large red chili, deseeded and sliced
2 ins/5cm piece fresh turmeric
2 ins/5cm piece fresh ginger
3 candlenuts, roughly chopped
¼ teaspoon salt
boiled rice, to serve

1. To make the marinade, wrap the shrimp paste in foil, flatten it with your hand and place over a heat source – a gas flame works best. When toasted, combine the shrimp paste with the other marinade ingredients, then rub all over chicken, inside and out. Marinate for at least 15 minutes.
2. Make the spice paste by grinding the ingredients on a grinding stone or in a mortar until you have a thick paste.
3. Put the chicken and marinade in a pot, then add the spice paste, lemongrass, salam leaf and 2 cups water.
4. Bring to the boil then cover the pot, reduce heat to low and simmer for 1 hour.
5. Remove the chicken and divide into serving portions. Place in a serving dish and pour some or all of the flavoured liquid over. Serve with plain rice.

If salam leaves are not available, you can substitute a curry leaf.

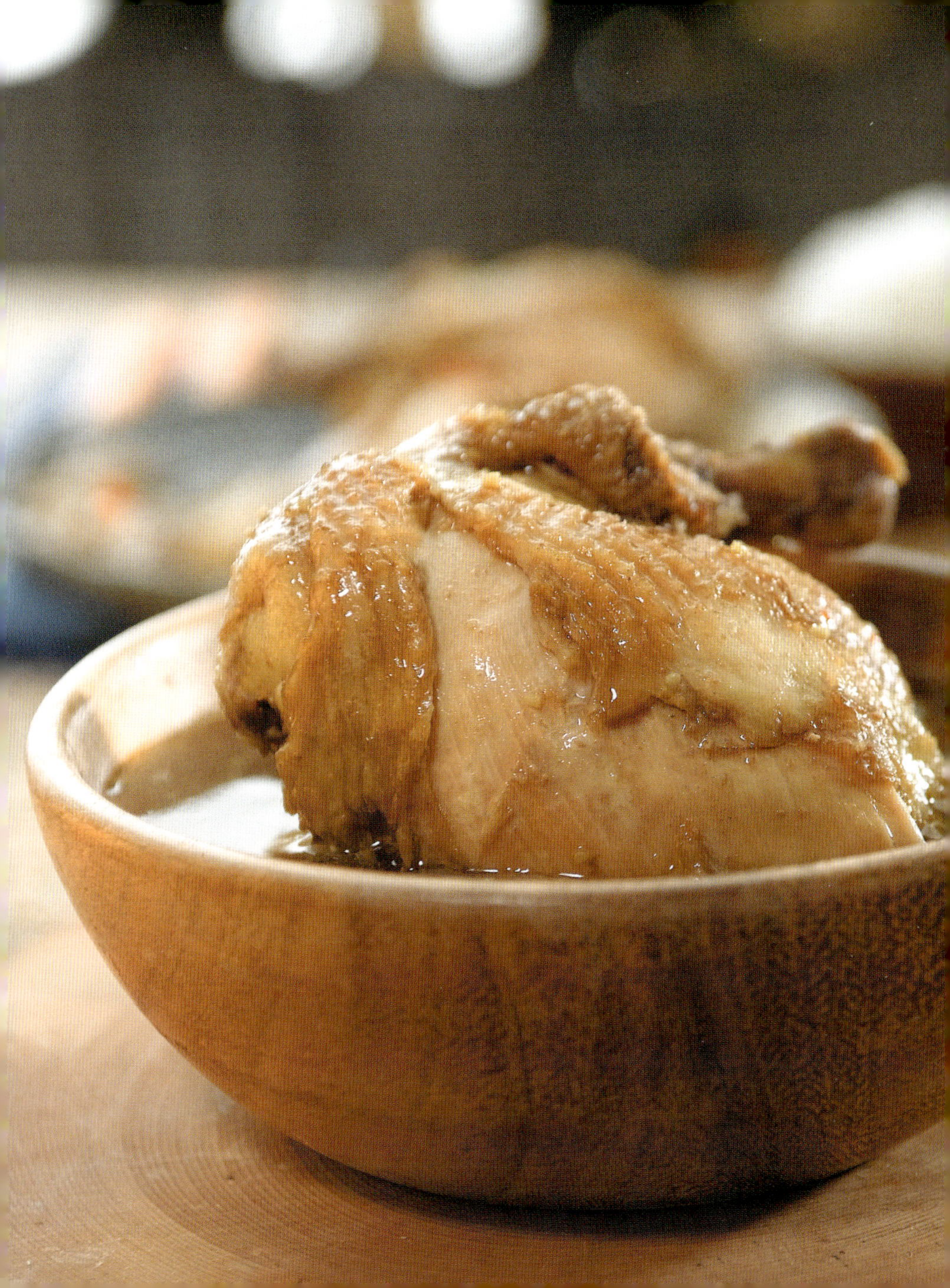

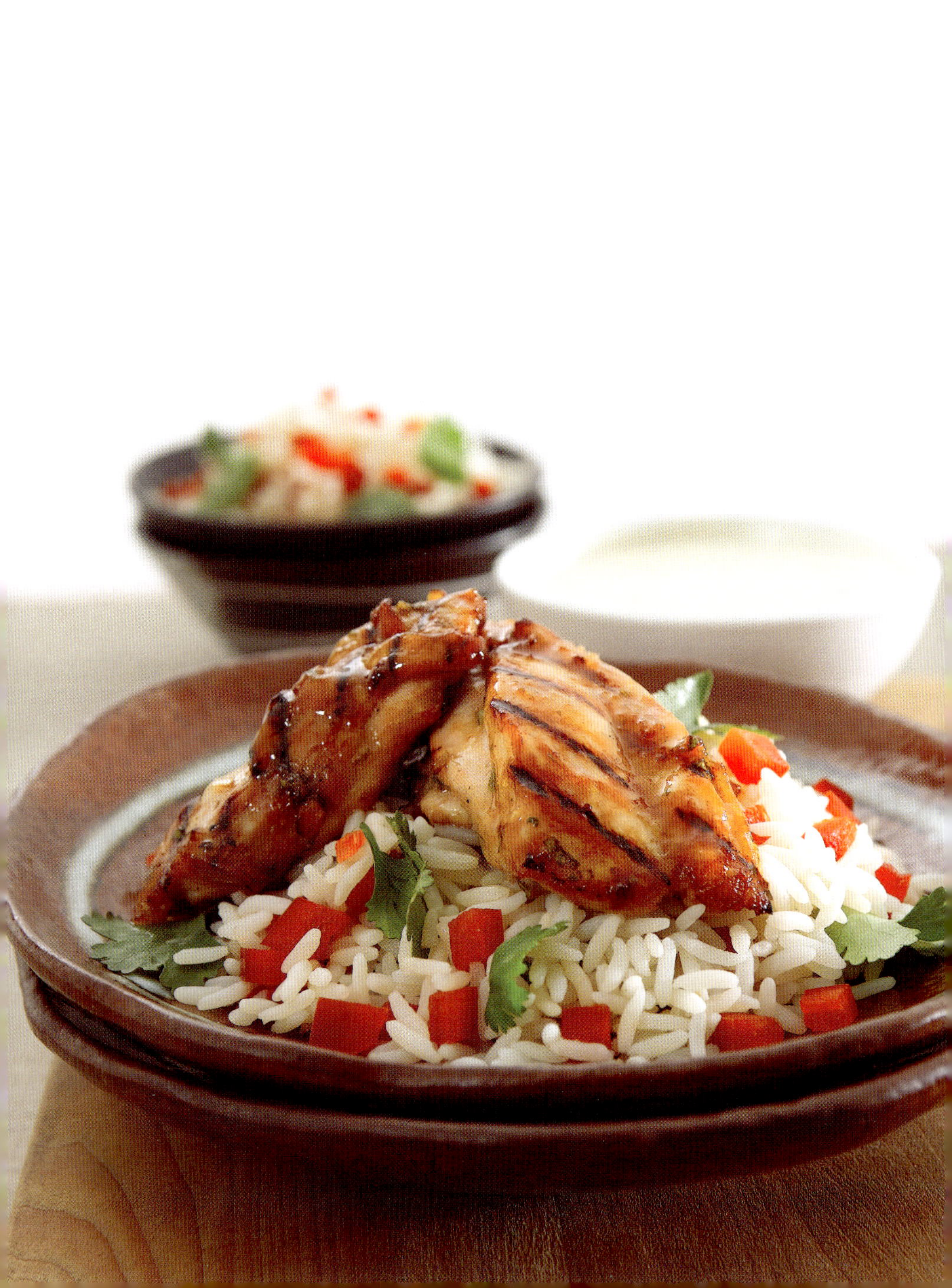

Barbecued chili lime chicken

SERVES 4

2 tablespoons chili oil
2 tablespoons honey
2 cloves garlic, crushed
zest and juice of 2 limes
salt and freshly ground black pepper
½ cup fresh cilantro/coriander, chopped
4 chicken thigh fillets

1 cup long-grain rice
½ red pepper/capsicum, finely diced
Chili Yoghurt Dressing
¾ cup Greek yoghurt
½ teaspoon chili oil
zest and juice of 1 lime
1 small red chili, chopped
salt and freshly ground black pepper

1. Combine oil, honey, garlic, lime zest and juice, salt, pepper and half the cilantro. Place chicken in marinade and coat well. Cover and set aside for at least 3 hours.
2. Combine the rice with 2 cups water in a saucepan. Bring to the boil, reduce heat to low, cover and cook for 15 minutes. Remove pan from heat, add red pepper and the remaining cilantro. Set aside and keep warm.
3. Remove chicken from marinade and place on grill or barbecue. Cook for 4 minutes on each side or until cooked through.
4. Mix dressing ingredients together then drizzle over chicken and rice and serve.

Baked chicken with cumquats

SERVES 4

4 chicken thighs
1 tablespoon olive oil
½ teaspoon salt
½ teaspoon freshly ground black pepper
½ teaspoon sweet paprika
½ teaspoon onion powder
2 cups orange juice
2 tablespoons apricot jam
2 tablespoons peach jam
2 tablespoons honey
1 tablespoon lemon juice
1 tablespoon lime juice
1½ cup dry white wine
1 onion, diced
9 oz/250g fresh cumquats
½ bunch basil, thinly sliced
steamed white rice, to serve.

1. Preheat oven to 390°F/200°C. Brush the chicken pieces with olive oil and sprinkle the chicken with salt, pepper, sweet paprika and onion powder. Bake for 30 minutes or until slightly golden.
2. Meanwhile, mix in a small saucepan the orange juice, jams, honey, lemon juice, lime juice, wine and heat until just about to boil. Whisk to remove any lumps. Place the peeled cumquats around the chicken pieces, sprinkle over diced onion and pour over the orange juice mixture. Reduce the temperature to 360°F/180°C and continue baking for another 30 minutes, basting every 10 minutes, and cook until the sauce is thick and the chicken is tender.
3. Sprinkle with the sliced basil leaves and serve with rice. Spoon extra sauce over the chicken.

If fresh cumquats are not available, you can substitute canned cumquats.

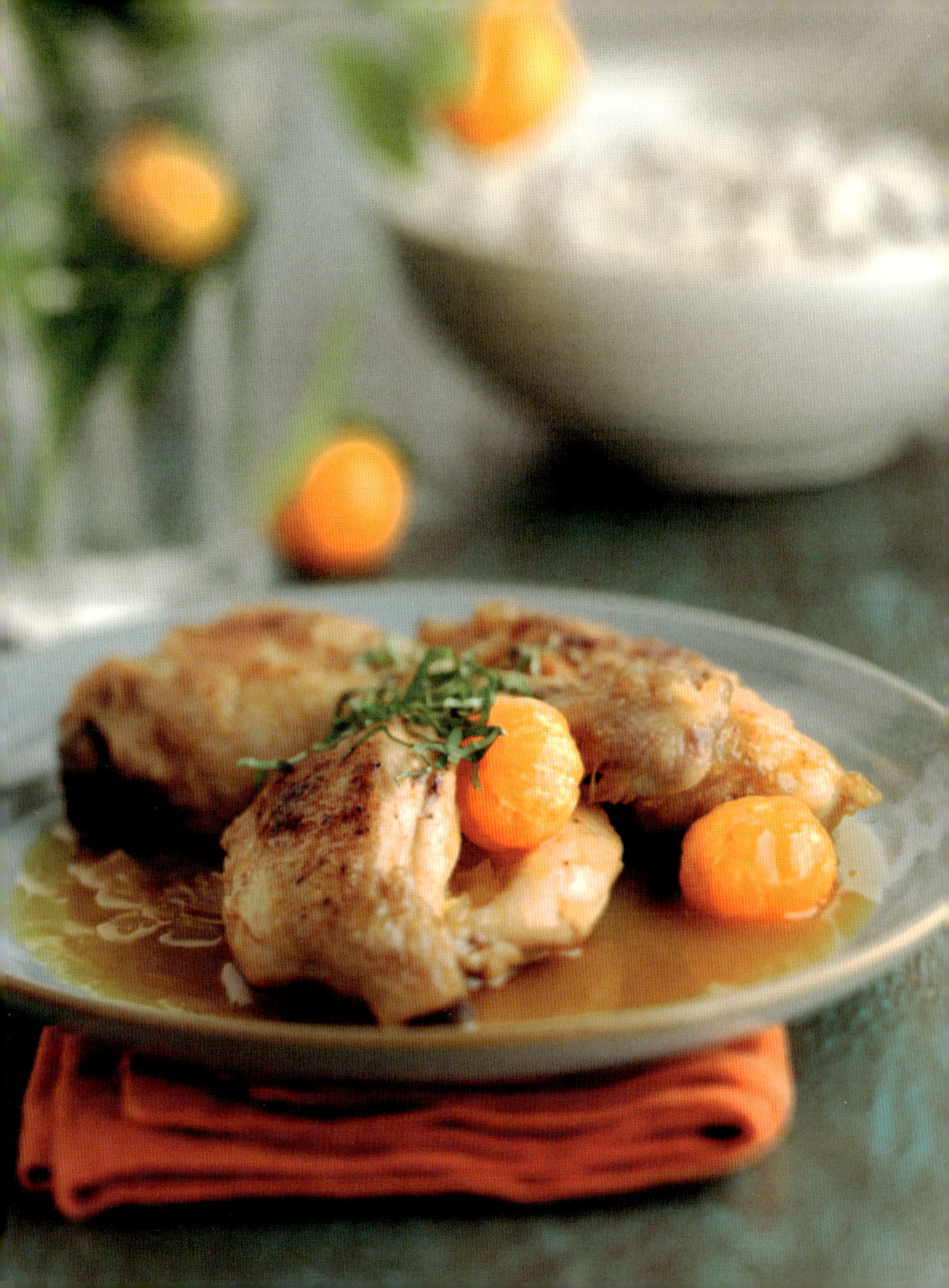

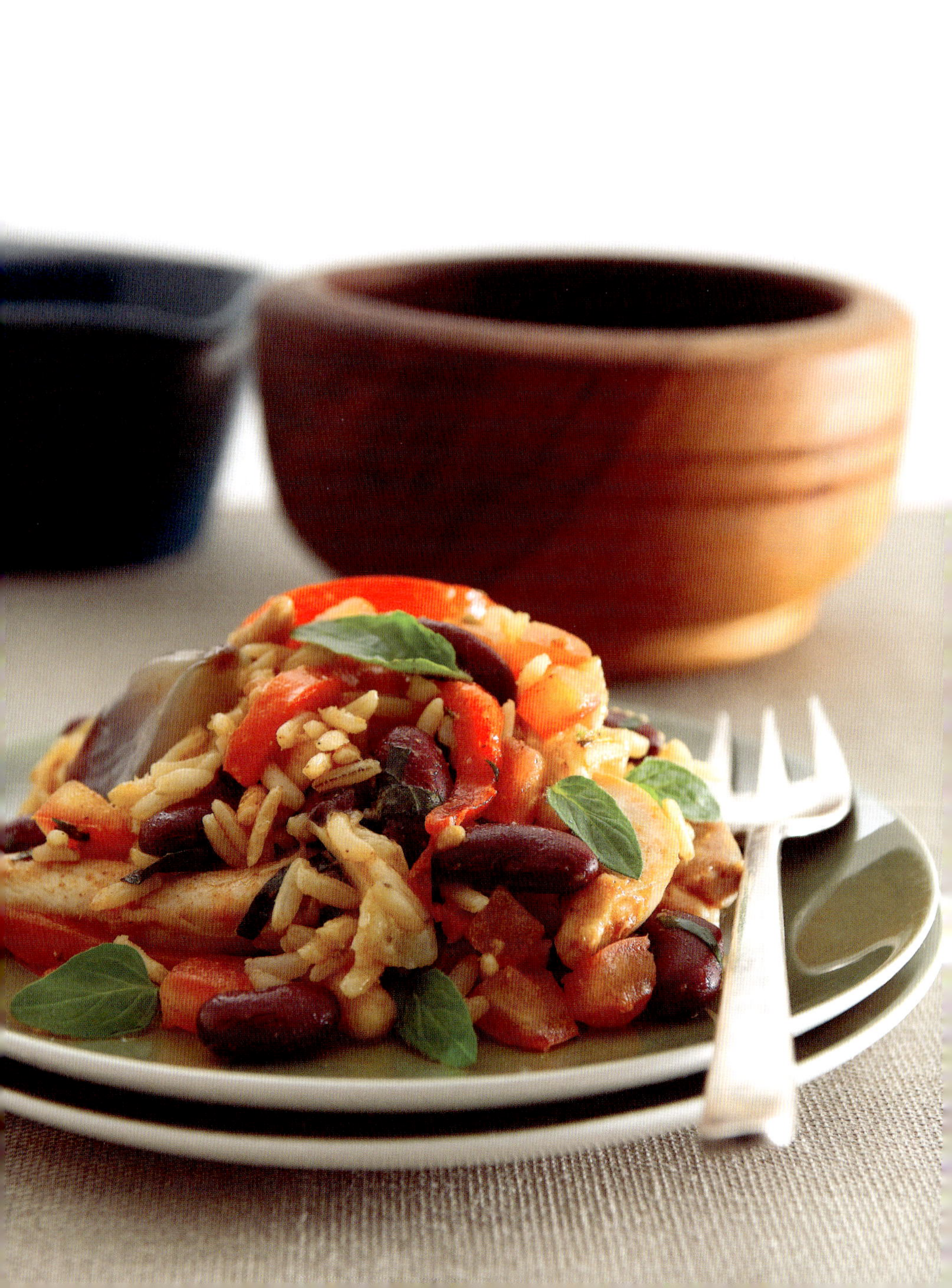

Mexican chicken rice

SERVES 4

2 red peppers/capsicums
6 shallots/escahlots
3 cloves garlic
2 tablespoons olive oil
4 chicken thigh fillets, sliced into strips
¼ cup sugar
1 tablespoon ground cumin
1 tablespoon paprika
1 teaspoon Tabasco sauce
3 tomatoes, diced
1 cup canned red kidney beans
salt and freshly ground black pepper
2 teaspoons chili paste
white rice, to serve
2 sprigs oregano, leaves removed and stalks discarded

1. Preheat oven to 390°F/200°C. Place red peppers, shallots and garlic on an oven tray and roast for 25 minutes. Once cooked, peel the roasted vegetables thinly, slice the pepper and set aside.
2. Heat the oil in a large heavy-based saucepan, then add the chicken and sugar. Cook for 1–2 minutes or until chicken has browned, then add the spices and fry until fragrant. Add the roasted vegetables, Tabasco and tomatoes and sauté for 5 minutes. Stir in the kidney beans and simmer for 30 minutes.
3. Season chicken with salt, pepper and chili paste. Spoon over rice and garnish with the fresh oregano to serve.

Mushroom and tarragon-stuffed chicken

SERVES 4

2 tablespoons olive oil
1 small leek, finely chopped
1 small courgette/zucchini, finely chopped
1 clove garlic, crushed
2 oz/60g button mushrooms, finely chopped

2 oz/60g oyster or shiitake mushrooms, finely chopped
4 sprigs fresh tarragon, chopped
freshly ground black pepper
4 skinless boneless chicken breast fillets, about 4½ oz/125g each
roast tomatoes, to serve (optional)

1. Preheat the oven to 390°F/200°C. Heat half the oil in a saucepan. Add the leek, courgette, garlic and mushrooms and cook for 5 minutes, stirring, until softened. Remove from the heat and stir in the tarragon and black pepper.
2. Place the chicken breasts between 2 large sheets of baking paper. Beat to an even thickness with a rolling pin. Spread the stuffing evenly over each breast. Roll up, folding in the ends, and secure with wetted toothpicks. Brush with the remaining oil and place on a non-stick baking sheet.
3. Cook in the oven for 30–35 minutes, until the juices run clear when pierced with a skewer. Remove the toothpicks and cut each roll into 1 ins/3cm slices, then garnish with extra tarragon. Serve with roast tomatoes.

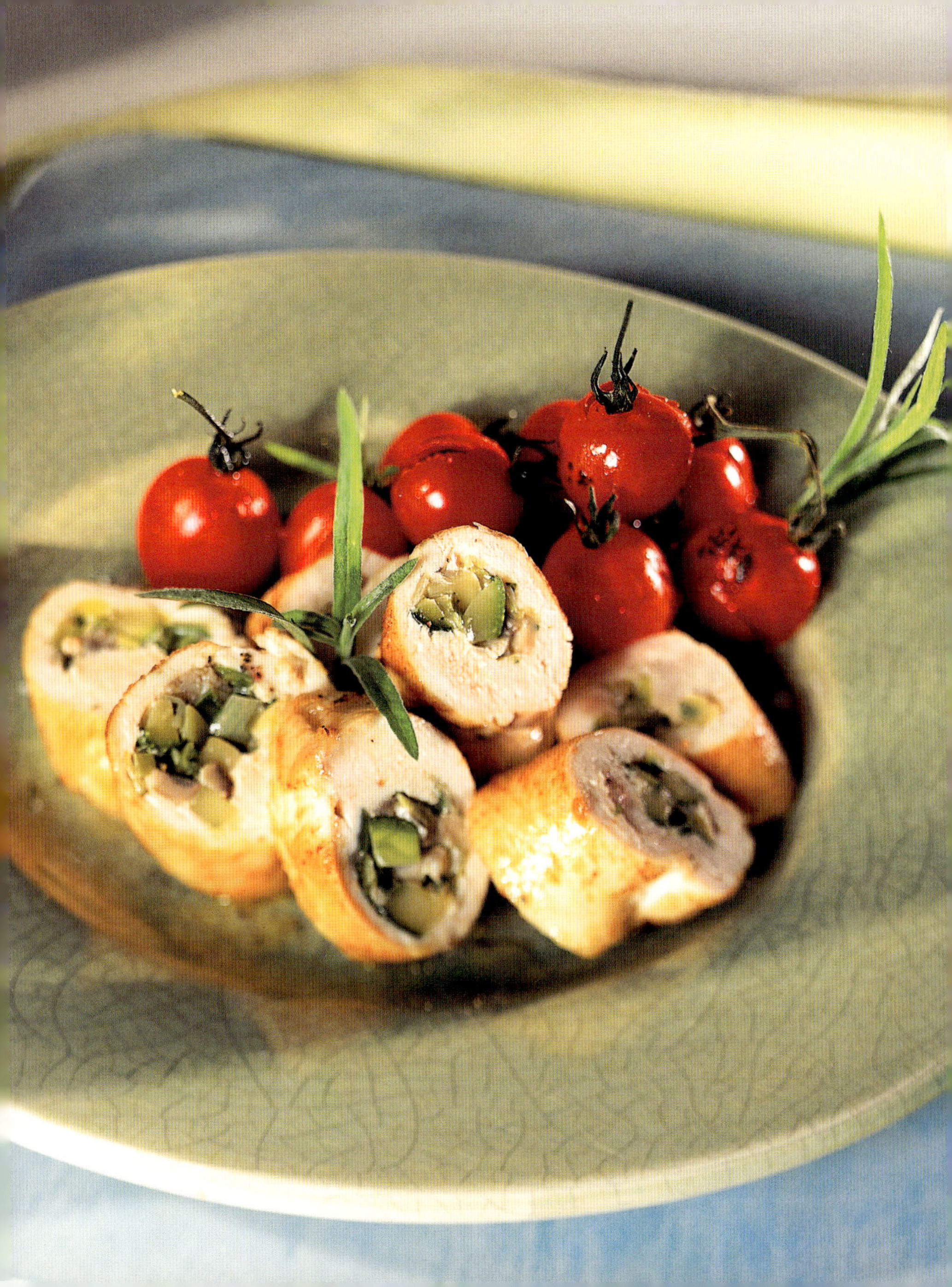

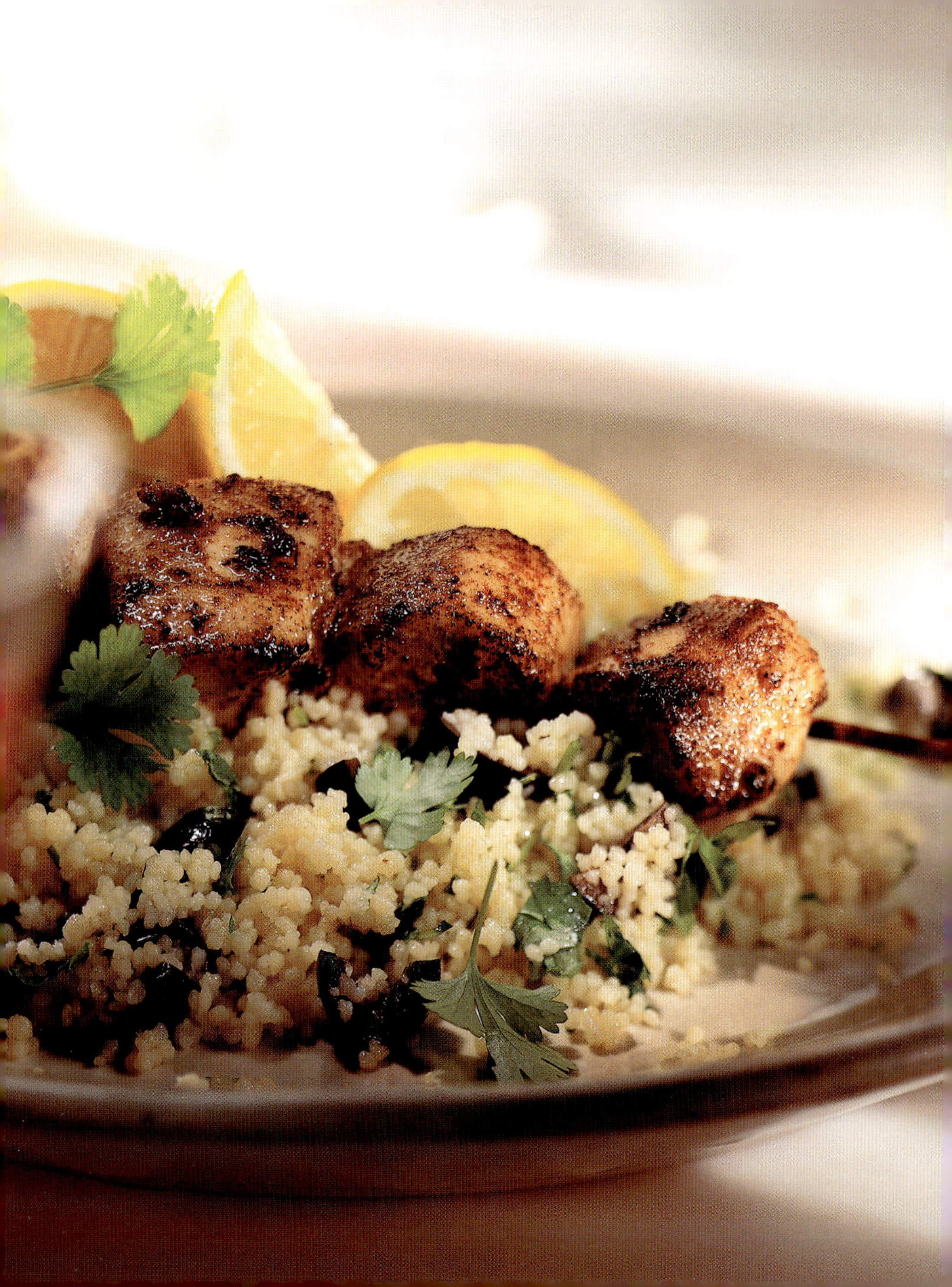

Chicken with lemon and cilantro couscous

SERVES 4

4 large skinless chicken breast fillets, cut into 1 ins/3cm cubes
1 tablespoon olive oil
1 clove garlic, crushed
1 teaspoon ground cilantro/coriander
1 teaspoon ground ginger
1 teaspoon ground cinnamon
pinch cayenne pepper
1 teaspoon salt

juice of 1 lemon
9 oz/250g couscous
1 oz/30g butter
¼ cup fresh cilantro/coriander, chopped, plus extra leaves to garnish
3½ oz/100g pitted black olives, chopped
freshly ground black pepper
lemon wedges to serve

1. Soak 4 wooden skewers in water for at least 10 minutes. Toss the chicken with the oil, garlic, ground spices, cayenne pepper, salt and 1 tablespoon of lemon juice until the pieces are evenly coated.
2. Preheat the grill to high. Thread the chicken onto the skewers and grill for 8–10 minutes, turning occasionally, until slightly charred, cooked through and tender. Keep warm.
3. Meanwhile, prepare the couscous according to the packet instructions, then fluff it up with a fork. Stir the butter, remaining lemon juice, cilantro and olives into the couscous and season. Transfer to serving plates, top with the chicken and drizzle over any pan juices. Serve with the lemon wedges and garnish with cilantro.

If you have extra time, marinate the chicken pieces for an hour or more so that they're really infused with the aromatic flavours of the cilantro, ginger and cinnamon.

Aromatic crispy game hens

SERVES 4

2 game hens/poussins
juice of 1 orange, plus
1 orange cut into wedges to serve
3 tablespoons soy sauce
1 piece preserved ginger, sliced into 4 pieces, plus 3 tablespoons syrup

1 teaspoon ground cinnamon
salt and freshly ground black pepper
1 oz/30g butter
4 cloves garlic, sliced
4 star anise

1. Preheat the oven to 430°F/220°C. Halve the game hens by cutting through the breastbone and backbone with heavy-duty kitchen scissors. Place, cut-side down, in a roasting tin.
2. Combine the orange juice, soy sauce, ginger syrup and cinnamon in a bowl. Pour the orange mixture over the poussin and season, then add the orange wedges to the roasting tin.
3. Place one-quarter of the butter on top of each game hen half, together with a sliced garlic clove, piece of stem ginger and star anise. Season with pepper. Cook for 25 minutes, basting occasionally, until the birds are browned and cooked through. Transfer to serving plates. Strain the cooking juices and spoon over the game hens.

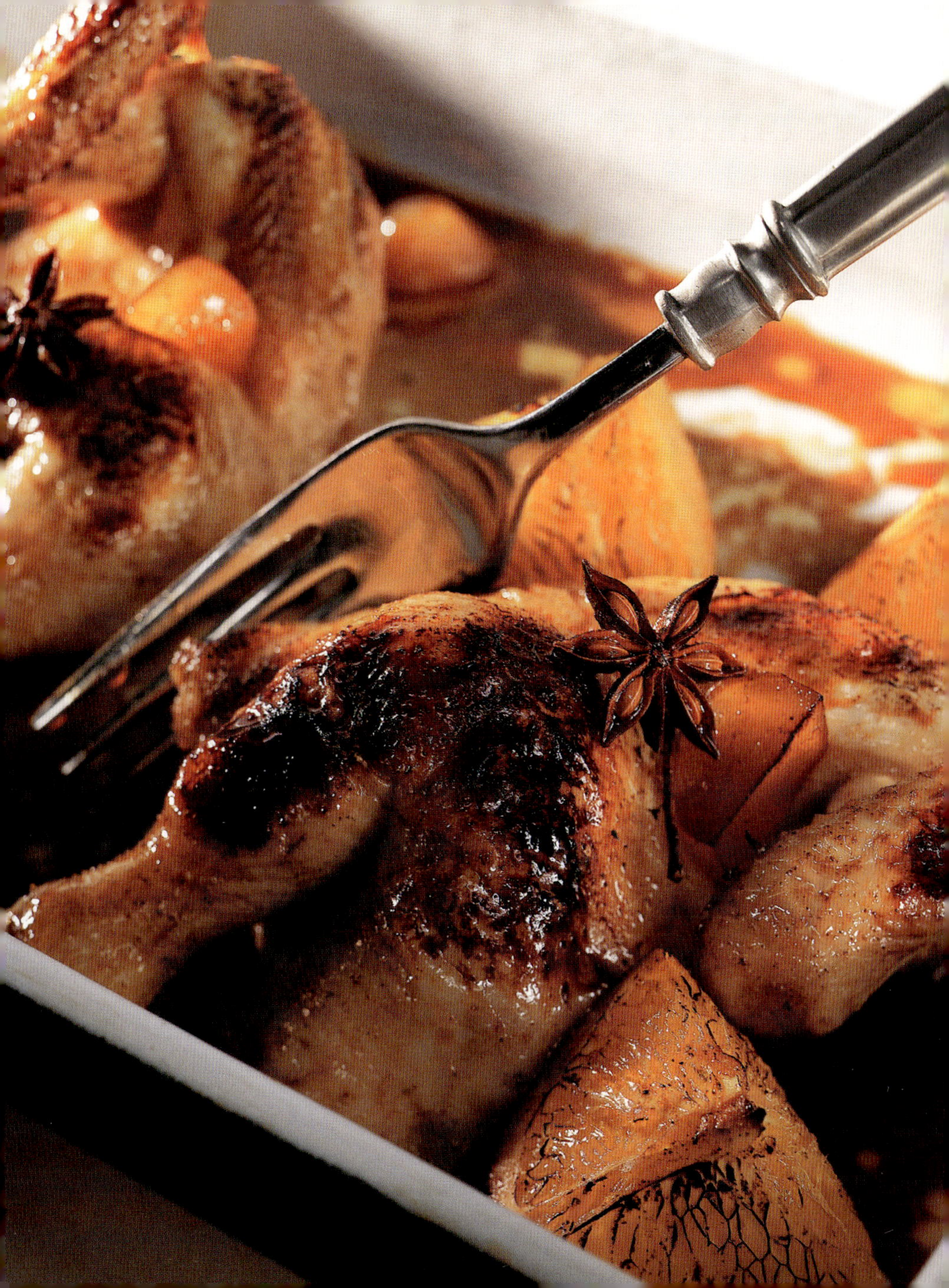

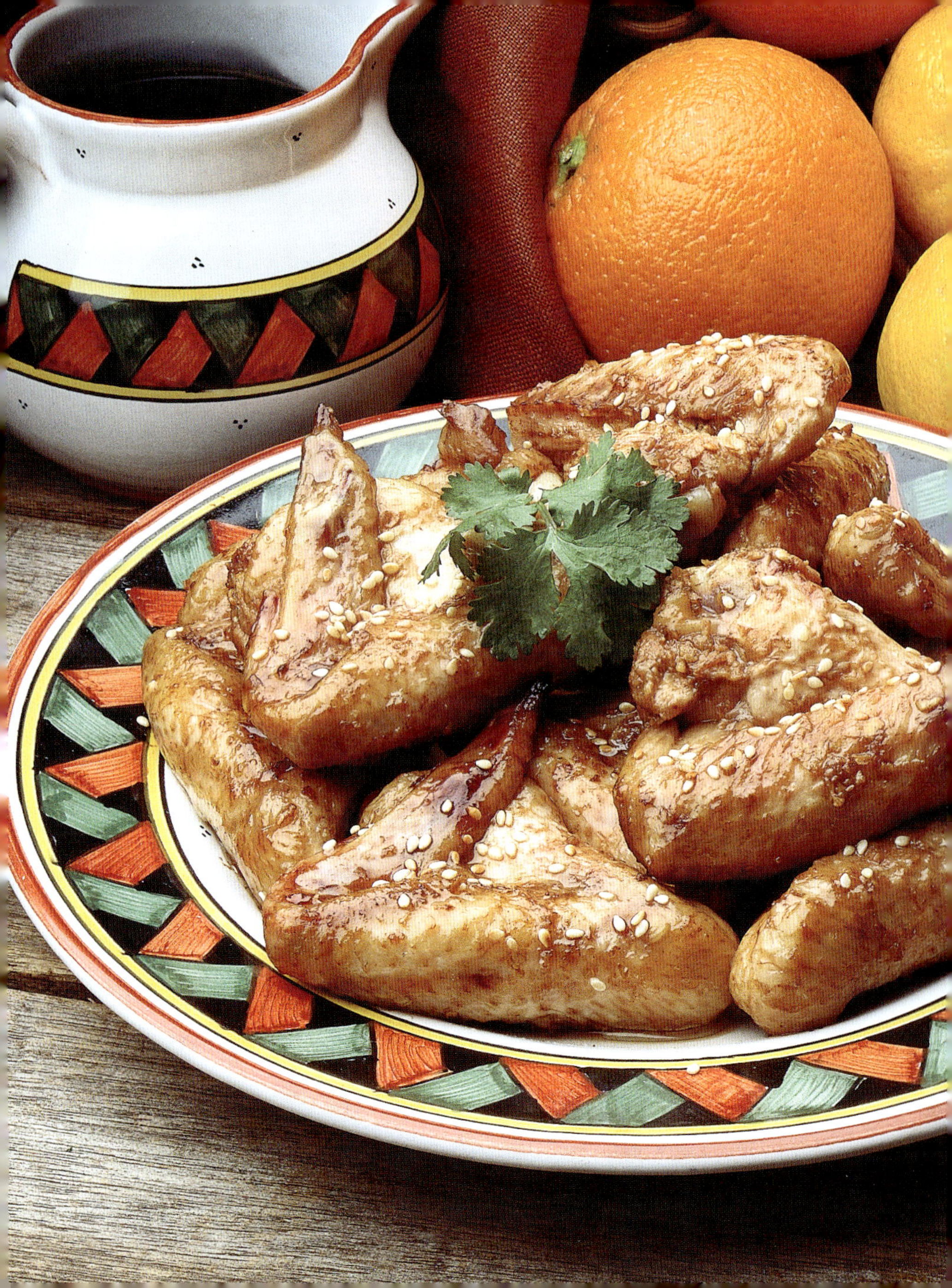

Ginger wings

SERVES 4

1 lb/500g chicken wings
1 tablespoon oil
1½ ins/4cm piece fresh ginger, grated
1 clove garlic, crushed

½ tablespoon soy sauce
1 tablespoon sugar
1½ tablespoons sherry
¼ cup toasted sesame seeds

1. Preheat oven to 360°F/180°C. Fold back the wing tip to form a triangle. Place wings in a large baking dish. Mix remaining ingredients together, except the sesame seeds, and pour over the wings.
2. Place in oven and cook for 25–30 minutes until brown and cooked through. Turn once during cooking. Remove from oven and arrange on a platter. Sprinkle over sesame seeds and serve.

Index

Apricot glazed chicken with savoury stuffing	126
Aromatic crispy game hens	186
Asian chicken curry	78
Avocado and chicken salad	51
Baked chicken with cumquats	178
Balinese chiciken	174
Barbecued chili lime chicken	177
Cashew nut butter chicken	82
Char-grilled chicken with mango salsa	165
Chicken and almond triangles	18
Chicken and endive salad with creamy dressing	55
Chicken and pear curry	81
Chicken and pear salad	39
Chicken and vegetable stew	109
Chicken and vegetable stir-fry	99
Chicken, baby corn and green pea casserole	110
Chicken balls with coconut and cilantro sauce	22
Chicken burger with tomato salsa	70
Chicken ceasar salad	40
Chicken curry with spinach	77
Chicken fingers	33
Chicken foccacia	65
Chicken in garlic sauce	121
Chicken, leek and mushroom flan	102
Chicken rogan josh	74
Chicken satay	169
Chicken sausage sticks	30
Chicken, spinach and cheese pastries	26
Chicken steaks with herb sauce	146
Chicken waldorf salad	44
Chicken wings Morroccan style	161
Chicken with lemon and cilantro couscous	185
Chinese five spice chicken	117
Crisp curried wings with steamed rice	134
Crunchy chicken and potato salad	48
Crunchy drumsticks	137
Curried chicken rolls	21
Curried chicken salad	52
Curry chicken	73
Drumsticks in dill sauce	158
Drumsticks in tomato sauce	149
Drunken chicken	173
Filo chicken pie	105
Finger food	13
Fried noodles with chicken stir-fry	95
Ginger wings	189
Greek chicken meatballs	106
Hawaiian poached chicken	153

Honey and sesame chicken	166
Honey balsamic barbecued drumsticks	118
Indonesian chicken rolls	154
Lavash rolls	58
Lemon and tarragon roast chicken	125
Main meals	101
Marinated chicken salad	36
Mexican chicken rice	181
Mini chicken pies	29
Moroccan roast chicken with herbed couscous	170
Mushroom and tarragon-stuffed chicken	182
Mustard chicken	157
Oven-baked chicken schnitzels	133
Piri piri chicken burgers	66
Poached chicken with tomato and mushroom sauce	150
Quick chicken cacciatore	162
Salads	35
Samosas	14
Sandwiches and wraps	57
Satay wings	141
Sauté Chicken with citrus and yoghurt sauce	89

Southern barbecued chicken	113
Southern-fried chicken drumsticks	145
Spicy chicken burritos	62
Spinach and almond chicken salad	43
Spinach and chicken omelette baguettes	69
Spring rolls (egg rolls)	25
Stir-fried chicken with almonds and broccoli	92
Stir-fry chicken	91
Sweet and sour chicken	96
Sweet mango chicken	86
Tandoori chicken	130
Tandoori chicken pockets	61
Tangy tenderloins	138
Teriyaki chicken with kinpira vegetables	114
Thai chicken curry	85
Thigh steaks with fruity mint salsa	142
Tuscan chicken with mozzarella and prosciutto	129
Vindaloo chicken nuggets	17
Vineyard chicken	122
Warm chicken and blue cheese salad	47

UK £9.99
US $14.99